The Practical Guide
to
Libel Law

The Practical Guide to Libel Law

NEIL J. ROSINI

PRAEGER

New York
Westport, Connecticut
London

Library of Congress Cataloging-in-Publication Data

Rosini, Neil J.
    The practical guide to libel law / Neil J. Rosini.
      p.   cm.
    Includes bibliographical references and index.
    ISBN 0–275–93782–8 (alk. paper)
    1. Libel and slander—United States.   I. Title.
  KF1266.R68   1991
  346.7303′4—dc20
  [347.30634]   91–9566

British Library Cataloguing in Publication Data is available.

Library of Congress Catalog Card Number: 91–9566
ISBN: 0–275–93782–8

First published in 1991

Praeger Publishers, One Madison Avenue, New York, NY 10010
An imprint of Greenwood Publishing Group, Inc.

Printed in the United States of America

The paper used in this book complies with the
Permanent Paper Standard issued by the National
Information Standards Organization (Z39.48–1984).

10 9 8 7 6 5 4 3 2 1

To Betsy

Contents

Preface

A primary function of the law is to reconcile competing social interests. The stronger the competition, the more difficult the reconciliation. Some interests are so powerful but lie so far apart that both society and the courts have extreme difficulty in charting a course between them. Issues like student busing, abortion, drug legalization, surrogate motherhood, animal rights, and genetic research all demonstrate the difficulty of accommodating positions at polar extremes. So does the law of defamation, which attempts to reconcile our society's deeply held belief in the value of a free press with its equally strong credo of individual rights and the value of reputation.

The nation's investment in principles of free speech under the First Amendment—which prohibits Congress from making any law "abridging the freedom of speech, or of the press"[1]—is fundamental. Our Supreme Court decisions have held time and time again, that "[t]he guarantees for speech and press are not the preserve of political expression or comment upon public affairs, essential as those are to healthy government." Instead, "[f]reedom of discussion, if it would fulfill its historic function in this nation, must embrace all issues about which information is needed or appropriate to enable the members of society to cope with the exigencies of their period." The benefits of those guarantees are not so much for the press "as for the benefit of all of us. A broadly defined freedom of press assures the maintenance of our political system and an open society."[2] Freedom to speak one's mind is therefore "not only an aspect of individual liberty—and thus a good unto itself—but also is essential to the common quest for truth and the vitality of society as a whole.''³

Against this background there exists ''a profound national commitment in this country to the principle that debate on public issues should be uninhibited, robust and wide-open, and that it may well include vehement, caustic and sometimes unpleasantly sharp attacks. . . . ''⁴ Of course, lies and false communications do not serve the ends of the First Amendment, but ''to insure the ascertainment and publication of the truth about public affairs, it is essential that the First Amendment protect some erroneous publications as well as true ones.''⁵ To punish ''error runs the risk of inducing a cautious and restrictive exercise of the constitutionally guaranteed freedoms of speech and press'' and any rule ''that compels a publisher or broadcaster to guarantee the accuracy of his factual assertions may lead to intolerable self-censorship.''⁶ Even the erroneous statement, inevitable in free debate, ''must be protected if the freedoms of expression are to have the 'breathing space' that they 'need . . . to survive.' ''⁷

On the other hand, the interests of individuals in the value of their reputations extend farther back than the invention of mass media. Around 880 A.D., the time of Alfred the Great, the minimum penalty for defamation was the loss of one's tongue.⁸ Over the following centuries, the high social value of a good reputation continued undiminished. In Shakespeare's *Othello*, Iago observed:

> Good name in man and woman, dear my lord,
> Is the immediate jewel of their souls:
> Who steals my purse steals trash; 'tis something, nothing;
> 'Twas mine, 'tis his, and has been slave to thousands;
> But he that filches from me my good name
> Robs me of that which not enriches him
> And makes me poor indeed.⁹

Over the last quarter century, the Supreme Court has repeatedly recognized that:

> The right of a man to the protection of his own reputation from unjustified invasion and wrongful hurt reflects no more than our basic concept of the essential dignity and worth of every human being—a concept at the root of any decent system of ordered liberty. The protection of private personality, like the protection of life itself, is left primarily to the individual

States. . . . But this does not mean that the right is entitled to any less recognition . . . as a basic of our constitutional system.[10]

The media cannot be permitted complete freedom to say what they will because "absolute protection for the communications media requires a total sacrifice of the competing value served by the law of defamation."[11]

The result of these clashing ideals has been a struggle "to define the proper accommodation"[12] between the need for a vigorous and uninhibited press and the legitimate interest in redressing injury to reputation. Recognizing that *ad hoc* resolutions of these competing interests in particular cases would not be feasible, the Supreme Court has attempted to "lay down broad rules of general application." But even the Court recognizes that these rules treat alike "various cases involving differences as well as similarities" and that "not all of the considerations which justify adoption of a given rule will obtain in each particular case decided under its authority."[13] As a result, the Court's approach to drawing lines and setting standards often seems unfair, or unpredictable and the results of defamation suits arbitrary and counter-intuitive. Without question, the Supreme Court's application of the First Amendment to the law of libel provides no means by which the press, the public, and the courts can resolve this tension between ideals with perfect consistency and accuracy.

But given the strength of those ideals and the distance which separates them, a perfect system of libel law will always elude us. Ultimately, the values of complete freedom of the press and the preservation of individual reputations are irreconcilable. One might argue over whether the Supreme Court has chosen the most efficient or socially beneficial way to distribute risks and benefits among the press, and public and private citizens. That discussion, however, would be nearly useless to the print and broadcast journalists, screenwriters, other writers, editors, publishers, broadcasters and motion picture producers*—and their lawyers—who must cope with the law as it is.

This book is not an attempt to reconcile the irreconcilable. Its more modest objective is to help the media guide itself though an imperfect system in a practical way.

*Instead of repeating throughout this book this litany of media professionals to whom this book is addressed, the words "journalist," "reporter," "writer" and "media professional" will be used interchangeably as a shorthand reference to everyone on the list. Similarly, references to "publishing" or "publication" of statements are meant in the broad sense of "making things public" and apply to dissemination of information by both print and broadcast media. The term "media" refers to all forms of mass media, both published and broadcast, including books, newspapers, theatrical motion pictures, broadcast television and cable television.

Acknowledgments

I gratefully acknowledge the support and encouragement of my partners at Franklin, Weinrib, Rudell & Vassallo, and especially that of Leonard Franklin, Michael Rudell, John Vassallo and Rose Schwartz. I am equally thankful for my wife Betsy's patience, endurance and assistance throughout the longer-than-expected gestation of this book. I also thank Paulette Strauss, Deborah Friedman, Iris Cohn, and Donna Chevannes, who typed the manuscript, in their "spare time," with care, patience, and sometimes unaccountable good humor. And to Eve and Ed, thanks for everything.

Introduction

You're at your desk one day feeling a little better than usual because one of your pieces, just out, is creating a stir: a report on some legal troubles the mayor is having.

The phone rings—it's a lawyer. You hate lawyers—even your own, who did nothing but discourage you from using your best material and charged so much you fired him. But this is not *your* lawyer, and he has a very unpleasant tone in his voice. It seems his client, the mayor, is suffering great mental anguish because of your report and particularly because of two allegations: first, that a "well-placed insider" (your words) said the mayor filed no tax returns for three years; and second, that the mayor is involved in a scheme to defraud the government.

You remember the first statement which was the focus of your story and you are not greatly concerned. After all, you had two sources *and the mayor is undoubtedly a public official* which, as far as you know, means you can say what you please about him. But you have no idea where the second charge comes from and just before you can ask, the lawyer says his client is suing for $10 million and hangs up.

The following day the process server arrives at your home and hands you a legal complaint. Sure enough, it demands $10 million for each of two claims. The second claim, which mystified you the day before, is based on the following quote from your report:

> This is not the first brush with accusations of criminality that the mayor has had to deal with in recent days. He is reportedly under investigation along with his brother-in-law, who was accused within the past month of

defrauding the government of millions through bogus sidewalk construction contracts.

So, they think you accused the mayor of acting with his brother-in-law to defraud the government! All you meant was that the mayor's brush with the IRS made him the subject of an investigation even while his brother-in-law was being investigated for the separate charge. How can you be held responsible if the mayor misinterprets your recap of his legal woes?

You have no choice but to talk to a lawyer. First she asks if you have insurance. You do not; it was dropped after premiums tripled[14] in recent years. Even when you were insured, the policy carried a $25,000 deductible and the limit of coverage was only $1 million.

Next your lawyer asks about the allegation from the "well-placed insider" that the mayor failed to file tax returns. "Who is the well-placed insider?" she asks.

You proudly show her the notes of your telephone call with a man who said he worked at the mayor's office and personally heard him brag that only "the little people" pay taxes. Your lawyer's eyes narrow. "You based this solely on an anonymous phone call?"

"Of course not," you respond with a trace of indignation. You heard the same allegation from the widow of the mayor's former accountant at a hearing of the Board of Ethics the day before your talk with the anonymous caller. You didn't put much stock in her testimony at the time—no one else at that hearing did—until the telephone call corroborated it. Your lawyer asks why you did not mention the Board of Ethics hearing in your story. After you ask why, she says the anonymous phone call is worthless, but if you had identified the allegation as a report of testimony at the hearing, it would be privileged even if untrue. "In other words the mayor would have no claim," she says. You regret that this idiosyncrasy of the law had not earlier been brought to your attention.

"But he's the mayor!" you protest. "This is a free country!" You say you thought you could write anything about public officials as long as you didn't make it up.

"You were wrong," she says.

You ask about the second claim in the legal complaint. Surely you cannot be held responsible for an alleged defamation that you didn't even see, or intend? Your lawyer shakes her head sadly, which both annoys you and makes you want to cry.

Because you have no proof of fraud at all, she gives you a 50/50 chance to beat the claim. "It would have been a lot easier had you caught the language and deleted it, wouldn't it?" she observes. You resist the temptation to hit her on the head with the large book at the corner of her desk.

Over the next year you, and most of the people you work with, spend a good part of your time working on the defense of the suit—answering interrogatories, meeting with your lawyer, producing papers, reviewing papers, preparing for, giving and attending depositions—and all of you have correspondingly less time to work on anything else. As the rules of libel litigation require, the mayor and his lawyer embark on long and complicated "discovery" involving detailed investigation of the workings of your office, the development of the story and the state of mind of you and your publisher. This kind of litigation is very expensive and the cost of defending the suit climbs to $150,000. Your lawyer assures you her fees are reasonable: recent studies have shown that the average cost of defending libel actions in the United States runs between $150,000 and $200,000.[15]

The case goes to trial. Unfortunately, the mayor has retained copies of every tax return he filed for 35 years, and no filing has been missed. He also demonstrates effectively that he has not spoken to his brother-in-law for 20 years. After the mayor's lawyer finishes a blistering cross-examination of you, he has convinced even you that your report showed "a reckless disregard for truth or falsity." You lose and the jury awards the mayor $2 million, mostly in punitive damages.

Your lawyer tries to reassure you by putting your loss in context: on average the media wins only about two in five of the libel cases which go to trial[16] and the average jury award had been $2 million a few years back[17] and is still about $500,000.[18] Even worse, punitive damages are awarded in 60 percent of all cases won against the news media, with some awards so large that yours seems molecular by comparison.[19] A Pennsylvania jury recently awarded $34 million in damages—including $31.5 million in punitive damages—based on a story that questioned a prosecutor's handling of a homicide case.[20] A Texas jury recently awarded $29 million, including $17.5 million in punitive damages, because of a series of news broadcasts investigating the activities of a local heart surgeon.[21] You are not consoled.

About a year later, on appeal, the mayor's claim regarding the brother-in-law connection is thrown out and the jury's verdict is reduced to a mere $400,000. (As your lawyer duly notes, a high percentage of judgments are either reversed or modified when appealed.[22]) After paying the judgment and another $50,000 in legal fees, you are free to put your life in order. This will not be easy following your divorce. And your career is in ruins because everyone considers you a walking liability.

This parable demonstrates two things: that libel litigation is a nightmare and that, in many instances, it can be avoided by those who act knowledgeably.

The nightmarish quality of libel litigation has long been recognized. Libel suits have frequently threatened and sometimes dealt terrible blows to the ledgers and reputations of writers and publishers throughout the country. Large corporate defendants like CBS, Inc., The Washington Post and Time, Inc.—who respectively defended suits brought by U.S. General William C. Westmoreland, William P. Tavoulareas, President and Chief Executive of Mobil, and former Israeli Defense Minister, Ariel Sharon—know this well enough. The attorneys' fees alone for the Westmoreland and Sharon libel cases exceeded $15 million.[23]

The threat of litigation is all the more harrowing to the many smaller news-gathering organizations, publishers, and individuals who lack the financial means to defend against a major libel assault. In one well-publicized instance, a small newspaper in Illinois was forced to declare bankruptcy after $9.2 million in damages was awarded in a libel suit against it.[24]

Furthermore, the conservative leanings of the current Supreme Court have heightened fears that the standards of accountability for journalists may soon be tightened. According to some observers, the Court's majority has an "instinct" to read the First Amendment as narrowly as possible; further reduction of the broad protection afforded journalists for the past 25 years seems inevitable.[25] But the rules of libel litigation need not even change for this to occur. The existing standards set by the Supreme Court are often applied loosely by lower courts to favor media defendants. The next libel case could be the one in which the rules are either changed or interpreted more stringently.

The penalties for not learning the lessons of libel law are potentially immense. The resulting pressure is felt acutely by those who every day, under deadline, must make decisions with potential consequences severe enough to cripple both their own careers and the organizations that employ them. They must therefore learn the basics of libel. Even those who can afford expensive legal reviews realize that by reducing the lawyer's job, they also reduce the cost of review. Simple accurate answers about the rules of libel and practical suggestions for limiting risk are absolute necessities.

But libel law is complex. There are confusing terms like "actual malice," "public official" and "public figure" which carry legal meanings that do not match conventional usage. These terms and the rules that accompany them do not easily inform the decisions of lawyers, much less those of lay persons. Rather, they constitute a set of abstract principles that lawyers and judges can contemplate and argue about in the context of lawsuits. The difficulty with the rules is further compounded by the courts' lack of uniformity in their interpretation and application—even when facts are apparently similar. Because of this unpredictability, a clear set of rules must anticipate the vagaries of the legal system *and* allow enough safety space to deter potential claimants at the outset from bringing legal action.

THREE STEPS

The purpose of this book is to furnish that set of rules by training media professionals to avoid potential problems in three steps *before* defamation is published. This book is not an analysis of the law applicable to any particular state. The emphasis will be on general practical approaches to coping with defamation law applicable in all states. Nor is this book limited to the law's imponderable gray areas; the emphasis will be on practical solutions (though some imponderables must be noted along the way). Moreover, this book is not a diatribe against the "chilling effect" that libel litigation has left on the work of journalists. (As one federal judge has noted, a "megaverdict" by a jury "does more than chill an individual defendant's [First Amendment] rights, it deep-freezes that particular media defendant permanently.")[26] Instead, the book will focus on what the law is (and will likely be), and how writers can make use of practical methods to stay within its bounds.

For obvious reasons, the best time to deal with potential defamation comes before a statement is made public. Therefore, the function of this book is to furnish a practical guide for limiting or avoiding defamation lawsuits at the stage when stories are researched, written and edited.[27] This book is not meant to supplant the use of skilled attorneys who can apply the legal rules to a prepublication review with more subtlety and precision. This book will, however, include the general rules of law, the critical areas in which the law is unpredictable and most importantly, it will show how the risk of being sued can be limited or eliminated: *first* by using practical ways of identifying a potential problem, *second* by gathering the proper measure of factual support, and *third* by writing the story to take advantage of the law. These are the Three Steps.

All three are key to avoiding litigation, or at least shortening the length and cost of lawsuits by improving chances of dismissal. This book is organized in three sections to teach each step, one at a time, in order— just as one should prepare and review every story before it is printed or broadcast. In the illustration used above, legal trouble could have been avoided at *each* of the three steps:

First, the journalist could have identified the "sidewalk fraud" libel and avoided it completely. The first section of this book entitled "What to Look For" will show how to identify a libel. The rule here is straight-forward—anything that damages a reputation is potentially libelous not-withstanding the status of the subject, the quality of the source, or the number of sources who say it. Even a journalist's innocent intentions have no bearing insofar as the definition is concerned. Spotting libel takes practice—defamation can hide. Potential defendants and their attorneys must therefore be watchful, particularly for libel's more dangerous va-rieties. Then, they must either eliminate the libel or make sure the proof is adequate.

Proceeding to the second step, the writer in the illustration could have postponed publication until—and unless—he obtained a proper measure of proof. The law forgives mistakes by the media but only when a requisite level of support was in hand at the time of publication or broadcast. This basic requirement applies whether the subject is a private person, a public figure, a public official, or a corporation. The second section of this book entitled "How Much Proof" discusses how much proof is necessary to support a potentially libelous statement. Through examples, the book will show that a common-sense rule is the best: factors such as the degree of potential damage to the subject, the number and reliability of the sources checked, the importance of the story to the public, and the availability of corroboration all must be taken into account.

At the third step, the writer could have avoided the "sidewalk fraud" claim in the illustration had he known enough to cite a special category of source: the administrative or judicial hearing. This is an example of what the third section of this book, "What to Write," will show. It will demonstrate how to write a story—after sufficient proof has been ob-tained—in ways that make the most of available legal defenses. Simple precautions like citing legislative or judicial records and disguising the identities of subjects are but two examples.

This book will discuss, illustrate and emphasize each step so that writers will know what to do almost reflexively under the pressure of deadlines without having to ponder the complexities of the law. Although much of the book recommends the conservative path, the objective is not to restrict journalists to dry and desiccated versions of their former work. Instead, the purpose of this book is to strike a balance between risk and reward and to assure that when journalists choose risk, they do so knowledgeably. Moreover, as Section III discusses, the law makes extra allowances for journalistic color and verve in a variety of circumstances. The journalist simply needs to recognize those circumstances.

There are ''Quick Questions and Short Answers'' in the Appendixes for ready reference at deadline time plus a list of simple Do's and Don'ts. Along the way, the book will offer examples, mostly taken from actual cases, which will illustrate the rules and help them sink in. The examples all have two parts: first the facts accompanied by a question about how the law will be applied and then the answer. Pausing to think about how the rules apply to the facts before proceeding to the answer will enhance considerably what you derive from this book.

As the examples show, libel is serious business but trouble is avoidable. Moreover, the facts of libel cases are often amusing—for everyone not involved in them.

SECTION I

What to Look For

Media professionals know that defamatory language can ignite multi-million dollar litigation, but many have only the vaguest idea of what constitutes a defamation. Journalists may have heard the dictionary definition: defamation is that which brings ill fame, dishonor, disgrace or shame upon another. But many believe exceptions exist depending upon whom the statement concerns, or who makes the statement, or perhaps whether the subject of the defamation is named in the statement.

For example, some writers believe that the mere act of quoting another, as opposed to making a disparaging statement in the context of an editorial, avoids liability; or that citing a source (rather than maintaining anonymity) accomplishes the same; or that citing a particularly knowledgeable source or a public official—or making a statement about a public official or public figure—or recording the opinion of a man-on-the-street—will affect the issue of whether a statement is defamatory or not.

These are all misconceptions. Although privileges exist for publishing defamatory statements—particularly if they are true—none of the factors described above bear upon the fundamental question of whether the statement itself is defamatory. And the writer must realize that all defamatory statements are *potentially* actionable; a reporter may not learn whether a privilege or legal defense exists until after the statement is published. Sometimes it takes a year of pretrial discovery and then a trial and then an appeal before anyone knows for certain.

Identifying defamation is therefore the first order of business. Unfortunately for the writer, defamation is broadly defined, ubiquitous and in many instances, camouflaged. Statements which are not defamatory on their face become so in light of extrinsic facts. Statements which seem innocent standing alone become possessed of defamatory implications when juxtaposed with other facts. Statements can defame without intent. They can defame even without using real names. Statements which allege crimes; diseases; dishonesty; sexual misconduct; religious, racial or ethnic bigotry; poor financial health; unsavory companions; or professional incompetence are both commonplace and particularly risky.

The task of recognizing defamation in all its guises may seem intimidating at first. Much of what journalists write is negative or critical, and much that is negative or critical is potentially defamatory. Intimidation, however, is not the purpose of this first Section. Instead, its aim is to alert writers to the many ways that reputations can be injured so that potentially defamatory statements first can be identified and then given the extra attention they deserve. If the statement is unnecessary as written, it should be modified or removed; if the statement is to be published as written, it should be supported by sufficient proof. Nothing in this first Section is meant to suggest that journalists cannot or should not publish defamatory statements; without them, the Fourth Estate would be dispossessed. Instead, the fundamental principle is that journalists must learn to recognize potentially defamatory statements and treat them with immoderate care—beyond that which applies to nondefamatory facts for which journalistic standards may require only a modicum of support.

Two good reasons compel such treatment. In the first instance, concern for others figures prominently; defamation can hurt people, and the law puts it in the same category of civil law as hit-and-runs and assaults. The second reason is born of self-interest: in many instances, the law will excuse defamatory statements which prove to be false, even when they cause severe injury to people or businesses, but only if the journalist has collected a good deal more than a modicum of proof. The levels of proof required for absolution are addressed in Section II of this book.

Recognizing defamation is the starting point for reducing its risks. A defamatory statement cannot be eliminated, corroborated, or written in a way to take advantage of legal privileges if it passes undetected. A three-step procedure for dealing with defamation therefore begins with ''What to Look For.''

DEFAMATION BROADLY DEFINED

Libel is written defamation. Slander is oral defamation. Defamatory statements made in a television or radio broadcast usually qualify as libel because, like writings, they have broader and longer exposure than the fleeting spoken word.[28] What is defamation?

The definition of a defamatory statement usually contains four elements:

1. It is a statement of fact.

2. It has a tendency to injure reputation or diminish the esteem, respect, good will, or confidence in which the subject is held by at least a substantial and respectable minority.

3. It is made about a living person, corporate entity, or other business unit, without its subject's consent.

4. It is "of and concerning" someone—that is, the subject must be identifiable to a legally significant group even if not explicitly named.

The first requirement, that a defamatory statement be one of "fact," leaves out statements which no one takes seriously, or which cannot be proven true or false. Name-calling, humor and hyperbole, which are not to be taken literally, as well as pure opinion, are not defamatory. Where fact leaves off and this safety zone begins, however, is not always readily apparent. (These distinctions and the legal issues they imply are discussed in Section III, "What to Write.")

The second criterion, respecting injury to reputation and the like, is broad enough to embrace a wide spectrum of statements. Some courts have further embellished this element to include whatever exposes a person to "public hatred, shame, obloquy, contumely, odium, contempt, ridicule, aversion, ostracism, degradation, or disgrace" or otherwise induces "an evil opinion of one in the minds of right-thinking persons and [deprives] . . . one of their confidence and friendly intercourse in society."[29] Added to the list are all statements which deter third persons from associating or dealing with the subject[30] and even statements which merely "excite adverse, derogatory, or unpleasant feelings or opinions" in readers or viewers.[31] Moreover, the standard of what injures reputation, diminishes esteem, respect, good will, or confidence is a moving target to some extent: it can vary from one place to another and from one year to the next.

Whether a statement defames also depends on the sort of people who would give it a defamatory interpretation; if just the subject's friends, or some group with either extreme or insular ideas of what constitutes a good reputation finds it defamatory, the statement may not qualify. On the other hand, everyone in a community—or even a majority—need not think less of a person to make a statement libelous because virtually no conduct is universally disapproved. In fact, even if a very small number of recipients understand the statement to be defamatory, a defendant may still be liable.[32] It takes only an "important and respectable part of the community" reacting reasonably for a statement to fuel a lawsuit; "liability is not a question of a majority vote."[33]

The reputations of the dead are not legally protected;[34] a defamatory statement must concern a living person or, in some instances, a corporation or other business entity. Moreover, if the subject of the defamatory statement has offered it for publication, or otherwise consents to its use, there can be no sustainable lawsuit; consent is a complete defense.[35]

As the fourth criterion indicates, a person can be defamed even if not specifically named. As discussed later in this Section, inadequate disguises and references to groups of people without even naming individuals can result in as much trouble as naming names.

Notice that there is no limitation regarding the form or context of the statement. Cartoons, editorials, photos, headlines, sidebars, photocaptions, promotional excerpts, "teases," letters to the editor, op-ed articles, graphics, classifieds, and display advertisements may all contain defamatory statements. Whether or not the source of the statement is reliable also has no bearing on the definition; a better source, given credit, generally makes the statement *more* damaging. Even a direct quotation which is self-critical, or one which makes a speaker seem mean-spirited or arrogant or unprofessional, can defame.

Note also that truth or falsity of the statement does not bear on the definition. A true statement can be as damaging to reputation as a false one—it is just more deserved. At least when matters of public concern are involved, truth *is* an absolute defense in a libel action against a media defendant, so the media will escape liability either when a report is proven true or (more often) not shown to be false.[36] Yet truth is often elusive, and it could take prolonged litigation and an appeal before the truth wins out, if it wins at all. In short, the writer must hunt down and identify potential defamation even when it is demonstrably true; perhaps the statement is unnecessary to the story, or the *implication* of the true statement cannot be supported by proof, or the statement might be written in another way to avoid the defamatory impact.

Whether or not the subject is a public or private person also has nothing to do with the definition of defamation. Famous persons can be defamed as easily as private persons. General William Westmoreland proved the point to CBS a few years back and Ariel Sharon delivered the same message to *Time* magazine. Whether the subject of the statement is Ralph Nader or Frank Sinatra, the president of the United States or the janitor in an office building has nothing to do with the definition of defamation. Whether the person is public or private pertains only to the standard by which a media defendant might avoid liability (that is, avoid paying damages) if the statement can be proved false. But the rules for avoiding liability come into play only after a lawsuit begins. The first objective must be to avoid inadvertent or unnecessary defamation and thereby avoid litigation completely.

Also notice that the definition makes no mention of whether or not the media defendant is the source of the defamatory statement or is simply quoting someone else. The usual rule is that a repeated statement is "adopted" through repetition, as if the party quoting another had originated the statement. A statement can be just as defamatory—and result in a lawsuit just as surely—whether it appears in a voiceover or in the mouth of an interview subject. For example, Dick Cavett and his program's production company were sued by Lillian Hellman after Mary McCarthy, a guest on Dick Cavett's show, said that everything Ms. Hellman wrote was a lie "including 'and' and 'the.' " Cavett said nothing offensive, but that fact did not save the production company from potential liability.[37]

Whether the work containing the defamation is fictional, based on fact, or nonfiction makes no difference either. If the statement is about a person who can be identified, it presents a problem. In a case based on the motion picture *The Bell Jar*, the plaintiff alleged that a character portrayed as a lesbian in the film was identifiable as herself—even though the character commits suicide and the plaintiff was still alive. The case was ultimately settled but the lesson remains that "fiction" based on the lives of real people requires effective disguises, not just superficial changes.[38] (This too is discussed further in Section III.)

Finally, note that the definition does not require knowledge or intent.

The fact that a writer does not detect a defamatory statement offers no consolation to the person whose reputation has been ruined. Even a media defendant who is completely unaware of the potential for defamation in a report because his values differ from those of some "important, respectable minority" conceivably could be held liable. A media defendant acting without fault will often be excused but the defense of "I didn't mean it" or "I didn't see it" generally offers no easy escape. (See Section II.)

The central point is that any statement which has potential for defaming another (a very broad category) is potentially the basis of a libel suit and must be detected. Then, if the potential defamation is merely the result of an inadvertent juxtaposition, the writer should fix it and if the statement is gratuitous or expendable, the writer should remove it. On the other hand, if the statement is intentional, it may be left undisturbed as long as the writer takes the precautions described in subsequent Sections "How Much Proof" and "What to Write."

The best way to learn the rules of libel is to apply them. In the first instance, we visit the offices of *Defamation Digest* where the *non*defamatory statements are difficult to spot.

"Defamation Digest"

On the list of new monthly magazines is *Defamation Digest* which brings its readers the best of the media's recent defamatory reports. Which of the following does not belong in the magazine?

1. A story about a right-wing group refers to its founder as "the leading anti-Semite in the country." He is also said to resemble Hitler physically and emulate his mannerisms. The article is based on many prior articles (assume 10,000 for purposes of discussion) with the same two allegations. The founder is undisputedly a public figure.

2. Another article about the same right-wing organization includes an interview with a free-lance journalist who says the group's founder "conducts his business by way of conference calls from a public telephone."

3. An article about a woman who sat on a jury in a murder case in which the defendant was acquitted, names the juror and reports that she decided to vote "not guilty" a day or two before jury deliberations began.

statement can also be defamatory, however, in combination with extrinsic facts known to the members of the community who hear or read the statement.[42] The first type of defamation is both easier to spot and more dangerous because when false statements are defamatory on their face, a plaintiff can win his or her case and collect substantial damages without demonstrating any out-of-pocket loss. Mere mental anguish (plus the requisite level of fault on the defendant's part) will entitle the plaintiff to damages.

Among statements which are defamatory on their face there are eight categories which represent time-tested exemplars of statements that defame, and courts are extremely unlikely to accept that statements of this kind do not injure reputation.

Eight specially sensitive categories of defamation are statements which:

1. Impute to another a loathsome disease (like leprosy, VD or AIDS).

2. Accuse another of serious sexual misconduct (this category traditionally applied only to women; it is well on its way to becoming unisex).

3. Impugn another's honesty or integrity.

4. Accuse another of committing a crime, or of being arrested or indicted.

5. Allege racial, ethnic or religious bigotry.

6. Impugn another's financial health or credit-worthiness.

7. Accuse another of associating with criminals or other unsavory characters.

8. Assert incompetence or lack of ability in one's trade, business, profession or office.

Statements imputing loathsome diseases are easy to spot. Statements in the second category, which charge sexual misconduct, are also easy to detect but not every writer recognizes their risk. Some believe that in these sexually liberated times, the defamatory sting of such remarks has been neutralized. Do not count on it. At the very least, a statement imputing adultery or even premarital sex is likely to go to a jury to determine its effect on the relevant community. And the vote of a jury is never a certainty.

Statements which impugn honesty or integrity or allege arrest or indictment are usually apparent. But statements which allege criminal activity are sometimes less obvious than one might think. Though crimes like murder, bribery, theft, and embezzlement jump off the page, there are many other crimes in the book. A recent case involving *Penthouse* publisher Robert Guccione illustrates the point and also shows why charges of adultery should not be treated lightly.

When *Hustler* published that Guccione was both married and had a "live-in girlfriend," Guccione sued. A federal court in New York City held that having sexual intercourse with another person when one has a living spouse violates New York Penal Law, Section 255.17 and Guccione was therefore defamed by the accusation of a crime. *Hustler*'s lawyers argued that while adultery is indictable, the offense is "so commonplace and so infrequently enforced that it should not be considered a crime for the purposes of libel law." The federal judge sitting in the modern Sodom refused to accept that adultery was "so insignificant" until "either the courts or legislature of New York indicate otherwise." (An appellate court did reverse the decision, but only because in Mr. Guccione's case, the statement was substantially true and, in view of his notoriety, did no harm to *his* reputation.)[43]

Allegations of bigotry, financial instability, and unsavory social companions are not difficult to find. On the other hand, injuring others in their trade, business, or profession is a deceptively broad category. For example, to assert that a section of a new hospital is "plagued with air conditioning problems relating to the design of the system" would injure the building's architect in his profession.[44] And suits based on statements in this category frequently come from unexpected sources. For example, a high school football coach sued a daily newspaper which assailed him for verbally abusing his players from the sidelines with exhortations like "Come on, get your head out of your &!(!!(&." The coach successfully argued that the description of the abusive, vulgar and profane language attributed to him was false and defamatory in that it cast doubt on his "fitness for his profession." The fact that the coach was considered a "public figure" for purposes of the suit did not alter the defamatory character of the newspaper's statement.[45]

In another celebrated case, a newspaper cartoon was found to be defamatory which depicted a professional psychic in a bizarre costume, seated in bed with charts on her lap. The court said the cartoon implied that the plaintiff had no skill in her chosen profession.[46] In New York, two ABC executives were accused by a lawyer of trying to embarrass the president of the company to gain better jobs for themselves. The executives filed claims and successfully argued that the lawyer's statements injured them in their profession by raising questions of ''professional impropriety.''[47]

Professional integrity can also be damaged indirectly. Consider what can go wrong when key facts are misstated:

"The Overpaid Expert"

A research physician testified as an expert witness in a lawsuit brought by persons with birth defects blamed upon a controversial drug. In an article written in *Science* magazine, the fee for the physician's appearance was quoted at $5,000. The article contrasted the fees paid to other experts: $250 to $500 a day, or, at most, $1,000 a day.

The doctor was actually paid $1,116 per day. Why does he have a libel claim?

"The Overpaid Expert"
(Answer)

An appellate court in the District of Columbia said the reporting of the fee was potentially libelous, particularly because of the direct comparison with the other experts. The court reasoned: "It is possible that a reader might conclude that plaintiffs' case was so weak they had to pay that much to get any expert to testify, and hence that Dr. McBride's testimony was for sale."[48]

The careful professional would have noticed first that the statement about the fee—if incorrect—would impugn the scientist's professional integrity. The next step should have been double-checking the facts.

The same procedure applies regardless of the subject matter of the article, be it a lawsuit over a drug, or a report on a political race:

"Who's The Boss?"

The chairman of the executive committee of the third largest drug store chain in the country resigned his job to run for governor. The candidate, whom we will call Lew, had been with the chain 18 years and served as president during eight of them.

Lew's former brother-in-law, Alex, who founded the drug store chain, had always held the position of chief executive officer. Alex sued for libel after reading the following quote from an interview with a man who had formerly been associated with the chain:

> Lew took a sleepy little company and breathed life into it. ... It was Lew's genius that took [the drug store chain] from being nothing into being really big. This is a pattern for companies. Many people play key roles but it was Lew who made it go while Alex minded the store back home.

What if anything is defamatory?

"Who's The Boss?"
(Answer)

A federal court found that the words quoted in the interview "clearly could be understood to disparage [Alex] in his business." The judge decided that a reader could reasonably interpret an assertion that Lew was the key to the tremendous success of the drug store chain and that Alex was "simply the plodding, uncreative bookkeeper who 'minded the store back home.' " Calling the chain a "sleepy little company" suggested it was "financially stagnant at the time [Lew] joined it and, more important, that it would not have become the success it did had [Lew] not come along." A reader could therefore "reasonably conclude that [Alex's] talents as a businessman were lacking and that his position as chief executive officer ... was little more than that of a figurehead."[49]

That Alex took offense should have surprised no one; that the article defamed him might have surprised its authors; that he brought a lawsuit must have put some people into shock. The point here is that each potentially defamatory statement must be located and weighed before it is printed—particularly when it falls into one of the clear-cut categories. Can it be eliminated? If so, eliminate it. Otherwise, make sure it is both supported by proper proof and written to take advantage of whatever legal privileges may exist (as discussed later).

STATEMENTS NOT DEFAMATORY ON THEIR FACE

Lawsuits based on statements which are not defamatory on their face and require extrinsic information to establish defamatory meaning are more difficult for plaintiffs to win. In such instances, the plaintiff must show actual out-of-pocket loss as a result of the statement instead of the mere mental anguish and embarrassment which suffice for statements which are self-evidently defamatory. Though media defendants may derive some advantage from this requirement, they may lose at least as much ground as they gain because statements of this kind can defame even when they appear innocent of disparaging content.

A classic illustration is the statement "Ms. Ledbetter is pregnant." If at least a respectable minority of the community knows that Ms. Ledbetter is unmarried, this extrinsic fact would make such a seemingly innocent statement defamatory. Furthermore, the statement would fall into one of the eight particularly sensitive categories by imputing sexual misconduct. One might argue, of course, that the stigma of having children out of wedlock is a thing of the past and the statement lacks defamatory meaning. But as noted above, this question could be one for the jury—not the writer. The writer must be on guard to identify the potentially defamatory statement and act to reduce the risk of liability.

Since a 1974 Supreme Court decision,[50] the media have enjoyed an additional advantage with respect to this type of defamation: the complaining plaintiff must show some measure of *fault* on the part of the defendant. Therefore, if the content of a factual misstatement does not warn a reasonably prudent editor or broadcaster of its defamatory potential, the defendant might be relieved of liability. However (as discussed further later on) issues like what a reasonably prudent editor or broadcaster should have spotted are the stuff of lawsuits,[51] and *potential* for litigation should be avoided whenever possible.

Sometimes particular prudence is required of those who report about specialized areas such as business, finance, law or medicine. Consider the following hypothetical example:

"The Guarantee"

Pop's Grocery Store, which had been faltering in recent years, owed money to Wheelwright Dairy. A business reporter doing a story on the demise of small businesses in town interviewed Wheelwright who said he was not worried about being paid by Pop because the chief loan officer at National Bank guaranteed Pop's debts. The reporter included Wheelwright's statement in his article without further investigation.

The Chairman of National Bank read the article and promptly fired the loan officer; it appears the bank had a strict policy against guarantees of this kind. The loan officer, who denied making any guarantee, sued for defamation.

What happened?

"The Guarantee"
(Answer)

The statement that the bank guaranteed Pop's obligations is not defamatory on its face, but in view of the bank's rule against obligations of this kind, the statement defamed the loan officer by stating that he violated a company policy and caused his termination. The loan officer can therefore show direct pecuniary loss and overcome the first hurdle which applies to statements that are not defamatory on their face.

But was the reporter negligent in quoting Wheelwright without further investigation? In other words, should the reporter have spotted the potentially defamatory impact of the statement?

The answer is yes to both questions; business reporters should know that loan officers are not usually in the business of guaranteeing the debts of small grocery stores.[52]

Are reporters expected to be omniscient? As the Supreme Court has held, the First Amendment precludes this expectation. However, reporters are expected to find what is reasonably defamatory, and this requirement applies even when the words, standing alone, are not.

IMPLICATION

The writer must also beware of the implication of statements—that is, the interpretation which the reasonable recipient may be expected to give them. A writer can defame through implication even when the facts stated in the text, or headline, or photo caption, or voiceover, are true. The question becomes: Are the *implied* facts true?[53]

Defamation through implication tends to arise in three contexts, with some overlap among them: when the writer tries to guide the reader to a conclusion without stating it expressly; when the writer writes ambiguously, offering multiple meanings, of which at least one is defamatory[54]; and when the writer juxtaposes one message with another thereby creating an implication which is not always even intended. Each of these three contexts deserves careful examination.

Deliberate Implication

The first context often involves the reporter who tries to avoid an outright defamatory accusation by deliberately seeding a report with selected facts. The apparent expectation is that a defamatory conclusion not specifically made in the report will sprout in the mind of the reader or viewer. Many writers and editors believe this technique will shield them from liability. In most instances it will not.

For example, a newspaper reporting on the relationship between a legislator and the insurance industry said:

> [We have] learned that on June 7, 1983, Senator Williams opened an account (number 14952) at the First Federal Savings of Puerto Rico branch in St. Thomas. The initial deposit was $5,500. Over the next two months the bank balance rose to $85,000. The withdrawals from the account included a certificate of deposit (number 69054563) in the amount of $25,500. A Virgin Island's senator's yearly salary is $25,000.

Senator Williams filed suit, complaining that the quotation conveyed a defamatory implication that he had been "paid off." The court said he was absolutely right and concluded, "[t]he specific statement and the article in general clearly implied that . . . Senator Williams was receiving large sums of money from business interests seeking to affect the legislative process. The suggestion of corruption could easily be gleaned from the publication."[55]

''Being cute'' may bring ratings and readership, but not the avoidance of a libel suit. Consider the following two examples:

"Geraldo on Jai Alai"

Geraldo Rivera is reporting on jai-alai frontons in a story not so subtly entitled "Jai-Alai: License to Steal." Mr. Rivera, in reporting the destruction of a fronton by an arsonist, lists four "coincidences": (1) the insurance coverage "just happened to be exactly equal" to the estimate of the damage; (2) the owner of the fronton "just happened" to increase his coverage from $4 million to $8 million (the estimated cost of the damage) several months before the fire; (3) the insurance agent who sold the policy to the owner is the brother of the manager of the fronton; and (4) despite a finding of arson, the insurance company "paid up on the policy in full."

Nowhere in the report did Mr. Rivera directly accuse the fronton owner of committing arson. Are these statements defamatory?

"Geraldo on Jai Alai"
(Answer)

Of course these statements are defamatory! Together they imply that the fronton owner had committed arson-related crimes.

The trial court held that "a viewer might well understand these statements to mean that plaintiffs had participated in various crimes such as arson and burning to defraud. The deliberate ambiguity of the word 'coincidence' is telling: an obvious implication that these were *not* coincidences."[56] Note that the report also falls into one of libel's sensitive categories: accusation of a crime (see pages 9–10 above).

"For Whom Charges Loom"

A taxpayers' association led by Lawrence, the group's president, and Simpson, its secretary treasurer, conducted a campaign opposing a municipal appropriation for the construction of a new

firehouse. The group circulated petitions to force a public referendum and obtained over 5,000 signatures. Soon after, the local
newspaper received a telephone call from the city's Business Administrator. He said that there were "irregularities" in some of
the signatures on the petitions and that the City Prosecutor was
conducting an investigation to determine whether there were
incidents of forgery or false swearing in connection with the signatures, adding that the investigation included signatures wit-
nessed by Lawrence and Simpson.

Two days later the following headline spanned the entire eight
columns of the newspaper's front page: "CITY ATTORNEY RULES
ASSOCIATION PETITIONS IMPROPER; FORGERY CHARGES MAY
LOOM FOR LAWRENCE, SIMPSON." The accompanying article
said that the prosecutor "was asked to take action by city officials
against association leaders because of 'irregularities' in the petitions," and reported other disclosures from the Business Administrator.

Is this defamatory? Is it susceptible of more than one meaning?

"For Whom Charges Loom"
(Answer)

The court found that the article was indeed defamatory, accusing the defendants of having committed a crime (one of the
particularly sensitive categories). The court concluded that the
"unambiguous import" of the reports was to "cast doubt on the
reputations of the plaintiffs, Lawrence and Simpson," and the
statement that they "may be" charged with criminal conduct "diminishes their standing in the community" to about the same
degree as an assertion that they had actually been charged with
crimes. In short, the articles were not susceptible of a meaning
that was *not* defamatory.[57]

A media defendant also may be held responsible for quoting someone
else's implication. In one case, a murder victim's father had the following
to say about another murder victim's father: that he refused to be examined
while under a truth serum, that he had employed an attorney the year
before, that he and his attorney had refused to cooperate with the murder

investigation, and that, furthermore, "the Fifth Amendment in our Constitution [was not] . . . intended . . . as a technicality to hide behind in a matter as serious as this, when your own child has been murdered." The interviewee concluded: "The public is free to draw their own conclusion." The court also drew its own conclusion: that the language broadcast was "to say the least . . . susceptible of the inference that [the silent father] was either guilty of the murders of the teenagers or was withholding information relevant to the commission of the crimes." The interviewee "intended that the public draw a conclusion from the broadcast other than the literal meaning" of his remarks by saying "the public is free to draw their own conclusion."[58]

Note that the broadcaster derived no protection from quoting a third party, even one who was intimately involved with the investigation in question; also note that the interviewee accused the other father of committing a crime, which should have alerted the broadcaster at the outset.

Dual Meanings

A second type of implication is one that does not deliberately suggest a defamatory meaning but rather offers two or more meanings, at least one of which is defamatory. Many implications of this kind are intentional, as if the coy dual meaning could undo a defamation. Optimism of this sort is unfounded. Legally speaking, implications through dual meanings are no better than deliberate implications; when a jury is asked to decide whether or not the statement is defamatory, it is likely to find it so.

"Torture Alleged by Playboy"

An article appearing in *Playboy* magazine entitled "Thirty-Six Hours at Santa Fe" focused on a state corrections official who had been stationed in Uruguay and Panama during the 1960's:

[The official] had spent 17 years in the U.S. Office of Public Safety (OPS), a CIA-inspired program established in the late Fifties to advise foreign police in suppressing political dissent in Latin America and elsewhere—and then abolished . . . 20 years later amid well-documented charges of U.S. complicity in torture and political terror.

The article then described how the police tortured political prisoners in Uruguay, Brazil and elsewhere: "Stripped, beaten, sexually abused, tortured under water and on racks, burned with electric needles under fingernails, shocked with electrical wires . . . the victims described their agonies in accounts that repeatedly implicated the OPS." The article asserted that "numerous reports of atrocity" were collected during the period of the official's career and that his office "was on the first floor of the Montevideo *jefatura*, where torture reportedly took place and the screams of the victims reverberated, who by his own account had intimate and influential relations with the Uruguayan police. . . . " The article did not directly assert that the official participated in—or even knew of—any of the torture. Was the article defamatory?

"Torture Alleged by Playboy"
(Answer)

The court concluded that the statements were susceptible of defamatory interpretation. On one hand, they could imply "no more than that [the official] was in a position to know about torture conducted in the countries where he served," but on the other hand might be interpreted to charge him with "complicity in that torture."[59] This example also illustrates, once again, that it makes no difference in the definition of defamation whether the subject of the statement is a private individual or a public official.

Juxtapositions

A subspecies of dual meanings is the third type of implication: juxtapositions. These implications can be intentional or inadvertent and derive from combinations of words with words or words with pictures or pictures with pictures. Identifying inadvertent juxtapositions can require extremely close attention—the kind of attention that the persons portrayed will give to news reports.

One of the more common types of defamation through juxtaposition comes from the use of innocent bystanders to illustrate stories with which they would rather not be associated. For example, a candid photograph of a couple having their luggage examined by customs agents bore the caption "Customs Inspectors are on the job when ships reach port. They have an uncanny knowledge of hiding places." The photo appeared in a book entitled "Our G-Men" which was "devoted to the exploits of notorious criminals against the laws of the United States and the activities of Federal agencies engaged in law enforcement." There was no apparent intent to portray the couple as smugglers; rather, the caption writer probably wanted to illustrate a point being made in the article and casually chose a photograph of officers at work. Yet the juxtaposition of the innocent photograph with the accusatory caption resulted in a lawsuit. The court found that the couple had, in fact, stated a valid claim for libel because the caption could be read to imply that the customs inspectors had detected concealed merchandise in their luggage.[60]

Similar results can flow from an inadvertent substitution of one photograph for another or a misidentification. In a South Carolina court proceeding, a character witness appeared on behalf of a woman who pleaded guilty to bank embezzlement. Leaving the courtroom after testifying, the witness saw news photographers and covered her face. That night, the local television news aired the story about the embezzler's sentencing and showed the character witness hiding her face without identifying her. The witness sued, claiming an implication that she was the embezzler (and note the particularly sensitive category of criminal conduct). The witness recovered $45,000 in punitive damages and an appellate court affirmed the award.[61]

Shots of "local color" are another rich source of defamatory juxtapositions. Stories need visuals and a sense of the local community is often an integral element. But consider an article about a "lawless" gang of youths who spent much of their time "standing around on the streets, looking longingly through tavern windows" and were held responsible for beating two older men. Accompanying the story was a shot of three teenagers standing outside a printing shop with a relatively innocent caption, "Teens linger here until 11:00 or 12:00 P.M." If the teens depicted were not involved in beatings or youth gangs, they have a defamation action because the juxtaposition of the shot, the caption, and most importantly the topic of the story, could impute involvement in the gang.[62]

For local color purposes, it is tempting to pick a shot of a location related to a story no matter who is in it. Witty but sloppy captions invite further trouble.

"Small Fry But Not Fishy"

A local newspaper photographer took a picture of a fisherman while he was unloading a catch of crabs on the Boston Fish Pier. A few days later the picture appeared as a human interest item in the newspaper and the fisherman registered no complaint. Some years later, however, the picture reappeared in *Forbes* to illustrate a short article on the relatively weak presence of organized crime in wholesale fish markets outside of New York. The caption for the photo read: "The Boston Fish Pier: smaller fry in a fishy business." Is this juxtaposition, which draws attention to the location of the shot, a show of wit or a libel or both?

"Small Fry But Not Fishy"
(Answer)

Although a photograph of a fisherman unloading a catch of crabs is not itself defamatory, taken together with the caption and the subject matter of the article, it could be. A reasonable person might see no more than a stock picture of a fisherman on the Boston Fish Pier; but the context could suggest that the man was one of the "smaller fry" involved with organized crime. [63]

The risks of defamatory juxtapositions are compounded in television broadcast news. Cameras are rarely on hand when a news event takes place, and a story needs something visual besides talking heads. Stories with abstract subject matter must also be illustrated. Complexities multiply when broadcast stories are assembled: narration is constantly edited; visuals are often added or subtracted at the last minute; and the marriage of visuals and narration usually occurs at a relatively late stage of the process. Broadcast stories must be put together with great care notwithstanding the pressure of deadlines.

Take for example a medical report on the evening news about a disease affecting millions, illustrated with shots of passers-by. In the six o'clock report, no defamatory meaning was implied: the report began with a panning shot down a busy street in downtown Washington. The camera closed in on pedestrians standing on a street corner behind the reporter, and then zoomed in on one woman who turned and looked in the direction of the camera. At the conclusion of the shot the correspondent standing in the foreground began her introduction of the report on treatment of herpes.

When viewed as a whole, this treatment of the female passer-by who looked toward the camera would probably not cause a reasonable viewer to infer that she suffered from the disease. For the eleven o'clock report, however, an edited version was substituted: the on-the-street reporter was dropped and the anchor read a shortened version of the report illustrated with the footage of the same pedestrians. And just when viewers saw the close up of the same woman turning directly towards the camera, pausing, and walking away, the anchor made reference to "the 20 million Americans who have herpes." The passer-by sued (not overlooking the particularly sensitive category of imputation of a loathsome disease), and the court found potential defamation in the eleven o'clock report.[64]

The words and pictures or words and words juxtaposed in a story do not have to be precisely contemporaneous to achieve a defamatory effect. Sometimes the use of a photograph early in a story, combined with a voiceover or interview comment later on, will also defame. The journalist may find this type of juxtaposition more difficult to detect—or may, in fact, arrange the story this way under the mistaken impression that defamatory implications can be avoided.

"A Story About Prostitutes"

One of the networks broadcast a documentary entitled "Sex For Sale: The Urban Battleground." The program showed how sex-related businesses affect local communities, leading in many instances to an increase in street prostitution. At one point, the program focused on how residents of a middle-class community felt the impact of street prostitution in their neighborhood, and the accompanying visuals showed three women walking down a local street. Two were middle-aged and heavy-set, carrying packages. The third, a young black woman, attractive and stylishly attired, was subsequently shown alone in closeup while the voice-over stated: "But for black women whose homes were there, the cruising white customers were an especially humiliating experience."

Seconds later, another black female resident appeared on screen and stated: "Almost any woman who was black and on the street was considered to be a prostitute herself. And was treated like a prostitute."

Assume everything in the commentary and narration was correct. What, if anything, is wrong?

"A Story About Prostitutes"
(Answer)

The appellate court refused to find that these statements were *not* capable of having a defamatory meaning, given the program's topic (street prostitution), and the contrast between the attractive woman in the shot and the matronly figures who preceded her. The implication in the narration that the attractive woman was just a resident ("black women whose homes were there . . . ") was "negated" by the juxtaposition of the resident's comment which immediately followed about prostitutes. It was left for the jury to decide whether the broadcast was defamatory.[65]

Avoiding juxtapositions is therefore both necessary and difficult. Having reviewed a few simple examples, try the next one, which offers at least seven potential defamations, mostly from juxtapositions.

"The Story of Klondike"

Visuals	Narration
Still photo: Klondike walking a dog.	FRED KLONDIKE WAS SEEN MEETING WITH KNOWN MOBSTERS BEFORE HIS DISAPPEARANCE.

Home movie: Klondike entering restaurant with unidentified man.

BECAUSE NO ONE HAS SEEN KLONDIKE FOR FIVE YEARS, HE IS PRESUMED DEAD. THIS HOME MOVIE (WITH KLONDIKE ON THE LEFT) WAS MADE ABOUT FIVE YEARS AGO.

Four unidentified people standing around a gaming table; one of them is rolling dice.

MEANWHILE, IN KLONDIKE'S CASINO, HIGH ROLLERS HAVE BEEN DROPPING AS MUCH AS $20,000 IN A SINGLE NIGHT. IN A JANUARY REPORT, THE DEPARTMENT OF JUSTICE ESTIMATED THAT THE CASINO GROSSES $20 MILLION A YEAR AND THAT ONE THIRD IS SKIMMED OFF BY THE MOB.

Photograph of bald man in tuxedo (Jack Gold) carrying sacks through a reinforced door entitled "Cashier's Office."

IN KLONDIKE'S ABSENCE, HIS HAND-PICKED MANAGER, JACK GOLD, HAS BEEN OVERSEEING OPERATIONS. HE REFUSES TO COMMENT ON ALLEGED IRREGULARITIES AT THE CASINO.

Jack Gold gesturing menacingly toward the camera.

GOLD HAS NOT YET BEEN INDICTED AND REMAINS A HIGHLY VISIBLE FIGURE.

Crew exiting in haste.

IN FACT, LAST MONTH HE REMARKED PUBLICLY, "THERE ARE OTHER CASINOS IN TOWN WITH FRAUDULENT PRACTICES. GO BOTHER THEM!"

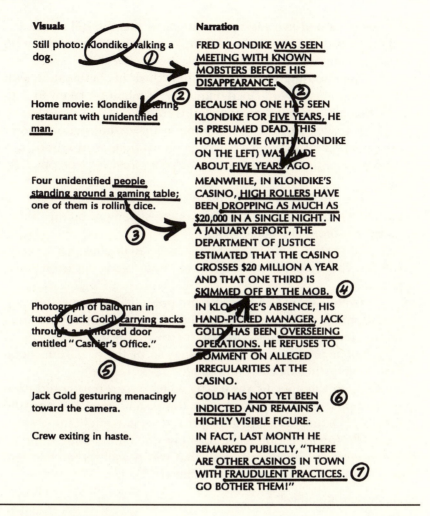

Visuals

Still photo: Klondike walking a dog.

Home movie: Klondike entering restaurant with <u>unidentified man.</u>

Four unidentified <u>people standing around a gaming table;</u> one of them is rolling dice.

Photograph of bald man in tuxedo (Jack Gold) carrying sacks through a reinforced door entitled "Cashier's Office."

Jack Gold gesturing menacingly toward the camera.

Crew exiting in haste.

Narration

FRED KLONDIKE <u>WAS SEEN MEETING WITH KNOWN MOBSTERS BEFORE HIS DISAPPEARANCE.</u>

BECAUSE NO ONE HAS SEEN KLONDIKE FOR <u>FIVE YEARS,</u> HE IS PRESUMED DEAD. THIS HOME MOVIE (WITH KLONDIKE ON THE LEFT) WAS MADE ABOUT <u>FIVE YEARS</u> AGO.

MEANWHILE, IN KLONDIKE'S CASINO, <u>HIGH ROLLERS</u> HAVE BEEN <u>DROPPING AS MUCH AS $20,000 IN A SINGLE NIGHT.</u> IN A JANUARY REPORT, THE DEPARTMENT OF JUSTICE ESTIMATED THAT THE CASINO GROSSES $20 MILLION A YEAR AND THAT ONE THIRD IS <u>SKIMMED OFF BY THE MOB.</u>

IN KLONDIKE'S ABSENCE, HIS HAND-PICKED MANAGER, JACK GOLD, HAS BEEN <u>OVERSEEING OPERATIONS.</u> HE REFUSES TO COMMENT ON ALLEGED IRREGULARITIES AT THE CASINO.

GOLD HAS <u>NOT YET BEEN INDICTED</u> AND REMAINS A HIGHLY VISIBLE FIGURE.

IN FACT, LAST MONTH HE REMARKED PUBLICLY, "THERE ARE <u>OTHER CASINOS</u> IN TOWN WITH <u>FRAUDULENT PRACTICES.</u> GO BOTHER THEM!"

"The Story of Klondike"
(Answer)

1. Accusing Klondike of consorting with known mobsters is potentially defamatory of Klondike, assuming Klondike is alive at the time the documentary is broadcast. (As noted above, the dead cannot be defamed.)

2. The implication here is that the "unidentified man" is a known mobster. Just before the man appears on screen, the narration states that Klondike was meeting with known mobsters just before his disappearance. The subsequent narration, referring as

it does to "about five years ago," suggests that the still photo was taken immediately preceding Klondike's disappearance, when he was meeting with known mobsters.

3. The photograph of the four individuals in combination with the narration is potentially defamatory: it might be taken to suggest that all four persons depicted were high stakes gamblers.

4. The allegation of wrongdoing at the casino is defamatory on its face and not because of juxtaposition. Attribution to a Justice Department report is very helpful, however (see pp. 129–134).

5. The juxtaposition of the picture showing Gold carrying money with the immediately preceding statement about "skimming" is potentially defamatory.

6. To say that Gold has not been indicted implies that he soon will be. This defamation arises from implication, not from juxtaposition.

7. To the extent Gold's comment potentially defames his own casino, the defense of consent ought to apply. But if there are a small number of other casinos in town, the comment about "fraudulent practices" might defame all of them. (Group defamation is further discussed on pages 32–33 below.)

Although the specific means by which this report could have been defused would depend on the visuals available and the results of factual research, an improved version might look something like the following. (The opening statement about Klondike is not changed on the premise that it is a well-researched fact which the journalist *intends* to publish.)

"The Story of Klondike"
(Revised)

Visuals	**Narration**
Still photo: Klondike walking a dog.	FRED KLONDIKE WAS SEEN MEETING WITH KNOWN MOBSTERS BEFORE HIS DISAPPEARANCE.
Home movie: Klondike entering restaurant.	BECAUSE NO ONE HAS SEEN KLONDIKE FOR FIVE YEARS, HE IS PRESUMED DEAD. THIS HOME MOVIE WAS MADE ABOUT FIVE YEARS AGO.

Four unidentified people standing around a gaming table; one of them is rolling dice.	MEANWHILE, KLONDIKE'S CASINO CONTINUES TO ATTRACT MORE THAN 5,000 PATRONS PER DAY. IN A JANUARY REPORT, THE DEPARTMENT OF JUSTICE ESTIMATED THAT THE CASINO GROSSES $20 MILLION A YEAR AND THAT ONE THIRD IS SKIMMED OFF BY THE MOB.
Photograph of bald man in tuxedo (Jack Gold) walking from his car into casino.	IN KLONDIKE'S ABSENCE, THE CASINO'S MANAGER HAS BEEN JACK GOLD. HE REFUSES TO COMMENT ON ALLEGED IRREGULARITIES AT THE CASINO.
Jack Gold gesturing menacingly toward the camera.	TWO YEARS AGO, A GRAND JURY REFUSED TO INDICT GOLD ON CHARGES OF BANK FRAUD. HE REMAINS A HIGHLY VISIBLE FIGURE.
Crew exiting in haste.	HOWEVER, HE USUALLY DECLINES TO GIVE INTERVIEWS TO THE PRESS.

In summary, context is critical. In searching for potentially defamatory statements, reporters must be alert to any nuance of offense and mindful of the particularly risky categories. There is more to the task than scrutinizing a report phrase by phrase, sentence by sentence, image by image. Statements must be read in the context of the story as a whole—just as readers and viewers will interpret them.

DEFAMING UNINTENDED PERSONS

As these examples suggest (and as noted at the outset), defamation does not have to be intentional to be actionable under law. In a lawsuit resulting from a defamatory statement, the plaintiff must show that the defamation is "of and concerning" him or her. Therefore, the question

"Whom was the statement about?" is primary. But the test is not "To whom was the statement intended to pertain?" but rather, "To whom does the audience think the statement pertains?"[66] This point is sometimes made with the observation, "[t]he question is not so much who was aimed at, as who was hit."[67]

The entire audience need not make the association before the aggrieved subject has a defamation action. The libel must merely designate the subject in such a way as to let those who know him or her or it make the identification. The whole world does not have to share in that knowledge.[68]

Statements can be defamatory even when they are meant to describe one person in neutral terms but are reasonably interpreted by a *respectable segment of the community* to apply to someone else. Returning for a moment to the pregnant Ms. Ledbetter: to say she is expecting would have no apparent defamatory meaning if she had a living husband. But if there are two Ms. Ledbetters in town and the writer correctly makes the statement about one but gives the address of the other, who has no husband, the consequences can be serious. Putting the wrong picture over the name of a crook, or (as described above) suggesting that an innocent witness is the person being tried, can lead to similar problems.

"The Ad in *TV Guide*"

TV Guide magazine accepted an advertisement submitted for publication by WXIA-TV of Atlanta to promote a special feature on the late news. The heading of the ad asked in bold letters: "Guess What Lori Found Out Today." A photograph of a diary in the middle of the advertisement answered the question with the following handwritten entry: "Dear Diary: I found out today I'm pregnant. What will I do now?" Directly below the diary was a photograph of a teenage girl embracing a young man. The bottom quarter of the ad offered details about the upcoming series on teenage pregnancies.

The girl in the ad whose name was Libby Sue (not Lori) sued the publishers of *TV Guide* and the station over the implication that she was pregnant. She asserted not only that was she not pregnant—and never was—but also that she never engaged in sexual relations with the young man in the photograph or, for that matter, anyone else.

In trying to have the suit dismissed, *TV Guide* argued that the girl's name was different, thereby avoiding identification, and the photograph, depicting as it did "two wholesome, smiling young people," was not offensive. Besides, the magazine argued, they saw no substantial danger to Libby Sue's reputation in the ad.

Was the advertisement defamatory?

"The Ad in *TV Guide*"
(Answer)

The Supreme Court of Georgia agreed with the trial judge that the ad was defamatory and the defendants were liable. Finding no merit in the "wholesomeness" argument, the court decided that substantial danger to reputation was apparent (whether *TV Guide* saw it or not), and that the photograph could be interpreted to depict Libby Sue as "Lori," notwithstanding the fictitious name.[69]

Note again the risky category of sexual impropriety, and that accepting a prepared ad from a regular advertiser did not automatically excuse *TV Guide* for the defamation.

In another case, the UPI reported an Iowa woman's arrest for indecent exposure and accurately named the woman, one Phyllis V. Hamilton. However, the story also said she was married to Jack Hamilton, owner of nightclubs in certain locations. Mr. Hamilton, who was not married to Phyllis, sued; so did his wife, Janyce D. (not to be confused with Phyllis) who was not arrested for anything. On the dubious principle that we are not judged on the behavior of our relatives, Mr. Hamilton's claim was lost. However, his real wife, Janyce D. Hamilton, stated a good claim because readers might think she was accused of the crime even though her name was not Phyllis.[70]

DEFAMING WITHOUT NAMING AT ALL

As certain of the examples above also illustrate, one need not name names to make a defamatory statement. Libby Sue, the couple waiting for the customs inspector, the women passers-by, the innocent witness, the fisherman unloading crabs in Boston, and the "other casinos" with fraudulent practices, were all defamed even without being named. The reason? A respectable segment of the community could identify them— that is, recognize the statement as "of and concerning" the complaining parties—without need for names.

Calling an unidentified policeman drunk on his beat at the corner of Madison and Main will defame him just as surely as if he were specifically named. To say that a health club is "totally mismanaged" entitles the manager to sue.[71] To assert that an unnamed theatrical producer reneged on his contract with a particular actress still defames the producer.[72] To use a model's picture without permission on the cover of a book concerning the Antichrist has been found capable of creating the reputation-wrecking impression that he was "branded with the 'Mark of the Beast' " even without the use of his name.[73]

As the real Mrs. Hamilton demonstrated, familial connections can also bridge the gap between defamatory statements and unnamed victims. To say a boy who died of a drug overdose was born out of wedlock would not defame him because the dead cannot be defamed; however, his living mother might have a claim even without naming her. Reporting that a suicidal son "might have fared better if his family had not abandoned him" will defame his surviving mother and sister.[74] And care must always be taken when a child or adult claims to be a victim of abuse even if the apparently responsible parent, spouse or significant other is left unnamed.

The potential for trouble exists even when the statement about the named family member (as opposed to the unnamed and defamed relative) might in some circles be considered complimentary.

"Elvis's No. 1 Girl"

Prior to Elvis Presley's death, a Memphis newspaper reported in its "People" column:

> FLICKERING FLAME: Back in 1957, Susanna Kent, who came from Jackson . . . was Elvis Presley's "No. 1 girl." This week as Elvis closed his month-long show at the Las Vegas Hilton, Miss Kent stopped by the hotel for what appeared to be a "reunion" of two old friends. Elvis recently filed for divorce from his wife of five years, Priscilla.

Susanna, who was not a single woman, and not in Las Vegas anywhere near the date reported, sued. Her husband sued too. Were they both defamed?

"Elvis's No. 1 Girl"
(Answer)

Both were defamed. Because of the implication that Ms. Kent was openly involved in a relationship with a married man who was not her husband, the article injured her reputation. (Note again, both the particularly sensitive category of sexual impropriety and the effects of implication.) Though her husband was one step removed from that implication, he too was defamed: the implication that he had been "cuckolded" exposed him to public contempt and ridicule, though not necessarily reflecting on his integrity or moral character. (This example also illustrates how a relative of the person to whom the article refers can be injured unwittingly.)[75]

As this example again shows, it can be difficult to foresee the range of targets who might be hit by a potentially defamatory statement, particularly if those targets are unnamed. But the potential defamation—like the implication of illicit affairs—can usually be identified and should be handled with care.

Another way of defaming unnamed persons is to disguise the subject of a defamatory story *without completely succeeding*. This may be accomplished either in fiction or nonfiction.

In nonfiction, the change of names for the subjects of anecdotal stories is a common device and a useful one. The author's objective might be to avoid legal difficulties, such as defamation, or to comply with an agreement to change the names and conceal the identities of the subjects of the story. In fiction—especially when writers draw from their own experiences—the goal is the same: to bury the identities of real people used as models in order to avoid trouble. In fiction or nonfiction, it serves no purpose to change names and a few biographical details if the story's audience can still recognize the subject from other clues. The key is to change identifying details so completely that no one can reasonably recognize the actual person. Otherwise, insofar as defamation law is concerned, the subject might just as well be mentioned by name. (Recommended ways of disguising identities are presented in Section III of this book at pages 123–128.)

GROUP DEFAMATION

Yet another way to injure someone without mentioning his or her name is to defame generally the group to which he or she belongs. Calling a five-member task force "rife with corruption" entitles each to sue. Asserting that a particular labor union is controlled by organized crime would certainly defame the officers of the union. Accusing all—or even most—of a 20 person night shift of using drugs on the job injures the reputation of each.

Not surprisingly, the rule is different with very large groups. Defamatory statements made about a large class of people cannot be interpreted to refer necessarily to any individual. And only individuals, not classes of people, can sue for damage to personal reputation. This principle has been established in a number of cases, including one in which a class action was brought on behalf of 600,000,000 Muslims to recover damages for airing the film "Death of a Princess." The group found the film, which depicted the public execution of a Saudi Arabian princess for adultery, insulting and defamatory to the Islamic religion. The claim was dismissed because the aim of defamation law is to protect individuals, and if a group is sufficiently large that a statement cannot reasonably be interpreted to defame *individual* group members, First Amendment rights would be impaired by permitting individuals to sue.[76]

Distinguishing a small group—which if defamed entitles all its members to sue—from a large group—which if defamed entitles no one to sue—is not always so simple. Some authorities have noted that in cases permitting recovery, the group generally has 25 or fewer members.[77] However, there is usually no articulated limit on size; suits have been permitted by members of fairly large groups when some distinguishing characteristic of the individual or group increases the likelihood that the statement could be interpreted to apply individually.

For example, a single player on the 60 to 70 man Oklahoma University football team was permitted to sue when a writer accused the entire team of taking amphetamines to improve its performance; the individual had a significant position on the team (he was a fullback) and had played in all but two of the team's games.[78] Twenty-seven out of a group of 53 unindicted police officers were permitted to sue when a newspaper editorial connected all 53 with the crimes of 18 who were indicted on charges of burglary, planting of evidence and other misconduct.[79] That the officers were employed in a small community—where people knew one another—was an important factor.

A prime consideration, therefore, is the public perception of the size of the group and whether a statement will be interpreted to refer to every member. The more organized and cohesive a group, the easier it is to tar all its members with the same brush and the more likely a court will permit a suit from an individual even if the group includes more than 25 members. At some point, however, increasing size will be seen to dilute the harm to individuals and any resulting injury will fall beneath the threshold for a viable lawsuit.[80]

DEFAMING CORPORATIONS AND DISPARAGING PRODUCTS

Corporations (and other business entities like partnerships and unions) cannot commit adultery and are not known to contract loathsome diseases. They lack feelings, too. However, they do have reputations and can be accused of dishonesty, criminal activity, incompetence in a business or profession, and most other categories of defamation. (See pp. 3–8 above.) In short, they can be defamed by most of the same means applicable to individuals.

A corporation can be defamed by an attack on its creditworthiness, ethics or business performance.[81] Imputing dishonorable, unethical, un-lawful or unprofessional conduct[82] or, in a more general sense, making any statement which tends to prejudice the corporation in the conduct of its business or deters others from dealing with it[83] can defame. So can defamatory implications, dual meanings, juxtapositions, and disparage-ment without names if the corporation is still identifiable. As with in-dividuals, care must be taken to avoid confusing separate subjects with similar names. With corporations, particular care must be exercised be-cause entirely different corporations in different states can have identical names; and even corporations which are apparently affiliated can still be operationally distinct so that a report accurately describing the misdeeds of one can trigger a lawsuit by naming the other.

As with the defamation of individuals, good intentions or public-minded subject matter will not make a statement any less defamatory. Brown & Williamson Tobacco Corporation won substantial damages against a television station and its reporter, who, in a commentary seg-ment, accused the maker of Viceroy cigarettes of aiming its advertising at children. The report was based on a study by the Federal Trade Com-mission which cited a memorandum by an outside market research firm hired to help develop a new advertising strategy for the cigarette. The firm's memorandum recommended an advertising campaign that would pitch Viceroy to "young smokers, starters" by presenting the cigarette "as part of the illicit pleasure category of products and activities" in the same category as "wine, beer, shaving, wearing a bra . . . and striving for self-identity." The television report quoted these portions of the marketing study and accused Viceroy of adopting a strategy to attract young people to smoking. In fact, Brown & Williamson had rejected the researchers' recommendations and never produced advertising of the kind to which the marketing study referred. Even though the tobacco company failed to show that it lost sales or profits or suffered any other identifiable financial loss because of the report, it was awarded $3 million in presumed compensatory damages (reduced to $1 million on appeal) and $2 million in punitive damages against the network plus an additional $50,000 against the reporter.[84]

"The Bear Bites"

Entrepreneur magazine published an article about the activities of separate companies operating in several states under the name Golden Bear Distributing Systems Inc. The parent company, Golden Bear of California, franchised the others. The article appeared in *Entrepreneur*'s monthly "Fraud" feature, which exposes instances of consumer and investor fraud. Much of the article's information resulted from an investigation by law enforcement officers into the companies' activities. Noting that "Golden Bear['s] promises were consistent throughout the country," the magazine reported that the California attorney general sued Golden Bear of California and described legal difficulties experienced by Golden Bear of Utah. To illustrate the company's advertising, the article took a sales pitch from the marketing director of Golden Bear of Texas. The Texas Company and Golden Bear of California did have common advertising and sales techniques, and the Texas company had to purchase vending machines and soda from the parent, but their stock was separately issued and owned, and each company had its own management.

The article did not expressly state that the Texas company had defrauded investors or that it was under investigation, but after the article came out, Golden Bear of Texas lost business and was eventually forced to file for bankruptcy. Golden Bear of Texas sued *Entrepreneur*. Did it win?

"The Bear Bites"
(Answer)

Because the article falsely imputed the fraudulent conduct of Golden Bear of California to the Texas company, it was found to be defamatory. The jury awarded Golden Bear of Texas $30,000 in actual damages and $20,000 in punitive damages, affirmed on appeal.[85]

While false disparagement of product quality is technically not defamation, it is closely related.[86] Saying that a product is dangerous, or defective, or does not work, are typical forms of product disparagement. As with defamation, the journalist must be on the lookout for potential trouble regardless of the degree of disparagement. This point was recently underscored in a case appealed to the Supreme Court: the Bose Corporation proved that Consumers' Union disparaged one of its speaker systems by reporting falsely that the sound of instruments heard through the speakers wandered "about the room" rather than "along the wall" between the speakers, which would have been accurate.[87]

As with defamation, failure to detect product disparagement can bring costly litigation. In one case, the company founded by Charles Atlas ("The World's Most Perfectly Developed Man") sued Time-Life Books over an illustration caption in the book *Exercising for Fitness*. The caption accompanied a reproduction of the famous "97-pound weakling" advertisement for the Charles Atlas Dynamic-Tension body-building program, which appeared in eight languages over more than 50 years. The advertisement contained a nine-panel cartoon strip in which a very skinny man grows tired of having sand kicked in his face, takes up the Charles Atlas system, and ultimately avenges himself.

The caption in the book stated that the Charles Atlas program "touted isometric exercises" to be better than weight lifting. And the main text on the same page warned of the "extreme dangers of isometric exercises," calling attention to potential lung damage, reduced blood flow, fatal brain hemorrhages and other disagreeable consequences. The basis of the suit was that the caption's description of the Charles Atlas system was simply wrong: it was not isometric. The court agreed that the combination of the caption and the text could make a reasonable reader conclude "the plaintiff's exercise program is dangerous'' and that the facts established a cognizable case of product disparagement.[88]

SECTION SUMMARY

Defamation is broadly defined and any statement that would shock, anger or otherwise offend someone—*anyone*—should catch a writer's eye and it deserves attention. Is it a statement of fact? Does it have a tendency to injure reputation or diminish the esteem, respect, good will or confidence of that person? Does it make that person undeserving of respect or hold the person up to hate or ridicule? Does it attack the creditworthiness or honesty, efficiency or business performance of a company? Or impute unethical, unlawful or unprofessional conduct? Does it have anything to do with contagious diseases or serious sexual misconduct or dishonesty or criminal acts, or accusations of bigotry, or of poor financial health or unsavory companions, or harsh criticism of skill in a trade, business, profession or office? If the answer to *any* of these questions is in the affirmative, the statement is potentially defamatory and must be treated with appropriate care. There is no easy defense in the words ''I didn't mean it'' or ''I didn't see it.'' It is part of the writer's job (and that of his or her editor and attorney) to identify defamatory meaning.

Sometimes statements are not defamatory on their face but become so when readers or viewers are aware of additional information. Statements can defame through implication; clever dual meanings or even inadvertent juxtapositions can injure reputation and invite litigation. Defamation can be unintentional. It can occur if and when names are not used or identities affirmatively disguised—whenever the alleged victim is still identifiable. Each member of a group can be disparaged by disparaging the group.

The need for constant vigilance cannot be overemphasized. Soon it will come as second nature. All it takes is practice.

And while practicing, the writer should look beyond the main subject of a story to consider who else might be harmed by a statement. Every person, company or other entity in the story deserves close attention: Is there anything negative said or implied about them? The writer should scrutinize even secondary issues, the ''throw-away lines,'' for tangential or peripheral persons mentioned in passing. Libel suits often come from the least expected quarters, where no one is focusing.[89]

After being identified, each potential defamation in a story must be separately weighed. Is it unnecessary? Is it expendable? Does it pertain more to background and ''enrichment'' than to the subject of the story?

Can it be said in a less harmful way without detracting from the point being made? Is the statement inadvertently offensive? If the answer to any of these questions is in the affirmative, then eliminating the defamation also eliminates its risk.

On the other hand, the potentially defamatory statement that goes to the heart of a story, or otherwise deserves to survive this purge, should not be removed—but it should not be ignored, either. The writer's next step is to consider what proof supports that statement and to what degree he or she is persuaded of its truth. The next section of this book is concerned with that process: assessing the necessary quantum of proof and obtaining it.

SECTION II

How Much Proof

It is true that the media are often excused from liability when they make a false defamatory statement about a public official or public figure. Most media professionals have at least a general awareness of the special legal privileges that make it difficult for public figures and officials, and even private persons, to win defamation suits. A smaller number, however, have taken the time to study these legal rules which are surprisingly difficult to comprehend, even for lawyers and judges. Fewer still recognize that distinctions between public persons and private persons are not always obvious and that the ways in which courts apply these legal privileges are not entirely predictable. In fact, the limitations placed on the media's privileges to make defamatory mistakes, compounded by unpredictability in the courts' application of these privileges, can render them useless to the media defendant in a libel suit.

This Section will first review the legal privileges which may apply to erroneous defamatory statements by the media.[90] These privileges are based essentially on standards of factual support which the media must meet to avoid liability for false defamatory statements. The required level of factual support is lower for statements about public officials and public figures, and higher for statements about private individuals. Next follows a detailed look at the risks incurred by relying on the lesser burden applicable to the public categories: the lack of certainty in identifying public officials and public figures and the variables in the application of factual support standards.

Lastly, this Section will discuss the practical approach to coping with

all this uncertainty: journalists, publishers, broadcasters—and their lawyers—should usually not concern themselves with categorizing subjects
when preparing or reviewing a story. (If a lawsuit follows, there will be
ample opportunity to worry about it then.) Instead, the safest approach
in most instances is to meet the highest standard of factual support notwithstanding the status of the subject. That standard is the one applicable
to statements about private people and it is based on a common sense
balance of factors like the extent of possible harm to the subject and the
quality and number of sources for the statement.

Media lawyers who review stories for potential defamation have taken
this approach for a long time.[91] As this Section will demonstrate, it is
by far the most sensible approach for everyone.

STANDARDS OF FACTUAL SUPPORT

In the 1964 landmark case of *New York Times Co. v. Sullivan*,[92] the
Supreme Court held for the first time that the First Amendment of the
United States Constitution limits the liability which states can impose on
the media for defamatory statements which prove to be false. Until that
decision, states were free to hold media defendants strictly liable for
injury caused by false defamatory statements no matter what level of
apparently factual support had persuaded them of its truth.

In the *New York Times* case, an elected Commissioner of Montgomery,
Alabama, who supervised the police force, brought suit over a full-page
political advertisement which criticized police conduct in a civil rights
demonstration.[93] Noting the importance of free and uninhibited debate of
important public issues like civil rights, the Supreme Court reasoned that
the media needed "breathing space" to promote freedom of expression
on public questions—particularly with respect to criticism of the official
conduct of public officials. After placing the commissioner squarely
within its definition of "public official," the Supreme Court required
dismissal of his claim in the absence of proof that false statements in the
ad were made with a high degree of journalistic fault that the Court named
"actual malice." Three years later, the Court extended the same constitutional "breathing space" to defamation of public figures.[94]

In 1971, a divided Supreme Court next suggested that the constitutional
"actual malice" rule should extend to defamation of *any* individual,
public or private, as long as the defamatory statements (shown to be false)
involved "matters of public or general concern."[95] This approach shifted
the focus from the *status* of the subject to the *content* of the story, but

it did not last. In 1974, the Supreme Court scrapped this purely "content-based" approach and restored primary emphasis to the status of the subject. At the same time, the Court introduced both a tighter definition of "public figure" and a stricter standard for excusing the media from liability in suits brought by private persons. As a result, from then until now, the media have not been entitled to the constitutional protections of the "actual malice" standard simply because a story concerns a public issue, and the "breathing space" for making defamatory mistakes about private persons has been considerably constricted.[96]

What, then, are the current standards which the media must meet to be excused from liability when a defamatory report proves to be false? In the 1974 case described above and others which followed, the tests adopted by the Supreme Court for public and private persons are the following:

---

1. *The Actual Malice Standard*

For false defamatory statements made about (a) "public officials" (as the Supreme Court defines them) which relate to official conduct or fitness for office or (b) "public figures" (as the Supreme Court defines them): the persons responsible for communicating the statement (including writers, publishers and broadcasters) can be held liable only if there exists "clear and convincing" evidence that they acted with (a) knowledge of the statement's falsity or (b) reckless disregard of whether the statement was false or not,[97] which is a standard meant to be "marked out" and elucidated case by case,[98] but certainly includes a high degree of awareness of probable falsity[99] or serious doubts as to truth.[100] This degree of fault has been named "actual malice" though it is not equivalent to the hatred, ill will or unfounded desire to injure which are part of the conventional meaning of the term "malice." The Actual Malice Standard is a subjective one: it looks toward the defendant's state of mind. But in order to prevail, the defendant must possess enough proof prior to making the defamatory statement to persuade a jury of good faith reliance on its truthfulness. Assertions of good faith will not likely persuade when allegations are "inherently improbable" or there are obvious reasons to doubt the truthfulness of an informant or the accuracy of his or her report.[101]

2. *The Private Person Standard*

For false defamatory statements made about private individuals (that is, anyone who is not a public official or public figure): the persons responsible for communicating the statement (including writers, publishers and broadcasters) can be held liable only if they acted with a lack of care amounting at least to negligence.[102] Negligence is determined in one of two ways depending on state law: (a) whether a defendant's conduct is what a reasonably prudent person would have done in the same or similar circumstances (the "reasonable person" approach); or (b) whether the defendant departed from established standards of professional conduct, which usually involves comparisons between the defendant's actions and recognized journalistic standards (the "journalistic malpractice" approach). A negligence test is purely objective rather than subjective. Though the states are free to preserve defendants from liability to private persons when even less care than negligence is evident (e.g. actual malice), the vast majority of states apply the negligence test to suits brought by private persons.

These standards do not lead toward sharp and unambiguous interpretations. Is every public employee a public official? What about others on the government payroll? Will the standard apply to part-time officials? What distinguishes reckless indifference to truth or falsity from negligence? Who can say what a reasonably prudent person would do in the countless unique circumstances faced by journalists every day? And how well established are standards of professional conduct? Not all of these questions have complete answers. Courts have been struggling to provide them for more than 25 years with obvious difficulty and varying results.

IDENTIFYING PUBLIC OFFICIALS

We begin with the threshold question: who are public officials? Subsequent to the *New York Times* case, the Supreme Court advanced three principal criteria:

The "public official" designation applies to those among the hierarchy of government employees who

1. At the very least "have, or appear to the public to have, substantial responsibility for or control over the conduct of governmental affairs"; and

2. Hold a position which has "such apparent importance that the public has an independent interest in the qualifications and performance of the person who holds it, beyond the general public interest in the qualifications and performance of all government employees"; and

3. Hold a position which "would invite public scrutiny and discussion of the person holding it, entirely apart from the scrutiny and discussion occasioned by the particular charges in controversy."[103]

Furthermore, the false defamatory statement in issue must relate to the employee's official conduct[104] or fitness for office,[105] and, in most states, the employee's official position must be named in the story[106] before the Actual Malice Standard will apply. Otherwise, the Private Person Standard will determine the liability of the defendant.[107]

These standards give some guidance but obviously do not allow for a sure-fire identification in every instance. Moreover, the Supreme Court has not defined specific boundaries for the category of public official.[108] It has not determined how far down into "the lower ranks of government employees" the designation should extend.[109] It has not defined precisely what kind of statement properly relates to "official conduct" or fitness for office. What is clear, however, is that the public official designation does not and was never meant to apply to all public employees[110] or to all statements made about government officials regardless of rank.

Public Employee Positions That Qualify

Some public employee positions easily meet the test for "public official." Certainly elected officials qualify at the federal, state and local levels including senators, congressmen, governors, mayors, and town council members.[111] Judges and high-ranking appointed officials also fit the profile.[112] Law enforcement personnel such as police commissioners and police chiefs, police captains, police sergeants and sheriffs will qualify; even police at the officer level are usually deemed public officials[113] because of the significant authority they possess, like the power to arrest.[114]

Most public employees, however, hold positions in the lower ranks. They do not pass the Supreme Court's test for public officials and were not meant to. But in practice, lower courts have been interpreting the Supreme Court's standards broadly and without painstaking analysis.[115] Some state courts have adopted such an expansive view of the public official test that public employees can be so classified merely because of their governmental affiliation.[116] In fact, up to now, the list of government employees who have been held *not* to be public officials is relatively small.[117]

Many examples show how courts have bent the rules—and bent over backwards—to classify public employees as public officials. These "officials" are hardly what the Supreme Court had in mind:

• A chemistry teacher at a local high school.[118]

• A *receptionist* at a U.S. Army hospital whose powers ranged only so far as to make appointments for the pediatrics clinic.[119]

• A medical doctor who was not a government employee but contracted with the state to provide medical services for five jails. He would make visits twice a week; his assistants visited the jails six days per week. The Alaskan Supreme Court found he did not appear to the public to have substantial responsibility for or control over the conduct of governmental affairs; nor was his position one which would invite public scrutiny and discussion apart from the controversy in issue. However, his position was considered one of such apparent importance that the public had an independent interest in his qualifications and performance beyond the general public interest in the qualifications and performance of all government employees. In other words, the doctor's position fit within only one out of three of the principal criteria described by the U.S. Supreme Court, and he *still* qualified as a public official.[120]

In most of these instances, courts simply ignore the Supreme Court's standards. Other courts embellish the standards to make them less rigorous. For example, the Tennessee Supreme Court decided to extend the public official designation to "[a]ny position of employment that carries with it duties and responsibilities affecting the lives, liberty, money or property of a citizen or that may enhance or disrupt his enjoyment of life, his peace and tranquility, or that of his family."[121] It is difficult to imagine a public employee who sits outside this description; even the work of a street sweeper bears upon the "enjoyment of life" and "tranquility" of the local citizenry.

When courts *do* apply the Supreme Court's test with rigor to any but the highest ranks of government employees, the results are often close calls, at best. Take the position of a state inspector of boarding homes for the elderly whose job was to recommend whether new licenses should be issued or existing licenses renewed, and to check on complaints filed against licensees. When called upon to address serious charges, such as the abuse of residents, the inspector did not initiate an investigation himself, but coordinated the work of other personnel and then submitted a follow-up report recommending possible action. His other duties included checking resident records, monitoring the paperwork of licensees, explaining the state's regulations to boarding home operators, identifying deficiencies in licensed facilities and ensuring proper compliance with state standards.

A state appellate court refused to consider the employee a public official because he had little exposure in the general community and his position did not call for any ''special public scrutiny'' apart from the controversy generated by the defamation giving rise to the lawsuit. (Two local newspapers had reported that the employee made unauthorized physical examinations of the genitals of elderly residents.) Because the employee simply fell somewhere within the ''extended hierarchy'' of the Department of Health and Rehabilitative Services, the court concluded that he did not meet the Supreme Court's definition of public official for purposes of defamation.[122]

The following examples also show how difficult predictions can be.

"To Be One or Not To Be One"

The editor-in-chief at the *National Tell-Tale* is having a tough day. She has been presented with four stories involving defamatory statements about public employees from around the country. Each of the four journalists who wrote the stories is certain that his or her subject qualifies as a "public official" for purposes of defamation law. The editor is not so sure.

The stories respectively concern the following:

1. One of four assistant city managers in the state's capital who shares responsibility for the budget, for management services, data processing and personnel. He also acts on behalf of the city manager at meetings of the city council subcommittees and addresses city groups.

2. A supervisor of a county recreation area used principally as a ski resort whose responsibilities include handling the finances of the center.

3. A "junior social worker" who investigates child abuse charges and has the power to recommend to her supervisor that children be removed from their natural parents and placed in foster homes. Upon approval by her supervisor, she prepares documents for submission to the juvenile judge, accompanies law enforcement officials when the children are taken from their parents and later meets with the parents should they want to know how to get their children back.

4. A jailer with access to keys who unlocks cell doors, who is required to conduct periodic body counts of prisoners, to inventory and store valuables found on prisoners, and to ensure that prisoners have been properly searched by the police officer who books them. He is also required to know where alarms are located within the jail and to see that proper booking procedures are followed in each instance. He has access to a night stick.

Which of these public employees are public officials within the Supreme Court's definition?

"To Be One or Not To Be One"
(Answers)

1. An assistant city manager with this job description is a public official in at least one jurisdiction notwithstanding his secondary role within the city hierarchy. The court simply emphasized that the position invited public scrutiny apart from the controversy in issue without offering further analysis.[123]

2. Given the information above, even the U.S. Supreme Court did not want to say whether the supervisor of the recreation center was a public official. The Court instructed a lower court to get more information and figure it out.[124]

3. The social worker, in one court's view, is a public official notwithstanding the fact that she could only recommend to her supervisor that children be placed in foster homes as opposed to making the decision herself.[125]

4. A jailer with these job credentials was found *not* to be a public official. Even though abuse of his position would conced-

edly "affect the public interest," the court emphasized his relative lack of training, the lack of discretion afforded him in performing his duties, and that he possessed significantly less authority than a police officer of any rank.[126]

Even assuming the editor in this example accurately predicted each of these results in each subject's respective jurisdiction, the same result would not necessarily apply in a different city or a different state.

A conclusion emerges from all this: despite the current tendency of lower courts to find "public officials" at every level, this trend could change even without modifying the Supreme Court's tough three-tiered test. If lower courts simply paid closer attention to those standards, the outcome in many instances would be different, and not in the media's favor. Given the tendency of recent presidential administrations to appoint more conservative federal judges, this likelihood hardly seems remote.

In addition to interpreting the Supreme Court's three principal criteria with greater rigor, courts can also cut down on the number of government employees deemed to be public officials by giving more weight to premises underlying those three criteria. The Supreme Court has repeatedly observed in recent years that public officials—like public figures—have voluntarily exposed themselves to increased *risk* of injury from defamatory falsehood, and enjoy significantly greater *access* to the channels of effective communication to counteract false statements, compared to private persons.[127] The Court has not indicated whether these characteristics attach automatically to public employees who meet the other three tests, or whether they must be viewed as independent criteria. To date, most courts do treat both risk assumption and access to media as automatic characteristics, or ignore them completely. But the opportunity still exists for lower courts—and even the Supreme Court—to consider these characteristics as *additional* criteria which must be met as a *condition* of public official status, thereby restricting the category further. In some rare instances, this has already happened.

For example, the Supreme Court of New Hampshire expressed substantial doubt that a police officer was a public official for purposes of defamation, leaving the decision to a jury instead (inconsistently with the prevailing view which recognizes police officers as public officials). After reciting the three principal tests, the court focused on "the principal assumptions that underlie their policy": the public official's voluntary exposure "to increased risk of injury from defamatory falsehood" and "access to the media of communications," which allows the public official "to respond to defamation more effectively than the typical private plaintiff can."[128] After applying the three standard criteria *and* their "underlying policy" to the characteristics of a police officer's job, the court unsurprisingly refused to find the patrolman a public official "as a matter of law." Also noteworthy is that the opinion was written by Justice David Souter, a recent addition to the U.S. Supreme Court.[129]

There always exists the possibility that the Supreme Court will change the rules to give the media a greater or lesser chance to escape liability. But given the observed "instinct" of the current Supreme Court to read the First Amendment narrowly, the standards are more likely to be tightened than loosened if they are changed at all.

Types of Statements That Qualify

So far, this discussion of public figures has only addressed the issue of whether or not a public employee has sufficient influence in the affairs of society to qualify as a public official. Though the point has not always been recognized by lower courts, the Supreme Court also requires that the statement in issue pertain to the employee's official conduct or fitness for office in order for the Actual Malice Standard to apply—no matter what responsibilities come with the employee's position. What is the scope of such commentary? It is quite broad, particularly when "fitness for office" is concerned. Even the Supreme Court has recognized that society's legitimate interest in governmental officials extends to anything which might touch on an official's fitness for office. This includes characteristics like dishonesty, malfeasance, or "improper motivation," even if publicizing them will affect the official's private as well as public reputation.[130]

Yet even this generous description can be sidestepped by a judge who puts his or her mind to it. In a case involving a police officer who served on the vice and gambling unit and was accused in the press of assuming a "compromising position" when seen in an automobile with someone else's wife, the court decided that the statement was insufficiently related to the officer's official conduct—even though his line of work involved the control of everyone else's vice. The court conceded that the statement could *possibly* relate to the officer's *fitness* to be on the vice squad, but because it did not relate to his official *duties* or to his *performance* of those duties, it would not qualify.[131]

Past Public Officials

If a public employee has left office but would have qualified as a public official during his or her tenure, and the statement in issue pertains to the former employee's conduct in office, the Actual Malice Standard will usually continue to apply to defamatory statements which prove to be false. The vast majority of cases have found that the media's privileges are not dulled by the passage of a reasonable period of time.[132] For example, the fact that a supervisor of the county recreation area had been discharged before the defamatory article was published had no significance, especially because management of the recreation area was still a matter of lively public interest.[133] The same result applied to cases brought by a former city attorney,[134] a retired state court judge,[135] a former chief of detectives (six years afterward),[136] and a former agent of the U.S. Bureau of Narcotics (also six years afterward).[137]

The length of a "reasonable" absence from office will be decided case by case, and, by the Supreme Court's reckoning, limits do exist. The Court has observed that "there may be cases where a person is so far removed from a former position of authority that comment on the matter in which he performed his responsibilities no longer has the interest necessary to justify the [Actual Malice Standard]."[138] This shows again how a more stringent application of existing Supreme Court rules can tighten the standards for journalists.

To sum up: it is unwise to take for granted that a public employee qualifies as a public official for purposes of determining whether the Actual Malice Standard or the Private Person Standard applies, except for employees who are high in government's hierarchy. And even then, one must be sure that a potential defamatory statement relates to official conduct or fitness for office and that if the official has left office, he or she has not been gone for too long. When in doubt, the wiser course is to test a potentially defamatory statement against the more stringent proof requirements applicable to a private person, which is just what a public employee might turn out to be.

IDENTIFYING PUBLIC FIGURES

As already noted, if the subject of a defamatory statement is not a public official, only two other categories remain: public figures and private persons. And if the subject is not a public figure, the Actual Malice

Standard—the standard of proof more favorable to the media—will not apply.

What then is a public figure? Unfortunately, that question has perplexed even members of the Supreme Court. They have attempted to define a set of standards which, they admit, "necessarily treat alike various cases involving differences as well as similarities"; they further admit that "often . . . not all of the considerations which justify adoption of a given rule" will even apply to every case.[139] In other words, applying the rules was never expected to be easy.

As a result, a large measure of unpredictability comes with most attempts to distinguish between public figures and private citizens. *More than one* exasperated judge has adopted the maxim that defining public figures is like "trying to nail a jellyfish to the wall."[140] One judge even consigned his task of identifying public figures to the exclusive "class of legal abstractions where 'I know it when I see it'. . . ."[141]

In view of this confusion among the judiciary, the media's task of identifying public figures with certainty—in the absence of a specific judicial pronouncement—can be very risky. In addition to the fuzzy general criteria common to all public figures, there exist two subcategories to contend with, sometimes called "general" and "limited."

The Supreme Court has defined public figures by identifying the characteristics which distinguish them from private individuals. The two principal characteristics are the following:

1. *They have voluntarily exposed themselves to increased risk.* For the most part, those who are public figures have assumed roles of special prominence in the affairs of society through purposeful action of their own. (Involuntary public figures hypothetically exist but few have been identified.) They "invite attention and comment" and voluntarily expose themselves to increased risk of injury from defamatory falsehood.

2. *They usually have pre-existing access to the media.* Public figures usually enjoy significantly greater access to the channels of effective communication prior to the defamatory statement and therefore have a more realistic opportunity to counteract false statements than private individuals.

The two subcategories of public figures to which these characteristics apply are:

1. *General public figures.* Such persons occupy positions of

"persuasive power and influence," attain "pervasive fame or notoriety," and achieve "pervasive involvement in the affairs of society." By reason of their fame, they shape events in areas of concern to society at large and therefore are deemed public figures for all purposes. (This is a small and elite group which includes extremely well-known celebrities.)

2. *Limited public figures.* These persons have thrust themselves, or are voluntarily drawn into the forefront (or "vortex") of particular public controversies in order to influence the resolution of the issues involved. They thereby become public figures for only the limited range of public issues with which they become involved.[142] (Political activists, for example, fall within this larger group.)

The definition of public figures is therefore supported by the same two premises which help distinguish public officials from the private person: voluntary exposure to increased risk and greater access to media. In the case of public figures, however, these premises are central to the definition used by most courts. Private persons, on the other hand, have not assumed any "influential role in ordering society" and do not enjoy access to the channels of communication; they therefore have a greater interest in the protection of their own good name and a "more compelling call on the courts for redress of injury inflicted by defamation." By this logic, public figures are less vulnerable to injury and less deserving of recovery, so like public officials they must jump the higher hurdle of the Actual Malice Standard to prevail in a defamation action.

But how is prominence in the affairs of society determined? What constitutes persuasive power and influence or general fame or notoriety? What is a public controversy? How can one be sure an individual has voluntarily entered the "vortex" of the particular public controversy to which the defamatory statement pertains? How is "access to the channels of effective communication" measured? Such questions imply the challenge of identifying public figures.

Identifying General Public Figures

The general public figure in our society has been called a "rare creature"[143]—that is, in terms of number, not the frequency of encounter. These are people who have stepped into a spotlight of public attention so bright and so broad that every aspect of their lives is exposed to detailed inspection[144] (at least insofar as matters of legitimate public concern are involved; see pp. 55–56 below). By renouncing anonymity— and chasing publicity—they satisfy both the requirements of voluntary exposure to the increased risk of defamatory misstatements, and of access to the media. The press is expected to fulfill its role of reporting and criticizing matters of public concern by investigating the talents, character and motives of general public figures. By this rationale, the fame that brings "power, money, respect, adulation and self-gratification" also brings close scrutiny and adverse comment,[145] and even the occasional defamatory mistake.[146]

This explains why the press gets additional "breathing space" for reports about general public figures, and the Actual Malice Standard may be applied to *any* defamatory statement about their lives even if it has no direct bearing on their line of work, or the affairs of society in which they are involved, or any other particular characteristic of their public lives.[147]

With consequences as drastic as these, courts are notably reluctant to bestow on very many libel plaintiffs the title of general public figure. The Supreme Court's criteria for identifying the general public figure, and its underlying rationale, make this exclusionary practice easy.

As noted, the general public figure must enjoy notable persuasive power and influence, pervasive fame or notoriety, and pervasive involvement in society's affairs. One federal court has attempted to define "general fame" as "being known to a large percentage of the well-informed citizenry";[148] if the local population taken as a whole has never heard of the person, the "general fame" requirement is not satisfied.[149] And mere participation in community and professional affairs is not enough; involvement in the affairs of society must be pervasive.[150]

Other factors can also help determine whether a plaintiff has achieved the degree of fame and influence necessary to become a general public figure. No one factor predominates; the decision must involve "an element of judgment."[151] So, apart from asking prospective jurors whether they heard of the person, the judge can examine statistical surveys that concern name recognition, as well as the extent of prior media coverage of the person in question. The judge might also try to determine whether people in the community "alter or reevaluate their conduct or ideas in light of the plaintiff's actions," and whether the public's proven preoccupation with the plaintiff guarantees him or her ready access to media coverage for rebuttal of inaccurate statements. Another indicator is whether the person has endorsed commercial products or publicly supports political candidates or takes an open stance on public issues, all of which may show the length and breadth of their recognition and influence, and make close scrutiny by the press especially appropriate. Whether the plaintiff's prominence is voluntary is also important. Has the plaintiff shunned the attention that the public has bestowed—and if so, have those efforts been successful?[152]

The direction in which all these factors point is that a general public figure must be, prior to the defamation in issue, a voluntary "celebrity," with a name that people know as a "household word," whose ideas and actions are followed by an interested public.[153] Most general public figures will therefore be drawn from the ranks of athletes or entertainers or a very small group of well-known social critics who have made it their business to speak publicly and lengthily on public issues. In the first two categories are Johnny Carson[154] and Wayne Newton.[155] People like Dan Rather, Lee Iacocca and Reggie Jackson would probably also qualify.[156] Social critics William F. Buckley,[157] William Kunstler,[158] and Ralph Nader[159] are general public figures.

Can general public figures have local rather than national appeal and influence? The answer is yes. The Supreme Court requires only "evidence of general fame or notoriety in the community,"[160] so the issue becomes whether the individual has achieved the necessary degree of notoriety where the defamation was published and he or she was defamed.[161] However, a number of judges who have found persons of local prominence to be general public figures have not paid much attention to the range of factors described above. For example, in Montana, a plaintiff who had published various works, had been featured in two articles, run unsuccessfully for the U.S. Senate, attended a Republican political convention, gave a speech at the convention and at an economic conference, served as chairman of the state Republican party, and actively participated in the National Taxpayer's Union, was found to be a general purpose public figure.[162] So was a former state insurance commissioner who had run for various city and state offices 12 times in 20 years—successfully only 3 times—who had served as a member of the county library board and promoter of a respected drum and bugle corp.[163] General public figure status was also assigned to a former county attorney who practiced law for 32 years, was prominent in many business, professional and social activities, was former counsel to a board of commissioners in a dispute over the construction of a court house, and was censured publicly for agreeing to defend a well-publicized murder suspect on a contingent fee basis.[164]

"More Defamation Digest"

We return once more to the offices of Defamation Digest, where the editor-in-chief is reviewing defamatory articles about three persons who are highly visible in public life. But are they general purpose public figures?

1. *Elmer Gertz.* Mr. Gertz enjoys considerable stature as a lawyer, author, lecturer and participant in matters of public importance. He has long been active in community and professional affairs, having served as an officer of local civic groups, and of various professional organizations. After a Chicago policeman shot and killed a youth named Nelson, he represented the Nelson family in civil litigation against the policeman. In so doing, Mr. Gertz voluntarily associated himself with a case that was certain to—and did—receive extensive media exposure, but he did not discuss the suit with the press.

2. *Morris Dalitz.* For many years, Mr. Dalitz has been given a substantial amount of publicity in voluminous newspaper and magazine articles alleging his involvement with organized crime. There is no indication, however, that he sought any of that publicity.

3. *Carol Burnett.* Ms. Burnett is a well-known comedienne and actress who has appeared on many television programs and about whom countless articles and reports have been written.

"More Defamation Digest"
(Answer)

One out of three is a general purpose public figure:

1. Mr. Gertz does not qualify. Although he was well-known in some circles, he has not involved himself pervasively in the affairs of society and he achieved no general fame or notoriety in the community. None of the prospective jurors called at the trial of his defamation action ever heard of him and there was no proof that the general population knew him any better.[165]

2. Mr. Dalitz does not qualify either. Even a "shoe-box full" of clippings and reports spanning many years does not indicate the general fame required to raise him to general public figure status.[166]

3. Carol Burnett is a general purpose public figure.[167]

Like people, major organizations, corporations,[168] and even religious groups[169] can qualify as public figures. What about involuntary general public figure status? Involuntary public figures of any variety are considered "exceedingly rare,"[170] but involuntary *general* public figures are even more so. It would be difficult indeed to assume a position of fame or notoriety and prominence in society's affairs, to exercise persuasive power and influence, and enjoy access to the media, all without trying.

What is conceivable, however, is that today's general public figure might be tomorrow's hermit, seeking to avoid the spotlight of public preoccupation with a new-found cloak of anonymity. Though the Supreme Court has not decided "whether or when an individual who was once a public figure may lose that status by the passage of time,"[171] lower court decisions have generally refused to find a loss of public figure status through the passage of time.[172] A federal appellate court has also noted that persistent press attention caused by continuing public interest may thwart a general public figure's quest for privacy. In such a case, the person's power and influence would likely continue, so his or her actions would still invite attention and comment and media scrutiny would still be appropriate.[173]

To sum up: the standards for designating a general public figure are stringent and for good reason. A writer should not assume that a subject fits the profile in the absence of clear-cut qualifications or a judicial determination.

Furthermore, as tight as the criteria are, they might become more so. The Supreme Court has dropped some broad hints in recent years that it might take the next opportunity to limit general public figure treatment only to instances where the defamatory statement involves a matter of legitimate public concern.[174] If the Court took this step, the Actual Malice Standard would no longer apply to matters of purely private concern (which the Supreme Court has done little to define)[175] whether or not the statements pertain to general public figures and notwithstanding their interest to the general public. Defamatory statements which did not pertain to matters of public concern would probably fall under the same standards applicable to private persons.[176] (See pages 92–96.)

All things considered, the criteria for identifying general public figures do not allow for completely predictable results, and may yet become even less certain. The task of identifying a general public figure, however, is as doubt-free as a litmus test when compared to the even more exasperating job of spotting the limited public figure.

Identifying Limited Public Figures

The press's need—and duty—to report on governmental affairs as well as the activities of the general public figures who court its attention justify looser standards of media responsibility for misstatements about public officials and general public figures. By assuming a public status, general public figures have also assumed public accountability and the risk that the press may inadvertently make erroneous statements about them. This helps justify the constitutional "breathing space" for statements about general public figures that the Actual Malice Standard helps assure.[177] On the other end of the spectrum, most private individuals, by definition, have withheld themselves from generalized public exposure and retain the right to hold the press to a higher standard of care. Between these poles there lies one more category of persons who appear in the morning newspaper and the evening news and assume the same risks as general public figures by dint of their public status: the erstwhile private person who enters the public arena not generally but specifically. In view of society's interest in encouraging press reports about this group, and mindful always of the "tension" between "the need for a vigorous and uninhibited press and the legitimate interest [of the defamed] in redressing wrongful injury," the Supreme Court created the status of limited public figure.[178]

In telling us how to identify one, however, the Supreme Court refused to apply a purely content-based test. Instead of simply conferring limited public figure status on persons involved in matters of legitimate public concern,[179] the Court defined a test which is far more restrictive and complex.

The test begins by examining whether the person, by voluntary involvement in a public controversy, *assumed the risk* of defamatory errors. This analysis has two parts. First, the subject matter of the report has to be more than a mere "public concern"; as noted above, a private person becomes a public figure only after voluntarily becoming involved in a *"public controversy"*—a small subset of general public concerns. The second part of the test looks beyond the content of the report to focus on the individual's participation in the controversy: he or she has to have special prominence in the public controversy sufficient to justify an assumed risk of defamatory errors. The Court's test next examines the plaintiff's prior exposure in the media: a limited public figure usually enjoys *access to the media* prior to the defamation.

Obviously, the Supreme Court did not intend to make it easy for private citizens to lose the greater measure of media accountability which the Private Person Standard provides and the Actual Malice Standard does not. Many lower courts, however, have taken every opportunity to transform erstwhile private citizens into public figures. They do this enthusiastically with novel interpretations of the Supreme Court's gloss on the Constitution or new ones of their own. This section will review the Supreme Court's "classic" criteria for identifying the limited public figure: assumption of risk through voluntary involvement and special prominence in a specific public controversy to which the defamation pertains; plus pre-existing access to the media. This section, however, will also show how lower courts have interpreted and embellished those standards, frequently in the media's favor.

The Assumption of Risk Criterion

In applying the Supreme Court's criterion of voluntary exposure to increased risk of errors in the press, courts usually begin with the threshold issue of identifying a public controversy—or lack of one—to which the defamation pertains. Next follows the question of whether the plaintiff has special prominence in the specific public controversy in a manner that seeks to influence the resolution of the issue involved. Whether participation is voluntary or the plaintiff is "caught up" in a controversy is germane.

The Supreme Court considered these issues in four cases and in each one refused to find limited public figure status. Along the way, the Court provided examples of publicly prominent individuals who did *not* assume the risk the Court had in mind.

The first negative example involved a lawyer who had been retained to bring a civil action for damages by the family of a youth killed by a policeman. The lawyer also appeared at the coroner's inquest into the death of the youth but played a minimal role solely as a representative of a private client. A monthly periodical featuring the views of the John Birch Society began to warn of a nationwide conspiracy against law enforcement agencies by Communists. In 1969, the year after the youth was shot, the magazine published an article purportedly demonstrating that the testimony against the policeman at his criminal trial was false and that his prosecution was part of a Communist campaign against the police. The article falsely portrayed the lawyer as an architect of the "frame up," accused him of being both a "Communist-fronter" and a member of various Marxist organizations, and implied he had a criminal record.

Was there a public controversy in all this? The Court found one in the criminal and civil litigation against the police officer—not in the alleged Communist plot. But the Court's focus was on another point entirely: the attorney never "thrust himself into the vortex of this public issue, nor did he engage the public's attention in an attempt to influence its outcome." Accordingly, the assumption of risk which is characteristic of limited public figures did not apply to him.[180]

The next Supreme Court decision to tackle the assumption of risk issue again involved a plaintiff who caught the press's attention because of her involvement in a civil litigation.[181] The libelous article appeared in *Time* magazine and reported that Russell Firestone, the "scion of one of America's wealthier industrial families," obtained a divorce from his third wife on grounds of extreme cruelty and adultery. In fact, the divorce had been granted on the basis that "neither party [was] domesticated." Testimony at the trial made mention of the wife's "extramarital escapades," which were both "bizarre and of an amatory nature which would have made Dr. Freud's hair curl." For his part, Mr. Firestone was "guilty of bounding from one bed partner to another with the erotic zest of a satyr."

The Firestone divorce was a "cause célèbre." Mrs. Firestone herself conducted more than one press conference and the controversy between the parties was manifestly of great interest to the public. Yet the Supreme Court refused to find any "public controversy" for purposes of establishing Mrs. Firestone as a limited public figure. In the view of the Court, dissolution of a marriage through judicial proceedings was not the sort of subject matter which conferred limited public figure status no matter how interesting it might be to "some portion of the reading public." The press conferences made no difference because they "should have had no effect upon the merits" of the divorce proceedings, and were not so intended, even if the proceedings had qualified as a public controversy.[182] The Court also refused to accept that Mrs. Firestone had freely chosen to publicize the propriety of her married life because obtaining a divorce compelled her to go to court. So, not only was there no public controversy but Mrs. Firestone assumed no special prominence in the resolution of any public question. Emphasizing that Mrs. Firestone was drawn into a public forum largely against her will to obtain the only redress available to her, the Court concluded that she was not a public figure who might be assumed to have exposed herself voluntarily to increased risk of injury from defamatory misstatements.[183]

The third case also involved judicial proceedings and false allegations of Communist sympathies but added the additional spice of espionage. In 1974 the Reader's Digest Association published a book which listed the plaintiff as a Soviet agent in the United States based on events which occurred in the late 1950's. At that time, a special federal grand jury sitting in New York City was conducting a major investigation into the activities of Soviet intelligence agents in the United States. As a result, the plaintiff's aunt and uncle were arrested and later pleaded guilty to espionage charges. During the investigation of his relatives, the plaintiff was interviewed several times by the FBI. He was then subpoenaed to appear before the grand jury itself but failed to appear because of ill health, and a federal judge scheduled a hearing to determine whether he would be held in criminal contempt of court.

These events naturally attracted the interest of the news media and a number of news stories were written about them. The plaintiff did appear at the contempt hearing but when his pregnant wife who was called to testify on his behalf became hysterical, he agreed to plead guilty to the contempt charge and received a one-year suspended sentence plus probation for three years. By 1974, however, the plaintiff had long since returned to the private life he had enjoyed prior to issuance of the grand jury subpoena.

The Supreme Court considered whether or not a public controversy existed in 1958 when Soviet espionage in the United States was under scrutiny. This proved a more difficult question than it seemed; the Court concluded that it was "difficult to determine with precision" whether a public controversy existed because there was *little difference of opinion* "about the desirability of permitting Soviet espionage in the United States; all responsible . . . citizens . . . were and are opposed to it." In other words, in the absence of a "debate" there may be no public controversy for purposes of determining limited public figure status.

The Court did not feel constrained to dwell on this question, however, because even if this issue did constitute a public controversy, the plaintiff's role in it was minor. As with Ms. Firestone, the plaintiff's "mere newsworthiness" would not justify application of the "demanding" Actual Malice Standard. Rather, the Court emphasized that the plaintiff did nothing to engage the attention of the public ''in an attempt to influence the resolution of the issues involved'' nor did he assume any ''special prominence in the resolution of public questions.'' Had he sought to arouse any public sentiment in his favor and against the investigation or to use the contempt citation ''as a fulcrum to create public discussion'' about the methods being used in connection with the investigation or prosecution, the result might have been different. But there was no evidence that his failure to appear was intended to have or did have any effect on any issue of public concern.

Furthermore, his participation was hardly voluntary; he was ''dragged unwillingly'' into the investigation. As with the attorney who represented the family against the policeman and Ms. Firestone, mere association with a publicized legal proceeding—and especially an unwilling association—was insufficient to establish the voluntary exposure to increased risk of injury which is the hallmark of a limited public figure.

In this case the Supreme Court also specifically rejected the proposition that any person who engages in criminal conduct automatically becomes a public figure for purposes of comment on issues relating to his conviction. This echoed a similar conclusion in the context of civil proceedings in the *Firestone* case. The Court reiterated its reasoning that there appeared to be ''little reason why these individuals should substantially forfeit that degree of protection which the law of defamation would otherwise afford them simply by virtue of their being drawn into a courtroom.''[184]

The last case in this Supreme Court quartet involved a fleece, a senator, a scientist and monkeys.

"The Golden Fleece Award"

The plaintiff, a scientist, was director of research at the Kalamazoo State Mental Hospital and a state employee. The bulk of his research was devoted to the study of emotional behavior. In particular he sought objective measures of aggression, concentrating on the behavior patterns of animals such as jaw-clenching in stressful settings. Reports of his research were published in scientific journals and both NASA and the Navy were interested in its potential for resolving problems associated with humans confined in close quarters. Other government agencies also funded his work.

A research assistant of a United States senator, on the lookout for wasteful government spending, got his hands on some reports prepared by the scientist. The assistant's purpose was to identify the "fleecing" of government funds for the purpose of awarding a "Golden Fleece Award." The scientist's work seemed to qualify, so the senator's office sent a press release to 275 newspersons across the country, announcing the award and denouncing the research as "nonsense." The release accused the scientist of making a fortune from his monkeys and a "monkey out of the American taxpayer." It also spoke of the "transparent worthlessness" of the jaw-grinding study and urged an end to the funding. These criticisms were repeated on other occasions as well.

The scientist sued for defamation alleging loss of respect in his profession, injury to feelings and other damage. In response, the senator argued that the scientist was a limited public figure, citing his long involvement with publicly funded research, his solicitation of federal and state grants, the local press coverage of his research, and the public interest in the expenditure of public funds on activities like his.

Was there a public controversy here of the type required to create a limited public figure? If so, did the plaintiff have the requisite special prominence in the controversy?

"The Golden Fleece Award"
(Answer)

In the Supreme Court's view, this was not a public controversy. At most, there existed a "concern about general public expenditures," undoubtedly shared by most people, but insufficient to make the scientist a public figure. To say otherwise, the Court reasoned, would result in a subject-matter classification for the limited public figure test rather than one based on the status of the person defamed.

Even if this did qualify as the proper type of public controversy, the Court said the scientist never "assumed any role of public prominence in the broad question of concern about expenditures." His mere applications for grants and his publications in professional journals did not invite "that degree of public attention and comment on his receipt of federal grants essential to meet the public figure level."[185]

As these cases show, the Supreme Court's standards require that the controversy be a public one, that is "a dispute that in fact has received public attention because its ramifications will be felt by persons who are not direct participants."[186] Moreover, the absence of a real debate and clearly delineated contours to a public question means there is no public controversy, notwithstanding ample and legitimate public concern. And even when a pre-existing public controversy is manifest, the plaintiff must assume special prominence in the debate by seeking to affect its outcome. An individual's mere newsworthiness, or even criminal conduct, have little bearing on the ultimate outcome of the test. Participation must also be voluntary. There is little space in the limited public figure category for people "caught up" in a controversy who do not join in. When any of these elements are missing, a plaintiff simply has not invited the kind of attention and comment which voluntarily exposes himself or herself to increased risk of injury from defamation.

In identifying public controversies, have other courts assimilated these rigorous requirements? Yes, but not always. Some decisions, following the Supreme Court's lead, have refused to recognize public controversies because they were not specific enough, or not extant at the time of the defamation, or not sufficiently public, or not much like a debate. None of the following issues measured up:

• Violations in the recruitment of college athletes (not specific);[187]

• An investigation of the lending policies of the Farmers Home Administration (too unspecific particularly because the plaintiff was not among the targets of the investigation);[188]

• The financial health of a bank (no controversy prior to the report in issue which erroneously alleged poor financial health);[189]

• The plaintiff's role as a physician and his implied inaction in response to the collapse of a person in need (though newsworthy, not a controversy);[190]

• Solicitation of investors for a tax-exempt bond fund (a matter of public concern but not a public controversy);[191]

• A proposal for an intermediate care facility for mentally retarded children before a formal application had been made and before the public was afforded "sufficient information to make any judgment" (at such an early stage there was no identified opposition, no discussion by the town board, and no public debate);[192]

• Whether a man was manipulating young naval recruits into homosexual relationships against their wills under the guise of religious counseling (whether the plaintiff was a homosexual cannot be a public controversy and there was no public controversy prior to the defamatory article; furthermore, to find a public controversy would presuppose that the plaintiff was luring naval recruits into homosexual relationships, for which there was no evidence);[193]

• Whether otolaryngologists were qualified to perform plastic surgery (this may have been a pre-existing controversy, but it was not a sufficiently public one, being of interest chiefly to physicians who perform plastic surgery and "substantially private" in nature).[194]

This is not to suggest that pre-existing public controversies have never been identified under the Supreme Court's criteria. Those that have qualified include the following two examples: the heated public dispute over the role played by the drugs Thalidomide and Bendectin in causing birth defects;[195] and the investigation by a Congressional subcommittee into the activities of a large beef processing company which included a number of public hearings, was widely reported in the media, and caused a controversy owing primarily to the investigation's potential to generate new legislation that might have affected both the meat industry and consumers.[196]

In other cases, however, judges have brought an innovative approach to determining the existence of a public controversy by either reciting the Supreme Court's standards and modifying them, or by ignoring them from the outset. Each of the following issues was found to be a public controversy:

• Alleged involvement in a major drug smuggling ring two and one-half years after charges to that effect were dropped[197] (this decision not only bumped up against the Supreme Court's holding that criminal activity alone could not create public figure status, but also explicitly rejected the Court's observation that there could be no controversy in the absence of a public disagreement, as with the desirability of drug trafficking);[198]

• The arrest and conviction of a triple murderer (the court simply observed that particularly heinous crimes "are public controversies and automatically become matters of great concern to the public");[199]

• The plaintiff's association with various "personalities" who appeared themselves to be subjects of widespread media reports;[200]

• Any employment which attracts "massive public attention," such as playing professional football.[201]

Because of this range of interpretations, it can be difficult to predict how a given matter of public concern will figure in a limited public figure equation.

Moreover, the controversy question is only the first half of the assumption of risk analysis for limited public figures. After identifying a specific pre-existing public controversy, a court must still determine whether the plaintiff achieved *special prominence* in that controversy by seeking to affect its outcome and thereby invited attention and comment. Both questions must be answered in the affirmative, according to the Supreme Court's test, before the individual can be said to have assumed the risk—characteristic of limited public figures—of inadvertent misstatements in the media.

Remember that the Supreme Court acknowledged the hypothetical existence of involuntary limited public figures, [202] but rejected public figure status for Mrs. Firestone, the monkey scientist, and the alleged Soviet spy.[203] Those who qualify as involuntary public figures must therefore be extremely rare in the Supreme Court's view, if they exist at all.[204]

Cases which closely follow the Supreme Court's criteria for identifying voluntary prominence in a public controversy do sometimes find limited public figure status. For example, regarding the public controversy (mentioned above) about drugs and birth defects, a research physician qualified as a limited public figure because he had gained international respect and renown for his research in the field of such drugs. He had traveled from Australia to the United States to testify before the FDA and on behalf of plaintiffs in a civil suit in Florida. By speaking of how the drugs caused defects, he voluntarily achieved special prominence in this controversy and sought to influence the outcome of the dispute.[205]

The highest court in Rhode Island recently applied the Supreme Court's criteria and found that a group of plaintiffs involved in "interstate waste collection" were public figures. The public controversy involved allegations that toxic waste was being illegally dumped in the state, and that organized crime was involved in the scheme. (The plaintiffs were accused of involvement in the illegal dumping and of organized crime connections.) The court noted that the controversy had been the "subject of dozens of newspaper articles" in which the plaintiffs were prominently mentioned. Moreover, one or more of the plaintiffs had consented to be interviewed or made statements to the media relating to the controversy. The access to media and assumption of risk requirements were therefore satisfied.[206]

Not surprisingly, rigorous application of the Supreme Court's criteria usually achieves the opposite result. In each of the following cases there existed insufficient voluntary prominence in public controversies to justify public figure status:

- A former executive in a large beef processing company which was being investigated by a Congressional subcommittee, appeared under subpoena as a witness and cooperated with the subcommittee "as he had an obligation to do" by answering questions; before and after his testimony he conscientiously avoided the media by making no public comment;[207]

- A farmer and businessman who borrowed money from the Farmers Home Administration was one of the subjects of an investigation by the agency of its loan practices, there being some question as to whether he met the criteria for the loans he accepted. However, he neither took a role in an investigation nor attempted to influence its outcome by assuming any role of public prominence;[208]

- A reputed Mafia member who had attracted a substantial amount of publicity alleging his connections with organized crime, never sought publicity or acted in any way "calculated or destined to knowingly bring [him] publicity and notoriety";[209]

- A California man who was one of the 52 Americans taken hostage in Iran in 1979 and held for 444 days, who participated in a televised Christmas message urging the return of the deposed Shah to Iran, but who (needless to say) did not become involved in these events voluntarily, was not a public figure;[210]

- A cocktail lounge owner who was charged and convicted of arson but who won a new trial on appeal and gave an interview to a local newspaper on the day his conviction was reversed, and who was the subject of numerous articles relating to his trial, was still not a public figure. Though his interview allowed him to profess his innocence, it was primarily a reaction to the court's decision to reverse his criminal conviction and he took no other action seeking notoriety.[211]

"The Mistake About Misdiagnosis"

A 16-year-old youth named John became ill with the flu; because of the severity of his symptoms, the family doctor suspected that he was suffering from Reye's Syndrome and instructed the boy's mother by telephone to take him to St. John's Hospital, where he would meet them. The mother called the police for assistance, but the officers who responded suspected the boy was on drugs and insisted on taking him to Harrison Hospital, which handled drug cases, where Dr. Pesta was on duty. The doctors at Harrison failed to diagnose John's illness and the boy died.

Several years later, in a segment of the CBS program "60 Minutes," another doctor expressed the opinion that the doctors at Harrison Hospital made a "critical mistake" by failing to order liver function studies on the boy. Another statement in the segment suggested that John would have had an 80-90% chance of recovery if he had not been misdiagnosed in the emergency room. Dr. Pesta, who was also interviewed on the program, sued for libel.

Is Dr. Pesta a limited purpose public figure?

"The Mistake About Misdiagnosis"
(Answer)

Dr. Pesta is not a public figure. Although there was a public controversy (the dispute arising from the alleged medical mistreatment or misdiagnosis of the youth), Dr. Pesta did not invite public attention to his views in an effort to influence public opinion about the boy's treatment prior to the defamatory program. The mere fact that he submitted to an interview on "60 Minutes" did not mean he assumed any position of prominence in the public controversy itself. The court refused to let producers interview a private person in order to make a public figure out of him. And after rejecting "assumption of risk," the court also found that the plaintiff did not maintain "regular and continuing access to the media."[212]

That the Supreme Court's rigorous standard respecting voluntary prominence weighs heavily against recognition of limited public figures does not mean, however, they are infrequently found. In a good number of other cases, the Supreme Court's standards for identifying voluntary prominence in a public controversy have either been used creatively or ignored. It seems that many lower courts yearn for a content-based test for limited public figure status—the one rejected by the Supreme Court—which would make a public figure of anyone publicly involved in a matter of public concern.[213] The following cases exemplify this yearning:

- When a food cooperative's president was dismissed, a trade publication erroneously stated that the cooperative had been losing money and had been retrenching. The executive said the error damaged his professional reputation and sued. He was found to be a limited public figure because the food cooperative had undertaken trail-blazing marketing policies (like unit pricing, open dating and highly competitive advertising), and the executive had pursued these policies and other consumer-oriented activities. The plaintiff was therefore deemed prominent in two public controversies: one about the viability of cooperatives as a form of commercial enterprise and one about the wisdom of these various precedent-breaking policies.[214]

- The boyfriend of a woman who collapsed at a party from a drug overdose (and later died) falsely told *The Washington Post* that he had been alone with the woman and had called for emergency assistance when actually others were in attendance, possibly including officials of the city administration with whom the boyfriend had many social contacts. The court found that the boyfriend's "hobnob[bing]" with high officials caused him to run the risk that "personal tragedies . . . [would] place him at the heart of a public controversy" in which he would become embroiled. This conduct, which the court emphasized had occurred before any controversy arose, plus his false statements at the outset of the controversy which went "beyond an ordinary citizen's response to the eruption of a public fray around him," made him a limited public figure.[215]

- *Penthouse* magazine reported that "the typical new dope businessman is an attorney," and gave the example of a lawyer from the Philadelphia area who, according to *Penthouse*, "contributed down payments of up to $25,000 on grass transactions." The article also reported that "[c]harges against him were dismissed because he cooperated with further investigations." In fact, the attorney had been indicted for the crime of contributing $25,000 for the purchase of marijuana and the charges were with-drawn, but the attorney sued for defamation because the article suggested he was *guilty* of an offense for which he was only *indicted*. He also contested that the charges were dropped for the reason stated. There was no evidence that the attorney attracted attention to his clients or himself with regard to their legal relationship. But his voluntary social connection with motorcycle gangs "in conjunction with the intense media attention he engendered" made him a public figure "for the limited purpose of his connection with illicit drug trafficking," which was not proved. (Note also the broadly drawn public controversy.)[216]

• An executive director of a country club, owned by a pension fund with reputed organized crime connections, who never disputed his associations with various "personalities" who appeared themselves to be subjects of widespread media reports, sued for defamation when *Playboy* called him "a California mobster." Without any mention of any effort by the plaintiff to seek to affect the outcome of any controversy, the court found him a limited public figure because of his voluntary choice of associations amounting to a course of conduct "that was bound to invite intention and comment."[217]

• An insurance agent who became "agent of record" to the county was deemed a limited public figure notwithstanding the lack of a prior public controversy, the agent's lack of voluntary participation in a controversy, and his lack of access to the media, all of which were acknowledged by the court. However, because the agent assumed the position of selling insurance to a governmental body, he was deemed to assume a role of public prominence respecting a matter of public concern.[218]

• A man who was accused in the press of committing a triple murder—nine months before he was actually convicted for it—sued for libel. The court determined that the crime, heinous as it was, constituted a public controversy all by itself, and the killer's participation in the controversy prior to the defamatory article was demonstrated by: the intense media coverage of the murder investigation and its eventual focus on the then-suspect; his voluntary act of turning himself in to the police; and his subsequent arrest and indictment for the triple murders.[219]

This last example, like other cases, raises the question of whether intense media attention can create a public controversy all by itself. The Supreme Court answered this question in the negative first by saying that "mere newsworthiness" will not justify application of the Actual Malice

Standard,[220] and then by making clear that even when the defamatory report about the individual becomes a matter of controversy, the public figure test will still not be satisfied. The Supreme Court held, "[c]learly, those charged with defamation cannot, by their own conduct, create their own defense by making the claimant a public figure."[221] So, as noted above, the media could not invite a private person to submit to an interview in an attempt to make that person a public figure, either for the same report which contained the defamation[222] or afterward.

But what about a defamatory report which follows a long string of reports by other media which have created intense public interest and perhaps debate? In the case of the triple murderer, the court found that intensity of prior news coverage did create a public controversy without reference to voluntary prominence apart from the criminal act. By the Supreme Court's standard, however, even when a public controversy materializes, the issue of voluntary prominence in the debate still needs to be addressed. In another case which applied the Supreme Court's standard, a "voluminous amount of newspaper and magazine articles" suggested that a man was associated with organized crime, but his failure to enter that debate still prevented him from being a limited public figure.[223]

A journalist, therefore, needs the skill (and luck) to discern when a public controversy has presented itself and to identify persons who have voluntarily achieved enough prominence in the controversy to earn limited public figure status. Both determinations can be risky, depending often on whether the judge who gets the case chooses to follow the Supreme Court's rigorous rules.

And do not forget, there is still a third hurdle in the assumption of risk criterion for limited public figures. By the Supreme Court's standards, a palpable public controversy *and* a plaintiff's voluntary prominence in it, are *still* insufficient to establish a limited public figure. Additionally, the defamatory statement must fit within the context of the public controversy in which the plaintiff has prominence.[224] So, even when (1) there is definitely a public controversy and (2) the plaintiff is voluntarily prominent within that controversy, that plaintiff will be treated as a private person if the subject of the defamation is not connected to the controversy.

Prior to the suit brought by the former employee against the beef processor (see p. 65), the employee was busily sharing documents he had taken from the processor's premises with various individuals interested in the processor's business practices, in private meetings without publicity. But these efforts were not deemed related to the Congressional subcommittee's investigation of the company which was the only public controversy the court could identify.[225] (Had the contour of the controversy been considered broad enough to embrace all efforts to oppose the meat processor's power, influence, and practices, the former employee's efforts would have qualified for public figure treatment.)

Other cases show the opposite side of the coin, where the public controversy is defined with ample breadth—or stretched—to embrace the topic of the defamatory statement. In the case of the doctor from Australia who testified regarding the connection between certain drugs and birth defects (see p. 11), the defamatory statement alleged that he had received $5,000 per day to testify as an expert witness—well above money paid to other witnesses—when, in fact, he only received $1,116 per day. Having defined the public controversy as the debate concerning the drug, the court could have found that the amount paid the expert witness had nothing directly to do with the merits of the drug, as opposed to the merits of the expert. This would have placed the defamation outside the limited range of issues as to which this public figure assumed risk. Instead, the court found a sufficient connection and applied the Actual Malice Standard.[226]

The point to remember is that even if the defamation relates to a public controversy and the individual has special prominence in the controversy, if the defamatory statement is not germane to the controversy, there will be no limited public figure—at least by the Supreme Court's standards.

The Access to Media Criterion

A second justification for the distinction between public and private persons rests on the premise that public figures, both general and limited, usually have greater access to channels of effective communication and a more realistic opportunity to counteract false statements, making them less vulnerable to injury.

Of the four Supreme Court plaintiffs described above (pages 57–62), all of them except Mrs. Firestone (who resisted public figure status on other grounds) were specifically found not to satisfy the access to media criterion:

• The lawyer who represented the family of a youth killed by a Chicago policeman in a civil suit against the murderer accepted a case that was certain to receive extensive media exposure. (He was subsequently libeled as a Communist with a criminal record by a group which interpreted his representation of the family as an attack on the police.) In finding the lawyer a private person, the Supreme Court emphasized that he never discussed with the press either the policeman's criminal prosecution or the civil litigation against the policeman and was never quoted as having done so.[227]

• The man whose aunt and uncle admitted guilt to espionage charges, failed to appear for grand jury hearing and pleaded guilty to the contempt charge arising from his nonappearance and was later defamed as a Soviet agent himself. The fact that he ''never discussed this matter with the press'' also disposed of the media access issue.[228]

• The scientist who performed experiments on monkeys, who was defamed by a Senator's accusations that he was wasting government grants on worthless inquiries, also failed to satisfy the media access requirement. The Supreme Court noted that his access was limited to responding to the defamation and, most importantly, he ''did not have the regular and continuing access to the media that is one of the accouterments of having become a public figure.''[229]

By these standards, media access is sufficient only when it precedes the controversy to which the defamation pertains, and can be characterized as ''regular and continuing'' rather than sporadic or occasional. Media access which follows the defamation, say for purposes of responding, is not the right kind; the media exposure must precede the defamation to establish the individual as the type who can correct misstatements when and if they occur.[230]

Not surprisingly, lower court decisions which apply this criterion with rigor often result in private figure status for the plaintiff. An assistant basketball coach at the University of Pittsburgh, accused falsely of violating recruitment rules, occasionally received press attention prior to the defamation and hypothetically might have been asked for his views if the local media were to publish an article on ''some nationwide recruiting controversy.'' However, this level of access did not imply that the coach could ''have insisted his views be published'' and therefore did not rise to ''the level of the regular and continuing access'' characteristic of public figures.[231] The doctor who was accused of mistreating and misdiagnosing a patient (page 66), failed to cross over to public figure status by submitting to an interview on the program ''60 Minutes'' several years after the peak of the controversy.[232] An inventor's demonstration of his new invention to which he invited the media, similarly failed to establish ''regular and continuing access to the press.''[233]

Such cases reflect the Supreme Court's view that contact with the media is by no means the same as regular and continuing access. This distinction is not always self-evident.

"The Bond Seller"

Mr. Jadwin formed two corporations in order to create a tax-exempt mutual bond fund in the state of Minnesota. He was the president of both companies and the principal shareholder of one. In a promotional effort to attract investors to the fund, Mr. Jadwin placed advertisements in newspapers throughout the state and mailed 13,000 copies of a prospectus and supplemental sales literature to prospective investors. He also issued a 4-page press release to 30 newspapers and magazines to announce the creation of the tax-exempt fund.

A newspaper article later appeared which was highly critical of Mr. Jadwin's efforts. The article said he lacked mutual fund management experience and that the fund registration was approved only when he agreed to keep the fund's expenses "within legal limits." The article also accused Jadwin of misrepresenting his past employments.

Jadwin sued. Did he have sufficient media access to meet the Supreme Court's criterion for a limited public figure?

"The Bond Seller"
(Answer)

Though Jadwin did solicit media attention to his enterprise, he did not cross the public figure threshold. His efforts to solicit public investment were insufficient to satisfy "the rationale of access to rebut the alleged libelous publication that is a distinguishing feature between private individuals and public figures."[234]

In a rigorous application of the Supreme Court's test, press releases and even a few press conferences may not be sufficient media access to confer public figure status.[235] Most courts, however, have interpreted this standard far more broadly. One frequently cited case (see p. 67 above) involved an executive of a food cooperative. He was known in the trade for his innovations like unit pricing and was defamed by an article that said the cooperative he ran was losing money and retrenching. Although the executive was ''not frequently'' the subject of news articles, he had held press conferences to discuss the cooperative's policies and operations. The court therefore considered him ''somewhat familiar with press operation'' and on the basis of these limited ''prior dealings with the media'' (as well as the ''overall picture'' of other factors) the businessman's media access was found sufficient.[236]

Other plaintiffs have been declared public figures without satisfying the media access requirement simply because courts give it less weight than voluntary assumption of risk. One reason is the Supreme Court's own observation that the ''self-help remedy of rebuttal, standing alone,'' seldom suffices to undo the harm of defamatory falsehood.[237] To explain why the assumption of risk criterion is more important, a federal judge also offered the compelling logic that ''[a]lmost anyone who finds himself in the middle of a controversy will likely have enough access to the press to rebut any allegedly libelous statements.''[238] Some cases have done more than reduce the weight given access to media: they ignore the requirement completely.[239]

In short, judicial application of the media access factor is as unpredictable as application of the assumption of risk requirement. Uncertainty springs not only from interpretation of the Supreme Court's criterion, but also from whether the criterion will be applied at all. These cases illustrate once again how the media's ability to invoke the Actual Malice Standard can be reduced not only by a change in the rules, but also by a more rigorous application of those already in place.

Corporations, organizations, religious groups and the like can be limited public figures but in most jurisdictions, it is not to be taken for granted.[240] Likewise, executive status within a prominent and influential company will not in and of itself confer limited public figure status even when a public controversy exists.[241] A corporation, organization, or executive is capable of voluntarily entering a public controversy but the same limiting standards will usually apply. For example, a bank which engaged in an extensive advertising campaign did not become a limited public figure for purposes of false defamatory comments about its financial health; there was no ''correlation'' between the bank's promotional efforts and the defamation. The facts that the bank was part of a heavily regulated industry, or that the public had an ''ongoing public interest in the stability of society's financial institutions,'' or that the bank enjoyed a ''relatively high public profile,'' were insufficient to make it a public figure.[242] Other decisions, however, have demonstrated that high-profile factors like these increase the likelihood of public figure status for business plaintiffs. It has been estimated that in the aggregate, decisions are about equally divided between those conferring public figure status on corporations and those which do not.[243]

Although the Supreme Court has not expressly addressed the issue,[244] it does seem clear that a reasonable passage of time will not extinguish a plaintiff's limited public figure status as long as either the plaintiff or the controversy is still known to the public, and the plaintiff would have qualified as a public figure at the time the public controversy was current.[245]

In summary, in order to determine whether a libel plaintiff is a limited public figure (as opposed to a private person), the first question is whether the individual assumed the risk of defamatory misstatements in the press by voluntarily wading into a public controversy and assuming a special prominence by seeking to affect its outcome. Though lower courts frequently have been generous to media defendants, their burdens will multiply should those courts pay more attention to the existing Supreme Court rules. In some lower courts, controversies have been broadly defined and special prominence in controversies have been identified even for persons involuntarily caught up in them. But the Supreme Court's stricter standards are enforced in other instances. Moreover, the defamation must be pertinent to the person's participation in the controversy and the controversy must exist prior to the defamation. Mere newsworthiness of the individual—either before or after the defamation—is not enough. Intense public interest and saturation media coverage will not suffice to create a public figure under the Supreme Court's tests.[246]

Even with assumed risk by involvement in a particular controversy, the individual must usually also command access to media before limited public figure status will be conferred. Access must precede the controversy and be regular and continuing. This criterion is not as important as assumption of risk, and is not as frequently applied, but it is likely to figure into any rigorous application of the Supreme Court's standards.

APPLYING THE ACTUAL MALICE STANDARD

As already noted, the Actual Malice Standard is used to determine whether a defendant will be held responsible for a false defamatory statement made about someone the courts accept as a public official or public figure. The Actual Malice Standard also applies to private persons in important ways: in a handful of states, it must be satisfied by *private* persons as well as public persons to collect "actual damages" for out-of-pocket losses, embarrassment, humiliation and the like. (This is very rare; the Private Person Standard will almost always serve this function.) In all states, public *and* private persons must meet the Actual Malice Standard when the defamation involves a matter of public concern, before jackpot awards of presumed and punitive damages will be allowed.[247]

Otherwise, the Actual Malice Standard applies only to assessing the fault of a defendant who makes a defamatory statement about a public person which turns out to be false. Falsity is the point of departure; if the statement is either proved true or, in most instances, the plaintiff cannot prove it false, the defendant wins without ever reaching the Actual Malice Standard. This measure assesses the quality and quantity of proof obtained by the defendant before making a false statement as well as the defendant's belief in its truth.

Good faith and rudimentary good sense are starting points for the Actual Malice Standard, which is founded upon assumptions of *responsible* reporting and the benefits it brings to a free society. The Standard's higher burden for plaintiffs derives from the U.S. Supreme Court's interpretation of the First Amendment. The Court has determined that the constitutional interest in the flow of information about public affairs is so strong, and that discovering the truth about public persons can be so difficult—even with the best of efforts—that those who write and speak about them require "some breathing room." The Supreme Court has accepted that if the press must face potentially staggering damages for every published mistake which injures a reputation, the result would be an unacceptable degree of self-censorship. Though such restraint would prevent the occasional mistake in libel, it would also constrict the timely flow of news which may not be readily verifiable but is believed to be true. The press is therefore given a privilege to spread false information from time to time even if it damages someone's reputation as long as a certain level of care is demonstrated.[248] That level is defined by the Actual Malice Standard for statements made about public officials and public figures.

The Supreme Court's rules for applying the Actual Malice Standard are usually followed by other courts. They do not, for example, readily employ the same startling creativity which has delineated the limited public figure. As already noted, the Actual Malice Standard allows defendants to escape liability for a false defamatory statement unless they acted with (a) knowledge of the statement's falsity or (b) reckless disregard of whether the statement is false or not (at least in the sense of having substantial doubts as to the truth). In other words, the standard requires "deliberate or reckless falsity"[249] for the media to lose a case. Actual malice may not be inferred from mere evidence of personal spite, ill will or intention to injure.[250] Nor will an intention to boost circulation or ratings prove actual malice all by itself.[251] Evidence of improper motive, however, will sometimes become part of the actual malice inquiry if, when combined with other factors, it helps show that deliberate or reckless falsity was also at work.[252]

The Actual Malice Standard does not just measure the conduct of the defendant against what a reasonably prudent man or woman would have published or would have investigated before publishing.[253] A newspaper or broadcast station will not lose its privilege to publish the inadvertent false statement simply because its employees have been negligent by failing to employ "ordinary care."[254] Even inadvertent implications and juxtapositions which defame will not amount to actual malice.[255] However, like improper motive, the degree of care employed by a journalist can enter into the actual malice calculus when it combines with other factors to show deliberate or reckless falsity.[256]

A defendant cannot expect to pass the standard's test by appearing in court, conjuring up the sincerity of a seven o'clock news anchor, and protesting that he or she deeply believed the statement to be true. Having a clear conscience, and even some proof, will not prevail unless a judge and jury can be persuaded of a good faith basis for one's belief. Though the Actual Malice Standard is a subjective test looking toward the defendant's state of mind, a plaintiff can demonstrate an "incriminating" state of mind through circumstantial evidence.[257] And when a statement is inherently implausible, or a reporter otherwise has obvious reasons to doubt its veracity, professions of good faith might not win a lawsuit.[258] A reporter's version of what he or she was thinking can be ignored.[259]

"The Governor Molests Children"

A newsman named Myers receives a telephone call:
Voice: Hello, Myers? I want you to listen good.
Myers: Who is this?
Voice: Never mind. Just listen. The governor has a taste for little boys—likes to molest them. Take it from me—I work

in his office. I know. He's controlled himself since the election but I saw it happen this afternoon—and he's got another one lined up for tomorrow. Something's got to be done. (Click)

    Myers: Hello? Hello? (Dial tone)

Myers is ten minutes from deadline.

What is the significance of the governor's status as a public official? What should Myers do?

"The Governor Molests Children"
(Answer)

What Myers should *not* do is publish the allegation without further investigation.

First, the statement is definitely defamatory and, worse yet, it falls into one of the particularly sensitive categories because it imputes sexual misconduct.

Secondly, the statement comes from an anonymous source. That the anonymous caller characterizes himself as a highly placed source and the subject is the governor have no bearing at all. The allegation is a serious one and anonymous sources are among the least reliable in the eyes of the law. To publish the accusation without verification could amount to "reckless disregard of truth or falsity" resulting in substantial damages, notwithstanding that the governor is a public official and that the alleged sexual misconduct could affect his ability to govern (for example, by making him a target for blackmail).

Myers should obtain verification from one or more reliable sources before reporting the accusation.

This example (which recalls the example in the Introduction concerning the allegedly tax-dodging mayor) presents a pedigreed breed of actual malice: the unverified anonymous telephone tip.[260] It is tantamount to complete fabrication. Courts will not dwell on whether a defendant believed an anonymous tip to be true; when proof is this weak, the law assumes that the defendant had serious doubts about its truth.

During the discovery stage of a litigation, when the plaintiff is entitled to take depositions, demand documents, and propound interrogatories, the plaintiff's lawyer will burrow and probe for anything suggesting knowing or reckless falsity. A plaintiff can ask for the defendant's conclusions at each stage of research and investigation: What leads were pursued or not pursued and why? What were the defendant's conclusions about facts offered by sources? What was the defendant's state of mind with respect to the truthfulness of persons interviewed? To the extent the defendant reached a conclusion concerning truthfulness of persons, information or events, what was the basis for those conclusions? What conversations occurred between reporters or between reporters and editors about including and excluding material? And what were the defendant's intentions as demonstrated by a resulting decision to include or exclude material?[261] This process can obviously be lengthy, time-consuming and expensive—and worse yet, may afford the plaintiff an argument based on circumstantial evidence which was lacking at the outset of the suit.

Investigatory techniques which are "slipshod and sketchy"[262] or in some cases completely absent, may contribute toward inferences of actual malice. And impeccable research will be of little use if it does not pertain to that part of the writing or broadcast which is defamatory. "It is the individual allegedly libelous statement (taken in its proper context) rather than the accuracy of the publication as a whole, which is on trial," as one federal appellate judge has observed. "A falsehood published with actual malice is no less actionable for being surrounded by an array of well documented and carefully researched allegations." The truth surrounding the statement not only fails to eliminate the libel, but also increases its credibility.[263]

The most obvious examples of actual malice are false defamatory statements which are fabricated or spring from the imagination of the defendant without any proof at all.[264] Deliberate distortions of the truth are close behind. For example, a talk show host accused a candidate appearing on the show of passing a bad check on the basis that a $697 draft, issued to pay for political advertising on the same station, had bounced. The host knew, however, that the check came not from the candidate or his campaign organization, but rather from his advertising agency. The candidate lost the election but, proving actual malice, won his lawsuit against the host and the corporation which owned the station.[265]

A reporter can have sources and still be charged with knowledge of a statement's falsity. For example, in a Rhode Island case, the president of a YMCA board of directors, who is also a physician, was informed at a directors' meeting that a man who had just left the meeting collapsed outside. The physician asked if he could be of any help, but was told that two people were administering CPR and that an ambulance had either arrived or was on the way. A reporter at the scene assisted in administering CPR, which commenced shortly after the man's collapse. An ambulance arrived five to ten minutes afterward. Nevertheless, the man died.

The reporter then interviewed a friend of the dead man and the dead man's son, among others, and wrote two articles. One article accurately related the friend's criticisms of the physician for his failure to respond at the scene with aid. The second article accurately described the son's angry complaint that his father should have been given earlier medical attention, again implying the physician's fault. Both articles were inconsistent with the reporter's own eyewitness experience, but he never disclosed, either to the persons whose complaints he reported or to the newspaper's readers, that the heart attack victim had been promptly attended. The physician sued and demonstrated that, notwithstanding his sources, the reporter published the defamatory accusations against the physician with knowledge of their falsity, or reckless disregard of whether the implication was false or not.[266]

Actual malice can also be imputed in cases of extreme journalistic sloppiness. For example, when one reporter mistakenly wrote that two deputies were convicted of taking bribes (when they were convicted only of malfeasance for allowing an inmate to leave on weekends), the newspaper ran a retraction. In the following month, when the inmate was again arrested and another reporter wrote of his previous newspaper exposure, she repeated the misstatement about the deputies after obtaining the information from the paper's computer files. Her editors missed the error. The deputies sued, and an appellate court agreed with them that these facts could establish knowing or reckless falsity in publishing the second erroneous article.[267]

In another example of extremely sloppy work, a news reporter appeared one Monday at the city police department to go over "incident reports" accumulated over the weekend. One incident report pertained to a scuffle outside a local night spot; one of the persons involved had reported the incident to the police but did not swear out a warrant against the man who fought with him. The reporter apparently misinterpreted the form, failed to check the arrest docket (ostensibly because of deadline pressure), and reported incorrectly that the alleged aggressor had been arrested and charged with assault and battery. A jury's conclusion that the reporter acted with actual malice was upheld on appeal.[268]

Many cases have demonstrated that even in the absence of knowing falsity or extreme sloppiness, a publisher or broadcaster still needs more than just *any* proof of a defamatory statement—and usually more than a minimum of proof—to avoid a finding of "recklessness" in the actual malice sense. A defendant needs proof of sufficient quantity and quality to justify a belief in its truth.

Failure to verify a report, in and of itself, does not necessarily establish knowledge of falsity or reckless disregard for the truth.[269] As long as the sources of libelous information appear reliable, and the defendant has no doubts about its accuracy, a public figure or official will lose a lawsuit even if a more thorough investigation might have prevented a defamatory error.[270] However, purposeful avoidance of the truth may be *inferred* from inaction in the face of probable falsity, and will establish actual malice.[271] Furthermore, some courts have noted that the seriousness of an allegation, and the potential harm it could cause, should heighten the effort required to justify a belief in its truth.[272] For these reasons, a reporter usually cannot stop with the first source who walks through the door. At least some investigative effort will be required.

Also, if other factors come to light which suggest a reason to doubt the truth of an allegation, failure to verify can tip the scales toward a finding of recklessness. A newspaper reported police brutality based on the accusations of two alleged victims, even though one of the two accused policemen was known to have a good reputation, one of the alleged victims had reportedly apologized to the officers, and that same victim "didn't sound too swift" to the reporter. The reporter's failure to verify the allegations which "were clearly serious enough to warrant some attempt at substantiation" manifested actual malice.[273] The failure to investigate was not reckless disregard of the truth by itself, but it became so when other facts confronting the journalist created a basis for doubt.

"The Fix"

The *Saturday Evening Post* published a story accusing Wallace Butts of fixing a football game between the University of Georgia (where he was athletic director) and the University of Alabama. The article reported that Butts gave Georgia's plays, defense patterns, and all of the team's significant secrets to the coach for the opposing side. The source for the accusation was an Atlanta insurance salesman who, through an "electronic error," accidentally overheard a telephone conversation between Butts and the other coach one week prior to the game. The informer's credentials were not impeccable—he had been placed on probation in connection with bad check charges—but he had made notes of the conversation with "specific examples of the divulged secrets." He said that Butts outlined Georgia's offensive plays and told the other coach how Georgia planned to defend, mentioning both players and plays by name. During the game in issue, Georgia's players took a "frightful physical beating" and, according to the article, some sideline observers were aware that Alabama was privy to Georgia's secrets. For investigative assistance, the *Post* writer had persons involved in another suit brought by the Alabama coach against the *Post*'s publisher, but their investigation was limited and they had no substantial source of verification.

In the ensuing lawsuit, Butts was considered a public figure and the accusation was shown to be false. (The informer *did* overhear a conversation, but Butts demonstrated that it went no further than general football talk.) Was there actual malice?

"The Fix"
(Answer)

Yes, there was actual malice. The U.S. Supreme Court agreed with the jury that the investigation undertaken by the *Post* was "grossly inadequate" particularly in view of the seriousness of the accusation. Among the "elementary precautions" ignored by the *Post*, according to the Court, were the following: The story was published without "substantial independent support" even when the *Post* knew that the informer had been placed on probation with bad check charges; those assisting the writer in his investigation, involved as they were in the Alabama coach's lawsuit, were deemed "unlikely to be the source of a complete and objective investigation." The Court also noted that the *Saturday Evening Post* was anxious to change its image by instituting a policy of "sophisticated muckraking," and the pressure to produce a successful expose might have induced a stretching of standards.

Though the jury returned a verdict for Butts in the amount of $60,000 in compensatory damages and $3,000,000 in punitive damages, the award was reduced to $460,000. This was still a substantial sum in 1967.[274] (The topic of what the *Post* might have investigated is taken up at pp. 100–101 below.)

The theme running throughout this case and others is that a reporter must continue research until obvious reasons to doubt the veracity of a source are eliminated. If more research suggests cause for further doubt, then either further research is required or the defamatory report should not be made.

Another illustration of this principle appears in another sports-related case. A newspaper reported that a basketball player recruited from high school had accused an assistant basketball coach at the University of Pittsburgh of offering him money if he came to the school. The transcript of an interview with the student showed that he never put the charge quite so specifically. For example, responding to a question of whether the coach was offering $100 or $1,000 or $5,000 the student athlete responded, "I was really kind of hesitate [sic] about talking about that because if I got to talking dollars and cents with him, then he would get the idea that at the right price, I could be bought to go to that school or whatever, so I didn't really get into that." The follow-up question was, "But do you feel like that was definitely what he was talking about?" which was answered by "Yeah. You know, just common sense on my part." The court found this exchange to be ambiguous at best, and that the newspaper's choice of the interpretation most damaging to the coach was sufficient to permit a jury to find serious doubt as to truthfulness.[275]

Bias in a source should put a reporter on special alert, though it need not disqualify a source completely. Persuading a judge or jury that such a source, even if biased, would not necessarily provide false information, might still avoid actual malice.[276] To trust in the power of that argument, however, with a single biased source, is a poor bet. The better approach is to use the biased source to corroborate unbiased ones.[277] Sole reliance on biased sources, or others who ought to raise doubt, constitutes a pure form of reckless disregard for truth or falsity.

"The Challenger and the Audio-tapes"

A lawyer (whom we will call Challenger) running for the position of municipal judge discovered just before the election that the chief court administrator of the incumbent municipal judge (whom we will call Incumbent) had been taking bribes to dispose of minor criminal charges. Challenger learned this from a witness named Patsy who said she had made cash payments to the administrator on 40 or 50 occasions. Challenger tape-recorded a lengthy interview during which Patsy detailed her accusations in the company of Patsy's sister, Alice, and seven of Challenger's supporters. After Patsy took a lie detector test and passed, Challenger delivered the tapes to the police and filed a written complaint against the administrator (who in due course was arrested, indicted and convicted).

On the day of the lie detector test, Alice, Patsy, Challenger, Challenger's wife and two of his supporters enjoyed a pleasant chat about a number of subjects. These included Challenger's plans to vacation in Florida with his wife after the election and the possibility that Challenger's wife might open an ice cream parlor some time in the future, at which Alice and Patsy might work as waitresses.

Several weeks later—just one week before the election—an article in the *Journal News* (which supported Incumbent) revealed startling accusations by Alice: that Challenger told her his purpose in taping the interview with Patsy was to get evidence with which to confront Incumbent privately and scare him into resigning; that Challenger promised to pay the expenses of a post-election vacation in Florida for Alice and Patsy; that he offered to set up their parents in the restaurant business; that he would provide jobs for the sisters; and that he would not allow knowledge of the sisters' involvement to become public. The *Journal News* did not fail to characterize these claims as allegations.

In preparing the article, the *Journal News* conducted a tape-recorded interview with Alice which later proved that her accusations had been accurately reported. The tape included Alice's explanation that she took offense at being called a "snitch and a rat" because of the sisters' accusations against the administrator and that she intended to "get that cleared up." She also said that when Patsy gave her tape-recorded interview to Challenger, he frequently turned off the recorder in order to ask leading questions without being heard. Her answers to questions were sometimes hesitant and unresponsive but she made clear her intent to prevent people from voting for a man who would use such dirty tricks and blackmail. At one point, Alice also assured the *Journal News* that Patsy would confirm everything she had said, but later suggested that Alice might be frightened or reluctant to do so.

Before publishing the story, the *Journal News* also interviewed Challenger, who did admit that at his meeting with the sisters on the day of the lie detector test, he may have speculated about what the Incumbent and the administrator would do if they heard the tapes (though he denied saying he would try to scare them into resigning); he admitted that he had told the sisters he hoped they could remain anonymous (though he said he never promised anonymity); he admitted that he and his wife had discussed the possibility that if his wife's dream of opening a gourmet ice cream shop should materialize, the sisters might work there; he also admitted referring to a possible Florida trip and a post-election victory dinner (but denied making any promises). Challenger's denials of the accusations and his contrary version of the events were duly noted in the article.

Before publishing the article, *Journal News* reporters also interviewed all of the witnesses to Challenger's discussions with the sisters, except Patsy; all of them were Challenger's supporters and corroborated Challenger. They said they missed Patsy because Challenger volunteered to have her get in touch with them, and he failed to do so. The reporters also obtained the tape of Patsy's interview with Challenger, but did not listen to it; they felt it would add nothing because the conversation to which Alice's charges referred was not on it. Soon after the interview with Alice, and before publishing her accusations (or interviewing the others), the paper ran an editorial expressing a distaste for dishonesty in campaign practices and predicting that further information concerning the integrity of the candidates might soon surface. After the article appeared, the *Journal News* endorsed Incumbent.

Challenger lost the election but sued the newspaper for libel. Because he was deemed a limited public figure, the Actual Malice Standard applied to his suit at trial. There were some discrepancies among the newspaper's witnesses as to the extent of the reporters' investigation; for example, it was unclear whether one reporter was directed by his editor to ask the police whether Alice had repeated her charges to them, and whether they considered her a credible witness. (In any event, no such inquiries were made.) The newspaper's employees testified that they believed Alice's allegations were all substantially true. Who won?

"The Challenger and the Audio-tapes"
(Answer)

Challenger won and was awarded $5,000 in compensatory damages and $195,000 in punitive damages, all affirmed by the U.S. Supreme Court. Although the *Journal News* reported Alice's charges as mere allegations, and included all of the Challenger's denials, the following reasons were sufficient to support the jury's finding of actual malice against the newspaper:

1.   The newspaper's failure to interview Patsy—the one witness who was most likely to *confirm* Alice's account—could reasonably demonstrate that the newspaper was committed to running the story before it began investigating. Denials by Challenger's supporters could be explained away but denials by Patsy could not.

2.   The prediction in the editorial that further information concerning the integrity of candidates might soon surface also indicated that the newspaper had decided to publish Alice's allegations before interviewing Challenger and the other witnesses.

3.   Six witnesses including Challenger unambiguously denied Alice's version.

4.   The reporters could have checked the veracity of some of Alice's peripheral allegations by listening to the tape of Patsy's interview, which they chose not to do. For example, they could have determined whether Challenger did selectively turn on and off the tape and avoid speaking when the recorder was running. (The Court also noted the strange lack of journalistic interest in the allegations of corruption against the Incumbent's court administrator, which were also on the tape.)

5.   The newspaper editorial focused its indignation on dishonesty in campaigning rather than dishonesty in the administration of the municipal court.

6.   Discrepancies in testimony by the newspaper's witnesses also may have given the jury the impression that the failure to conduct a complete investigation involved a deliberate effort to avoid the truth.

7.   Alice's charge that Challenger intended to confront Incumbent to scare him into resigning, and not disclose the tapes publicly, was not only highly improbable but inconsistent with Challenger's arranging for a lie detector test and delivering the tapes to the police.

8.   Alice's hesitant and sometimes unresponsive answers to the newspaper's questions also raised obvious doubts about her truthfulness.

In short, the Court said the jury must have believed Challenger, disbelieved the *Journal News*, and concluded that the newspaper had made a deliberate decision not to acquire knowledge of facts that might confirm the probable falsity of Alice's charges. Although failure to investigate alone will not support a finding of actual malice, "the purposeful avoidance of the truth is in a different category." Every Justice on the Supreme Court agreed with the results.[278]

Both this case and the example with coach Butts show how direct or circumstantial evidence of an intent to run a story regardless of the results of investigation can help prove actual malice.

These cases also demonstrate the advisability of verifying a story with the most likely sources of information, which frequently include the person about whom the defamatory statement is made. As long as other factors do not generate doubt about the truth of a statement, and thereby suggest a need to verify with its subject, failure to do so is not reckless disregard of the truth.[279] However, whenever a defamatory statement turns out to be false, and other factors do indicate some cause for doubt (which frequently occurs), failure to interview the subject of a story can be counted against the defendant in the actual malice calculus.[280] In a case against *Newsweek*, the magazine argued that if the subject had been interviewed, he would have responded with "unhelpful, blank denials." But the court dismissed this argument as speculation; "*Newsweek* never asked the questions, and it cannot know whether the answers would have provided information which would have been helpful in determining what really happened."[281]

At first glance, this may seem a no-win proposition. If a journalist fails to ask the subject of the statement for a response, and other factors point toward reasons for doubt, actual malice may be found; if the journalist does ask for a response from a subject who denies everything (as they usually will), would that result in actual malice too? Courts have answered this question with a "not necessarily." If the person defamed furnishes "specific, verifiable facts contradicting the allegations so directly as to cause any reasonable person to conduct further inquiry," actual malice might be demonstrated in the absence of further inquiry; but general denials or unspecific demands for retractions, standing alone, will not suffice to show actual malice.[282]

Remember that the same issue of verification applies to everything which is published or broadcast including stories accepted from third parties, advertisements, letters to the editor, editorials, and sidebars.[283] Although absence of deadline pressure at the time of publication does not necessarily make a journalist "more accountable," it does make failure to verify more difficult to explain when his or her state of mind (i.e. belief in truth) is being scrutinized. As one federal court put it, "when an article is not in the category of 'hot news,' that is, information that must be printed immediately or it will lose its newsworthy value," then "actual malice may be inferred when the investigation for a story . . . was grossly inadequate in the circumstances."[284] The court's logic is that when a reporter has the luxury of time to investigate a story, failure to do so (assuming the existence of any doubt-causing factor) is more easily construed as "willful blinding" to the truth.[285] On the other hand, the overriding test is still knowing or reckless falsity even when the news is hot. Rushing to publish or broadcast a breaking story despite serious doubts as to truth will still constitute actual malice.[286]

Is there any dispensation for live programming such as a call-in show? There is no reason to expect one; this is why a seven-second delay and screening procedures are prudent.

Turning now to another anonymous phone call:

"Another Anonymous Phone Call"

On Sunday, a television reporter received two telephone calls from a male voice who identified himself only as the son of a senior officer of an international company with headquarters nearby. The caller told the reporter that a scientist at the company planned to leave for Taiwan to sell documents and the company had gone to court to stop her. He disclosed the full name of the scientist, where she lived and worked, that she was working on a blood sugar device, and that she had been caught copying trade secrets which she planned to sell for a million dollars or more.

On Monday, the reporter went to court and obtained a copy of a legal complaint filed by the corporation against the scientist. The complaint alleged that sensitive materials had been discovered in the scientist's office and at the photocopying machine in close proximity to the office. It indicated that the scientist had access to and misappropriated protectable trade secrets and that she was preparing for a meeting in Taiwan with potential competitors of the company at which the secrets would be "discussed and disclosed."

The reporter concluded that because the legal complaint had been filed after 6:00 P.M. on Friday, when the court was closed to the public, the tipster had to have inside knowledge. The reporter also telephoned the scientist who confirmed she was soon departing for Taiwan though not, she insisted, to sell trade secrets. The scientist declined an opportunity to be interviewed on camera on advice of counsel, and her lawyer would not discuss the case at all. The reporter made no further efforts to verify the story; she did not, for example, try to speak to anyone at the company.

That evening, the reporter broadcast the story including the tipster's assertion that the scientist had been offered one million dollars for trade secrets about the blood sugar device, which neither the legal complaint nor any other source of information supported. The scientist sued. At trial, the reporter testified that she accepted the tipster's word because she had verified other parts of the story and nothing he said had been shown to be false.

If the allegations were false, was this actual malice?

"Another Anonymous Phone Call"
(Answer)

According to the court which considered this case, no actual malice was demonstrated even though the reporter failed to confirm from a second source everything the tipster told her. The reporter did attempt to verify her source's claims and everything she did verify suggested that the source possessed inside knowledge and that he was relaying his knowledge accurately.[287]

Would all courts agree that the anonymous tip plus a view of the complaint demonstrated a lack of serious doubt as to truth or falsity? There is no certain answer to this question or others like it.

Reliance on memory alone without reviewing written material or performing original research can be risky. Some cases say it is not necessarily proof of actual malice in the absence of "obvious inaccuracies."[288] However, other cases have found misplaced reliance on memory to be sufficient evidence of actual malice to be submitted to a jury. For example, a reporter attending the sentencing of a convicted criminal reported that the criminal's brother "spewed obscenities" about the judge who had done the sentencing. She did not ask anyone to confirm the speaker's identity, however, and relied on her recollection that an individual whom she believed to be the defendant's brother had been pointed out to her in the courthouse some years before. The man doing the spewing, however, was not the criminal's brother. The actual brother sued and the court agreed that the reporter's failure to confirm could establish actual malice.[289]

An employer such as a newspaper or television station will be held responsible for the actual malice of its reporters, along with the reporters themselves. However, when a newspaper or station accepts a report from a third party whom it neither employs nor controls, the station or newspaper must be independently guilty of actual malice to be held responsible.[290] The same rule applies to taking stories from previously published sources[291] like books and newspapers, and from reputable wire services.[292] However, even when accepting stories from freelance reporters or prepublished sources or the Associated Press, a publisher or broadcaster is still required to investigate when the source raises any doubt as to truthfulness. For example, failure to corroborate obvious errors,[293] or sole reliance on a "sensationalizing" tabloid, can trigger liability for a journalist who repeats a report.[294]

"Hemingway's Friend"

The plaintiff Hotchner is an author and was a friend and companion of Ernest Hemingway. He wrote a memoir entitled *Papa Hemingway* and adapted the works of Hemingway for radio, television, and motion pictures. He is deemed a public figure because he injected himself into the public controversy surrounding the latter years of Hemingway's life. He claims to have been a close friend of Hemingway up to the day he died.

The defendant is an important Spanish novelist, and one of the most important journalists in Spain. He wrote a book in which he described Hotchner as a manipulator, a "toady," and a "hypocrite," who exhibited "two-faced behavior" toward Hemingway's true friends and "put up a very good front as [Hemingway's] mild-mannered, obedient servant." The book also characterized Hotchner as an "exploiter of [Hemingway's] reputation" who was "never open and above board."

Doubleday decided to translate the defendant's book and to publish it in the United States. After reading the book, an editor noted that the author did not like Hotchner very much and that the book contained "side-swiping." A contracts manager observed that the book ridiculed Hotchner and impugned his reputation and character, and moreover that the statements in the book were probably incapable of being substantiated in any way. Doubleday also found factual errors in the Spanish edition.

But the writer had produced several pictures of himself with Hemingway, and both the writer and his Spanish publisher had sterling reputations. The book itself also "seemed to indicate" that the writer's opinions of Hotchner were based on personal observations. So, trusting in the writer's claims that he was a close friend of Hemingway, Doubleday published the book, including all the statements quoted above. Doubleday made no effort to verify anything with Hemingway's widow or with other persons present in Spain. In fact it made no effort whatever to double-check the accuracy of the statements.

The jury found the statements about Hotchner to be false and defamatory. Does Doubleday's conduct amount to actual malice?

"Hemingway's Friend"
(Answer)

Doubleday did not have cause for serious doubts regarding the truth or falsity of the underlying facts. Moreover, the writer's allegations were "not of such an extraordinary nature as would suggest a high probability of falsity"; for example, there was no claim in the book that Hotchner had engaged in any unusual or outlandish conduct. The writer's obvious animosity toward Hotchner and the fact that Doubleday failed to conduct an elaborate investigation, did not demonstrate actual malice on Doubleday's part.[295]

To sum up: this case and all the other examples in this Section show that the Actual Malice Standard is not predictable in its application. Though it focuses on the subjective state of mind of the defendant, it does not necessarily accept the defendant's description of his or her beliefs when circumstantial evidence indicates either knowing or reckless falsity. This leaves plenty of room for actual malice on the part of a reporter, notwithstanding sources which seem to be reliable (at least at the time) and the best of intentions. In close cases will a jury agree that the assembled evidence leaves no room for serious doubt? To be sure, there are decisions in which courts bend over backwards to find justifiable reliance upon questionable sources.[296] But most cases show that the media would be reckless to rely on so favorable a result.

IDENTIFYING PRIVATE PERSONS

Private persons include every individual, corporation, or other entity which is neither a public official nor a public figure, either general or limited. As already noted, the definitions of public officials and public figures are highly specialized and sometimes counter-intuitive. The private person category, therefore, embraces not only individuals who usually relish their privacy and lead ordinary lives but also everyone else who has fallen through the cracks of the other definitions. This means that public employees who lack sufficient responsibility to be deemed public officials and people in the public eye who are well-known but not quite household names or who have not become involved in any public controversy are all private persons in the eyes of the Supreme Court.[297] As a result, the private person category embraces most people in this country and even a large percentage of newsworthy people.

Unlike public officials and public figures, private persons do not usually enjoy regular access to media channels. Having less of an opportunity to rebut false statements, they are considered more vulnerable to injury and "the state interest in protecting them is correspondingly greater."[298] Moreover, private persons by definition have not run the risk of closer public scrutiny which public officials and public figures are assumed to have accepted. They have not "voluntarily exposed themselves to increased risk of injury from defamatory falsehood" by accepting any influential role in ordering society; and having relinquished no part of their interest in the protection of their good name, they have a more compelling call for redress of injury from false defamatory statements. Balanced against these factors, the media's First Amendment interests are not as strong as for reports on public persons. In short, private persons are not only more vulnerable to injury but they are also more deserving of recovery.[299]

All this solicitude for the private person does not mean that the First Amendment has abandoned the unhappy media defendant who falsely defames one. There is still a margin of error for making inadvertent statements which prove to be false. However, to avoid liability to a private person, the media must meet a higher level of care—which often means a higher level of proof—than that which excuses false defamatory statements about public persons. That standard, called the Private Person Standard in this book, is defined at pages 41–42 above.

The following discussion of how the Private Person Standard is applied, pertains at the very least to defamatory statements which relate to matters of public concern (as opposed to purely private matters). As in the context of general public figures, the Supreme Court has dropped broad hints that constitutional protections may apply to stories about private figures only when matters of public concern are reported. (Remember that even now, statements about public officials must pertain to official duties or fitness for office; and statements about limited public figures must pertain to public controversies, which are clearly matters of public concern.) What would replace the Private Person Standard for statements about private matters? Strict liability is a possibility, which would hold the media responsible for the consequences of false defamation *irrespective* of the care taken to gather proof.[300]

APPLYING THE PRIVATE PERSON STANDARD

Instead of defining in detail the standard of media liability for defaming private persons, the Supreme Court allowed each state to define its own standard as long as it did not impose liability without fault on the defendant's part.[301] In other words, the press and broadcast media will pay damages for a false defamation only if they act with a lack of care amounting at least to negligence, though states are free to give defendants even more breathing space if they choose to do so.[302] Not all states have adopted a negligence test. A handful have elected to apply the Actual Malice Standard even to private individuals, frequently with the additional requirement that the subject matter of the defamation be of legitimate public concern in order for the lesser standard of care to apply.[303] New York has adopted a "gross irresponsibility" test which is somewhere between the Actual Malice Standard and a negligence test (this is described with more detail beginning on page 104 below). The vast majority of states, however, have adopted a negligence test to determine whether defendants have acted with enough "fault" to be liable for false defamatory statements about private persons.[304]

To assess whether a media defendant has been negligent in falsely defaming a private person, the states generally use one of two tests: the "reasonable person" test, or the "reasonable professional" test which is essentially a standard of journalistic malpractice. At the outset, bear in mind that under both tests, *everything* which amounts to actual malice also amounts to negligence; negligence is a stricter standard for the media which subsumes actual malice.[305]

Stated simply, the reasonable person test uses as its yardstick what "a reasonably prudent person would or would not have done under the same or similar circumstances."[306] When it comes to the question of "How much proof?" the press is required to act reasonably in checking on the truth or falsity of the communication before publishing it.[307] The primary question becomes whether the defendant, when judged by the objective standard of the reasonable person, should have known that the defamatory statement was false or that further investigation would have revealed that falsity.[308]

The "reasonable professional" test holds the press to the standard of "skill and knowledge normally possessed by members of [the] profession ... in good standing in similar communities."[309] In other words, this standard looks to the professional standard of care in investigation and reporting which ordinarily prudent persons in the same profession usually exercise under similar conditions.[310] In applying this standard, judges may permit experts to testify about what constitutes custom in the trade, but their opinions do not control the outcome.[311] The judge or jury still decides.[312]

Proof Measured Against Five Factors

Practically, it does not matter much to the journalist writing a story which type of negligence test is apt to apply: both of them may be narrowed to a question of whether the journalist had a reasonable quantum of proof to justify a defamatory statement at the time it was made.[313]

How much is "reasonable"? Courts will usually try to balance a number of factors to answer that question.

What constitutes a reasonable level of substantiation under a negligence test depends on the relative weight of these five factors in the circumstances of each case:

1. Whether the material was topical and required prompt publication or whether additional time was available for a thorough investigation of its contents ("the hot news" issue);

2. The newsworthiness of the material and the public interests in promoting its publication;

3. The extent of damage to the plaintiff's reputation should the publication prove to be false;

4. The proven reliability and trustworthiness of the source;[314] and

5. The availability of sources which were *not* used (particularly if they are obvious ones).[315]

There is nothing exotic about these factors. In essence, they reflect common-sense standards of responsible journalism.

The first factor, whether the defamatory statement is "hot news" or not, is often given special emphasis.[316] It stands to reason that more verification should be expected from a reporter who has no immediate time pressure. On the other side of the coin, however, publishing even "hot news" with *insufficient* verification, measured in the balance of the other factors, may still demonstrate negligence.

For example, in a Vermont case, a police inspector performed a brief investigation and erroneously concluded that two men who had recently come to town soliciting advertising sponsorship from local businesses were perpetrating a hoax. The inspector called the local newspaper at 11:45 A.M. to issue a press release warning merchants; he was eager to make the noon deadline for that afternoon's edition. A reporter who covered police matters tried without success to reach the company responsible for the advertising solicitation and made no independent investigation to verify the charge before publishing it at 1:00 P.M. that day. The accusation was false and the men accused of fraud, who suffered as a result, sued the newspaper. The perceived time pressure did not excuse the newspaper from liability, notwithstanding the laudable goal of protecting merchants from fraud.[317]

Lack of time pressure almost always works against a journalist who makes a report with insufficient corroboration. In a case where a *U.S.A. Today* reporter misquoted an interview subject, and failed to verify his own account of the subject's statements, the fact that there were four full working days to catch the error, and the means of verification was readily at hand (i.e., a telephone), made the mistake especially egregious in the view of the court.[318] When the event reported is relatively distant in time, and a matter of historical rather than topical interest, failure to obtain sufficient verification will often weigh heavily against a journalist.[319] This means that background information accompanying a story of current interest must also be reviewed with care.

"The Air-Powered Car"

A professor invented an air-powered car and revealed it at a demonstration to which the press was invited. Press releases were distributed. There was only one demonstration. Two years later, the professor was indicted on charges of attempting by fraudulent means to obtain financing for the development of a fuel-saving device for an automobile. The article which correctly reported this fact also reported erroneously that the air-powered car failed to start at the earlier demonstration. In fact, it actually started and ran one quarter of a mile, which was far less than its theoretical maximum range of nine miles. The mistaken paragraph was based on material in the newspaper's archives, apparently without verification.

Is the untrue statement defamatory? Is the professor a public figure? If not, what bearing does the passage of two years have on the question of negligence?

"The Air-Powered Car"
(Answer)

The statement is defamatory and falls into the particularly sensitive category of maligning one in his trade, business or profession. The single demonstration of the automobile was not sufficient to make a public figure out of the professor; he still lacked regular access to the media and the court could not identify any public controversy, both of which precluded limited public figure status.

In upholding the jury's finding of negligence, the court emphasized that the paragraph in issue "did not involve news of the day, but involved background information only peripherally related to the current news article." The court implied that had the news been "hot news," involving the pressure under which current news is assembled and published, negligence might not have been established.[320]

Historians and the writers of sidebars have a greater responsibility to verify than the reporter of fast-breaking news.

The second factor to be balanced in a negligence test—the newsworthiness of the material and the public interest in its disclosure—also has obvious significance. The media is not expected to verify a story of earth-shattering importance (assassinations, wars, catastrophes) with the same care applicable to defamatory details of comparatively small social significance (like someone's sexual preferences).[321] Most stories fall between these two extremes; they will be assessed according to their relative proximity to one pole or the other.

The third factor, which measures the extent of damage to the plaintiff's reputation should the publication prove to be false, is also one which most journalists should embrace intuitively. (Professional instincts combine with financial incentives: more damaging statements result in higher jury awards should they prove to be false.) For example, a charge that someone participated in the systematic torture of political dissidents requires more journalistic effort before publication than verifying the facts offered by sources; the *background* of the sources should also be checked.[322] A report of a housewife's sexual fantasies, accompanied by her photograph in the nude, requires more checking than a single telephone call to the phone number supplied with the photo and information (the source of which turned out not to be the housewife).[323]

Recognizing a lack of sufficient corroboration is relatively simple in cases like these, but often more careful attention and thought is required.

"The Truth About The Teacher"

A news article on the front page of the Sunday *Richmond Times-Dispatch* reported that a local high school teacher was "disorganized, erratic, forgetful and unfair." It further reported charges by certain parents and their children that she demeaned and humiliated students; returned graded papers weeks late; absented herself from the classroom for long periods; and insisted that students stick to the rules, while flouting them herself. The reporter who wrote the story interviewed and quoted a number of the teacher's colleagues and students, and the students' parents. One colleague of the teacher opined that she "might be out of her element." The father of one student, a physician and professor at a medical college, told the reporter that complaints about the teacher's performance had been delivered to the school's principal. Another parent, a minister, said that his son was "unreasonably and harshly treated." Two more parents were quoted with similar complaints. A student said the teacher "was patronizing . . . late for class and . . . missing from class a third of the time." Three more students quoted in the article claimed to be victims of the teacher's harassment.

When the teacher sued for defamation, the reporter proved that he had interviewed the complaining parents and students and also telephoned the teacher's principal and two of her colleagues. He obtained little information from the teacher, however, who was advised by the school board's attorney not to discuss details with the reporter. The school authorities also refused to give the reporter the names or the addresses of additional students in the teacher's classes. One student, however, gave the reporter the names of some other students, but he did not pursue interviews with them.

At trial, a number of other students, teachers, and school administrators—not interviewed by the reporter—contradicted the complaints of the parents and students who were interviewed. The jury concluded that the teacher was not all that bad and that she had been falsely defamed by the report.

Did the reporter adequately verify the accusations before publishing them?

"The Truth About The Teacher"
(Answer)

The jury found that the reporter was indeed negligent in publishing the charges and the reporter lost his appeal. The appellate court held that the students who appeared at trial and said positive things about the teacher were "readily available for interview" even without the cooperation of the school authorities, because their names could have been (and in fact were) ascertained from other students. In view of the substantial danger of injury to the teacher's reputation, the court determined that a reasonably prudent news reporter would have contacted a number of additional students to verify these accusations and this reporter should have done so.

The teacher was awarded $100,000 against the reporter and his newspaper. An additional award of punitive damages, however, was disallowed.[324]

The more serious the accusation—particularly from the point of view of the private person—the harder a journalist must work to test its accuracy.

The fourth factor in a test of negligence concerns the reliability and trustworthiness of the source, be it an earlier publication or an interviewee. Journalists must investigate whether sources are in a position to know what they claim to know. If sources have been used in the past, their proven reliability (or lack of it) is a good starting point but the journalist should also consider: Where do they get their access to information? What are their motives for revealing information? Do the sources have any personal interest in the subject of the negative comments? Do they bear a grudge? Are they inclined to have extreme views on the subject matter or otherwise to give false or defamatory information without sufficient basis?[325]

The major wire services have been recognized as sources of such proven reliability, they can be relied upon without further verification unless their information appears to be false. The highest court in Massachusetts has further held that the press would not be negligent in republishing a UPI or AP story of local importance without verification, even if local independent investigation would be "feasible" and the accusations were serious, in the absence of reason to doubt the accuracy of the report.[326]

The vast majority of other sources do not enjoy the same legal weight, and the police are among them. A tip, a statement, or even a press release from a local police official should not be published in the absence of further investigation (as demonstrated by the example about the advertising solicitors on pages 94–95.)[327] Information from less deliberate police sources is even less trustworthy. The Arkansas Supreme Court did not look kindly upon the report of a local television station which reported that two men had robbed a store at a shopping center based on uncorroborated monitoring of a "police scanner"—even when supported by the eyewitness account of a news reporter. (She did not know the surrounding circumstances of what she observed).[328] If police sources require corroboration, then along the spectrum of unreliability, so do most others, especially when there exists any basis to doubt their word.

The fifth factor concerns availability of other sources not tapped by the reporter (and particularly the most obvious ones). As discussed in the section on Actual Malice (see pages 86–87), failure to consult the most obvious sources will be held against media defendants in actions brought by public persons, and the same applies to suits by private persons in the negligence test's balance of factors.

Failure to verify with the subject of the article will usually not constitute negligence by itself, but in the balance of other factors it may be very damaging.[329] The usual journalistic practice is to give the target of accusations an opportunity to respond, to enhance the fairness and balance of a story. Legal reasons furnish extra motivation. The subjects of news stories are obvious sources of information to confirm or deny a defamatory report. As in the analysis of actual malice, a reporter does not necessarily have to accept the subject's point of view, particularly when denials are unspecific or patently unpersuasive. On the other hand, when the target of a defamatory statement provides convincing, detailed reasons to question the truthfulness of the statement, proceeding with publication would be negligent without substantial support to the contrary.

For similar reasons, a reporter should not fail to investigate obvious sources of information other than the subject of the statement. In the case of the allegedly incompetent teacher (described above at pages 96–98), failure to seek out and interview noncomplaining students weighed heavily in the balance of factors and resulted in a finding of negligence. Recall also that in the case of the Challenger for the judgeship (see pages 82–86 above), the reporter's failure to interview the most likely witness contributed to a finding of actual malice; if this same variety of neglect surfaced in a test of negligence, it would count even more strongly against the journalist.

Worse than mere sloppiness, failure to interview the most obvious sources of information may suggest deliberate blindness to the truth and perhaps a predisposition to publish a defamatory statement regardless of what the proof shows. Discerning the "obvious" sources of verification, however, sometimes takes careful consideration and in some cases, help by experts.

"The Fix Revisited"

Remember the insurance salesman who furnished the *Saturday Evening Post* with the contents of a telephone conversation between the football coaches of the University of Georgia and the University of Alabama which he accidentally overheard because of a "crossed line"? (See pages 80–82 above.) The *Post* was found guilty of actual malice for failing to obtain any independent support for the salesman's allegations of game-fixing.

What if the *Post* had decided to act conservatively and gather enough proof to meet even a negligence test? Particularly since the news was not "hot," what sources should it have checked at a minimum? And what other factors should it have balanced to assess the proof?

Bear in mind two additional facts: The salesman was not alone when he heard the coaches' conversation; another man, John Carmichael, was present, though he did not listen in on the call. Also, the salesman took notes and presented them to the *Post*; they were not examined by the magazine's personnel, however, and did not contain support for all his claims.

"The Fix Revisited"
(Answer)

First, the *Post* should have considered that time pressure was not critical, the social fiber would not unravel in the absence of this story, and the accusations would have severe consequences for the career of the coach, attacking as it did both his integrity and professional standing. Furthermore, the source (despite his notes) was less dependable than others who were not on probation for passing bad checks.

In deciding this case, the Supreme Court declared that the following paths of investigation should have been followed by the *Post at a minimum* to avoid actual malice; the Court's imperative would apply even more strongly in a negligence test:

1.   The *Post* should have taken a close look at those notes. Was it reasonable to believe the salesman's claims that were not reflected on them?

2.   The man who was with the coach when the phone call was overheard should have been interviewed. What did he hear and observe?

3.   The salesman's story should have been checked with someone highly knowledgeable about football (which the *Post* reporter was not) to see if the "divulged secrets" were actually of any value to the Alabama coach. (At trial, experts said that the information was either valueless or would have been evident from prior game films.)

4.   A film of the game should have been screened to see if the informant's information was accurate.

5.   The *Post* should have determined whether Alabama adjusted its plans after the alleged information was divulged.[330]

The mere existence of the five factors—time pressure, newsworthiness, severity of defamation, source reliability, and availability of other sources—points ineluctably toward one conclusion: there is no mechanical, hard and fast rule which can answer the question "How Much Proof?" A universal practice of obtaining verification from two sources or four sources or ten sources is not the winning approach. When news is "hot," the public need for quick disclosure is great, the extent of potential damage is slight, and a source is uniquely and utterly reliable, a reporter would not be negligent by quoting the first source and investigating no further. In the case of the football coach, however, it would have taken the original informant plus at least five sources to satisfy the Supreme Court.

The other lesson these factors teach is that determining the amount of proof required to publish a defamatory statement is largely a matter of *common sense*. (This distinguishes this exercise from most other legal analyses which in the main offer only even odds that common sense, conscientiously applied, will yield the legally-favored result.) Though simple common sense will not necessarily tell a writer who is a public official or what constitutes a limited public figure or what constitutes actual malice, when it comes to private persons and the negligence test, little more is required than reasonably good judgment and careful consideration. Most journalists would be expected to apply these standards intuitively. Certainly the rest of the population—when sitting on a jury to consider whether a journalist has acted with reasonable care—is apt to do so.

In the last analysis, basic common sense answers the question "How Much Proof?" to which this Section is dedicated. However, there are more ways to be negligent than by failing to gather or verify proof.

Basic Professional Care Also Required

To ask "How Much Proof?" as a means of avoiding negligence pre-supposes the observance of a basic level of professional care in recording and communicating the results of research and verification. Otherwise the risk of negligence—and liability to a private person—is no less threatening.

Avoiding negligence requires not only good researchers, but also good proofreaders, and some basic care on the part of the journalist as a matter of habit. For example, misreading, misinterpreting or miscopying published sources, or other documentary proof, or a newspaper's archive,[331] or even a reporter's own notes can be labeled negligence. So can forging ahead without a measure of expertise (or ready access to it) in any area where the assignment is the least bit esoteric. As noted earlier in this book (see pages 13–14 above), a writer's failure to understand the way a specialized industry works may blind him or her to the impact of statements which injure reputation among those in the know. Making inadvertent implications or juxtapositions which defame *can* amount to negligence.[332] So can misinterpretation of specialized information which can occur in any esoteric area; it frequently occurs in the area of law.

Legal documents like complaints, indictments, divorce papers, deeds and the like are often unintelligible to the lay person and for a journalist to assume a "logical" interpretation can be a grave mistake. For example, relying on his review of the pertinent docket page of the Juvenile and Domestic Relations Court, a reporter erroneously suggested that two parents had been accused of molesting their child. The information in column headings on the docket page, however, was not readily intelligible: from left to right they read "COUNSEL CA P W," "OFFICER/CMPLNT BSE," "CCRE DATE APPEAL DATE." The reporter copied the information in the columns but not the column designations, which, once translated, would have told him that the parents were not accused of molesting their own child. Rather, they had accused a third party to whom the docket sheet referred. The parents sued and won; the reporter was negligent for failing to ask someone knowledgeable about what the column headings meant.[333]

Another basic element of care is taking good notes (or making recordings of sources) and paying close attention to them. A reporter for *U.S.A. Today* interviewed a clinical psychologist at a Veterans' Administration Hospital who counseled veterans and their families. He was quoted in an article as saying: "We've become a nation of hand wringers . . . It's amusing that vets feel they are the victims when the Vietnamese had the napalm and . . . bombs dropped on them," among other comments showing a similar lack of empathy for his patients. In fact, the psychologist had said something quite different at the interview; he had quoted what he read in another news story which said that *Vietnamese veterans* of the war found it amusing that American veterans felt like victims when the Vietnamese had the napalm and bombs dropped on them. *U.S.A. Today* lost that case.[334]

Misplaced reliance on memory is another bad mistake which can lead to liability for negligence just as it can contribute to proof of actual malice. (See page 89 above.) A Louisiana newspaper reporter erroneously recalled, and reported as background to a current story without checking, that two deputies had been convicted six years earlier of granting a jail inmate weekend passes in exchange for stolen goods. Actually, the deputies had been tried and convicted of malfeasance, a lesser offense. They sued and a federal appeals court agreed that negligence was in evidence.[335]

When good notes are taken, and good research completed, a journalist should not then draw inferences which the notes and research will not support. As discussed in more detail below (see pages 114–123), rigorous limitation to exactly what can be proved is essential to non-negligent reporting.

Screening procedures must be set up to flag potentially defamatory statements requiring verification in all editorial and advertising content.[336] This also applies to live programming such as call-in shows, for which there is no logical exception. Editors are expected under the law to note potential sources of damage to reputation,[337] and they should be trained to meet those expectations. After procedures are put in place, they must be followed with care; failure to comply with one's own standards is another way of being negligent. For example, a reporter's failure to follow his newspaper's normal procedure to check the police blotter before reporting the details of an arrest was sufficient for a jury to conclude that he and his editor—who failed to enforce the rule—had been negligent.[338]

Establishing screening and verification procedures may occasionally work against a media defendant in this way; but such instances will be rare when compared to the many occasions where they will help avoid trouble.[339]

As with actual malice, questionable motives in making a story public can also persuade a jury of negligence by helping to demonstrate why a reporter failed to act with reasonable care. Bias, spite, or ill-will[340] on the part of the publisher or broadcaster, or economic motives like boosting ratings or circulation[341] will be welcome discoveries to a plaintiff's lawyer.

In short, basic journalistic standards must first be met before the question "How Much Proof?" can be intelligently addressed under the negligence standard.

New York's "Grossly Irresponsible" Test

The courts of New York have adopted a standard for defamation suits by private individuals which requires less care on the part of the media than a negligence test though theoretically more than the Actual Malice Standard. (In practice the difference is not that great.) Unlike the Supreme Court's tests for applying the Actual Malice Standard, the trigger for the New York "grossly irresponsible" test is content-based:

> [W]here the content of the article is arguably within the sphere of legitimate public concern, which is reasonably related to matters warranting public exhibition, the party defamed may recover; however, to warrant such recovery he must establish, by a preponderance of the evidence, that the publisher acted in a grossly irresponsible manner without due consideration for the standards of information gathering and dissemination ordinarily followed by responsible parties.[342]

In New York, the term "legitimate public concern" embraces a great many subjects—far more than the restrictive "public controversy" phrase which applies to the definition of limited public figures. Some decisions have interpreted the phrase very generously, including within the definition of legitimate public concern virtually everything which the press, acting responsibly, determines in its editorial judgment to publish or broadcast.[343] The category includes a political election,[344] the arrest of a public school teacher for unlawful possession of drugs and drug paraphernalia,[345] the practice of prostitution,[346] the emergence of the Italian neo-realist film movement,[347] and a dispute between a well-known Venezuelan actress and the producer who brought her to perform in New York.[348]

The grossly irresponsible standard of fault will be applied, like the negligence standard, to all kinds of conduct. Its most frequent use is assessing the amount of corroboration obtained for a defamatory statement which later proves to be false. In the following examples, grossly irresponsible conduct was found to be absent:

• A newspaper accurately reported that a public school teacher had been charged with criminal possession of a hypodermic instrument and of heroin, but incorrectly linked the teacher with others arrested at a party where drugs and beer were found. The judge noted that neither the police captain who had been interviewed nor the police record examined by the reporter supported the false statement; and that both the writer, the desk reporter and the copy reader missed the error; but the judge used these facts to prove the absence of gross irresponsibility because the "article was written only after two authoritative sources had been consulted and it was not published until it had been checked by at least two persons other than the writer . . . [thus showing] that the publisher exercised reasonable methods to insure accuracy."[349]

• Reliance on the accuracy of previously published statements, without any substantial reasons to question the accuracy of those statements or the trustworthiness of the reporter, is not grossly irresponsible.[350]

• A newspaper's publication of a defamatory article written by an experienced, reputable, free-lance author was not grossly irresponsible because the paper had no reason to doubt the accuracy of the author's material and its editor and production manager reviewed the article prior to publication.[351]

The media's room for error under the grossly irresponsible test does have its limits, however; in each of the following cases, the courts refused to reject the argument that the defendant could have been grossly irresponsible and submitted the issue for trial:

• A photograph accompanying an article about a group of juveniles who visited a state prison as part of the "Scared Straight" program identified the youths on the bus as having been "involved with the law." The reporter allegedly knew, however, that at least one youth was an observer and not a participant; the youth was identifiable in the photograph and had not been "involved with the law."[352]

• A reporter quoted a former paralysis victim cured by acupuncture to say that his "American doctor" had informed him that he would never walk again and "abandoned him." When the doctor sued (noting that the charge fell into the serious category of unprofessional conduct), he demonstrated that the patient's wife had provided much of the source material for the article, that other medical personnel were involved in the patient's care, and that the reporter had devoted limited efforts to verify the accusations. Because the reporter failed to obtain permission from the patient to speak with the doctor, or to determine if others provided treatment for the patient, the court agreed that the reporter's conduct could be "grossly irresponsible."[353]

Many of the same traps and pitfalls which can result in a finding of actual malice or negligence also apply to a grossly irresponsible test: potential bias of witnesses, bias of the reporter, failure to obtain precise answers to important questions, and failure to verify further after hearing a flat denial from the target of the statement. For practical purposes, the advice in the preceding section for avoiding negligence also applies to the journalist who wishes to avoid "grossly irresponsible" reporting.

A CAVEAT ABOUT CONFIDENTIAL SOURCES

More than half the states have shield laws[354] which, to varying degrees, permit reporters to keep their sources confidential; First Amendment considerations and the common law may also offer limited privileges.[355] Some shield laws apply absolutely even when the adversary in a libel suit demands disclosure.[356] However, in the absence of a shield law, and sometimes even with one, the media's privilege to withhold identification of confidential sources is qualified and may dissolve, for example, if the plaintiff exhausts all reasonable alternative means of identifying a source.[357] Having a shield law is also no guarantee that a confidential source will be of any use in a libel litigation, even if disclosure is not compelled; in Rhode Island, for example, if a reporter tries to defend himself or herself by professing good faith reliance on an undisclosed source, the legal shield crumbles into dust and the court may compel disclosure.[358] Failure to disclose a source when disclosure is compulsory can result in contempt of court and fines or jail or, in the worst case scenario, a default in the lawsuit.[359]

With or without a shield law, and even when disclosure of a confidential source cannot be compelled, refusing to reveal a source at the trial of a defamation suit has varying ramifications. At the very least, unwillingness to disclose is more than likely to influence how a judge and jury weigh other factors in an actual malice or negligence test. It may be more difficult, for example, to dispose of the suit prior to trial; a judge may be unwilling to grant summary judgment when a source cannot be identified, leaving it for a jury to determine whether a reporter acted with actual malice or negligently.[360] At trial, the media defendant may be precluded from making any mention whatsoever of the confidential source, as if the source did not exist;[361] even if questioned about sources, the reporter could be barred from saying that the information came from a reliable or confidential source.[362] By failing to disclose sources, the press may also be precluded from offering at trial "evidence [obtained] through or relating to" such persons,[363] and even evidence about the reporter's reputation as a journalist when offered to help prove reliance on good, though confidential, sources.[364]

Another alternative, though less draconian, would still hobble a media defendant's defense. Reporters would be permitted to testify and be cross-examined at trial about all information they had at their disposal prior to publication of the defamatory statements, but any unnamed source could not be used, by itself, as proof of verification or evidence of responsibility on the reporter's part. Instead, the defendant would have to introduce *extrinsic* evidence to support the validity or the apparent reliability of the source's information and the plaintiff could offer evidence, or argument, to the contrary. The jury would then be free to believe or disbelieve the reporter's testimony concerning the credibility of the confidential source and reliability of its information.[365]

Clearly, confidential sources can be a handicap for defendants trying to prove that the necessary standard of proof and care has been met. Sources with secret identities should not be equated with reliable identifiable sources in a prepublication assessment of whether a defamatory statement should be published.

SECTION SUMMARY

To summarize, we return to the question which introduced this Section: "How Much Proof?" As the last 68 pages have illustrated, this question cannot be answered with a mechanical formula. The legal answer is a moving target and depends in the last analysis on the circumstances of the case and the particular jury or judge who considers them. One unimpeachable source may be enough; 12 rotten sources will always be insufficient. Instead of a mechanism, journalists must bring intelligence, judgment and care to answer this question whenever making public a defamatory statement.

The most conservative approach would require applying the common sense balancing of the negligence test to every potentially defamatory statement without trying to figure if the statement's subject is a private person, public figure or public official. This is the best way to limit risk from the vicissitudes of the legal process in the categorization of defamation subjects and in the application of the various standards for escaping liability for a false defamatory statement.

Somewhat less conservatively, but still within the bounds of acceptable risk, a journalist might attempt to apply the Actual Malice Standard in the most clear-cut instances—when potentially defamatory statements refer to public officials at the top of the hierarchy of government employees, or to celebrities or organizations in the household name category, as long as the statements pertain clearly to matters of public concern *and* *all* of the following tests are undeniably met with room to spare:

1. The journalist, the editor, the publisher or broadcaster and everyone else concerned is innocent of any knowledge of falsity regarding the statement;

2. The same group is free from any substantial doubt as to the truth of the statement;

3. The statement has no traces of inherent implausibility; and

4. The source or sources of the statement are exceptionally good (including reputable wire services, seven bishops and the like).

A reporter can be certain only under these limited circumstances that the Actual Malice Standard is the one to apply, and that its criteria will be met.

For every other defamatory statement, about every other class of individual, company, organization or other entity: publishers, broadcasters, and all their employees should usually assess the proof required for a defamatory statement through an exercise in ordinary care and common sense without wasting time on figuring whether the subject of the statement is public or private. This exercise must rest on a bedrock of journalistic rigor which does not allow for:

- Sloppiness in the interpretation of documents;
- Sloppiness in the interpretation of legal, scientific, or other exotic terminology;
- Lack of reasonable familiarity in the area to which the report pertains or failure to find an expert in the absence of that familiarity;
- Taking poor notes;
- Misplaced reliance on memory; or
- Unreasonably broad inferences or conclusions beyond those which the proof explicitly allows.

In other words, the point of departure is good training, good research, fact-checking, good editing, and generally rigorous attention to the basics of careful journalism.

Beyond these basics, the common sense approach will not allow for publication of defamatory statements which are known to be false or probably false, or contain any inherent improbability, or give rise to substantial doubt as to their truth. A statement must be believed to be true at the time of publication based upon reliable sources of proof.

The answer to "How Much Proof?" ultimately requires a common sense balancing of factors:

1. The extent (or lack) of real time pressure. In the absence of real topicality, the law expects that time be taken for more thorough investigation.
2. The importance of the disclosure. Newsworthy reports in the public interest receive more protection; matters of purely private concern which are not legitimately subjects of public concern are accorded less protection (and may soon be accorded even less).
3. The severity of the defamation and the extent of damage to the subject should the statement prove to be false.[366]
4. The trustworthiness of the sources relied upon. Past performance is an important factor.
5. The availability of other sources to offer further corroboration. The subject of the defamation and other obvious sources[367] should not be overlooked.

Confidential sources must be used with care; if they cannot be named, they may be useless when a judge or jury assesses the sufficiency of their proof.

Furthermore, publishing a defamatory statement without defensible journalistic motives courts disaster. Any kind of hidden agenda—like improving ratings or circulation, or "getting someone," or improving the chances of an adversary in a political race, or any species of spite or ill will—will result in an extra burden for the journalist when sufficiency of proof is being assessed.[368]

In addition to good training, good habits, good intentions and common sense, the media have other means of limiting risk. One way offered by the Supreme Court is the encouragement of frank discussion among reporters and editors to promote sound editorial judgment.[369] Another means is the establishment of error-avoidance procedures which emphasize the detection of potentially defamatory statements, and assure close editorial supervision in the gathering and assessment of proof. Once procedures are set in place, they must be followed; lapses will be cited as evidence of negligence.

As part of these procedures, editors (and in many instances, lawyers) must ask the right questions to assess the reporter's balance of these factors. These include:

1. Are the reporter's sources in a position to known what they purport to know? What is their access to information?

2. Have the sources been used before? Have they proven themselves to be reliable?

3. What are the motives of sources for disclosing information? Are they biased?

4. Does the story contain any inconsistencies or lapses or other indications of falsity?

5. Does the reporter really understand the story?

6. Does the reporter (or anyone else at the organization) know anything which suggests that the defamatory statement, or anything else in the story, is false?

7. Does the reporter have serious doubts about the truth or falsity of what is being published?

8. How much verification did the reporter accomplish? Why did he or she stop?

9. Was the subject of the statement given a chance to respond fully? Was the response included in the story?

10. Have any obvious sources been overlooked either intentionally or not? [370]

When all is said and done, the best defense is good sense at every level of journalistic endeavor. And, after all defamatory statements have been identified, and "How Much Proof" has been addressed for each, there remains one more stop on the risk-avoidance itinerary. "What to Write" is the topic of Section III, which follows.

SECTION III

What to Write

After journalists scour stories for potentially defamatory statements, discarding the unnecessary ones and ascertaining the amount of proof needed to support the rest (assuming, as always, a professional level of care in gathering and reporting facts), there awaits one more step on the path toward avoiding defamation suits and hastening the dismissal of those which cannot be avoided. This is writing the story to make the most of the proof obtained and of journalistic privileges which reduce the risks of publishing a potentially defamatory story.

For one thing, to make the most of the Actual Malice and Private Person Standards discussed in Section II, rigorous limitation of the facts in the story to those facts for which proof has been obtained is absolutely critical. Another means of limiting risk is disguising the identities of defamation subjects. As noted in Section I (pages 3–5), libel plaintiffs cannot win unless they demonstrate that the defamatory statement could reasonably be interpreted to apply to them. Changing names or avoiding names completely (as long as identification is avoided too) is a risk-limiting technique which should not be overlooked.

A journalist is often well advised to do more than collect good sources to corroborate a story; to make the most of legal privileges, those sources must be named in the text. This applies particularly to reports based on official proceedings. In some jurisdictions, a doctrine known as ''neutral reportage'' will also shield the media from liability when statements are based on allegations by particularly impeccable sources. These sources also must be identified or the privilege is lost.

The law also recognizes a privilege for opinions which can sometimes take the sting out of what otherwise would be defamatory. But libel does not become opinion by preceding it with "in my opinion . . . "; the premises of the opinion must be laid out, they must be truthful, and the opinion must not imply additional undisclosed facts. The law also finds a social value in criticism and comment about the foibles and failures of the socially or artistically prominent. The law does not require bland writing. It allows for colorful name-calling, for hyperbole, and for jokes and satire. These categories, which unfortunately cannot always be isolated with precision, are not defamation. Piloting what otherwise would be defamatory into one of these safe harbors may avoid the time, effort and expense of a lengthy libel litigation.

All these topics are discussed below in this Section, "What to Write."

THE NECESSITY OF RIGOROUS LIMITATION

The most important means of avoiding risk after identifying defamation and obtaining sufficient factual support with requisite journalistic care is to make certain that the words of the defamatory statement are rigorously chosen to reflect the factual support. The match must be exact. The lessons of imprecision are painful and all too common.

For example, it is very dangerous to leap to a defamatory conclusion which is not directly supported by the proof. Journalists must avoid any tendency to bridge the gap between the proof which sources have provided and what might be more suited to the flow of the story. So must any simplification of a source's information which renders the statement even slightly more damaging.

To take an obvious hypothetical: if a report by the Department of Justice states that a casino "is unable to account for large sums of cash and organized crime is presumably responsible," this should not be reported as "The Department of Justice has charged that organized crime skims money from the casino." There is no real accusation in the report and the story freights a mere "presumption" with more weight and more defamatory sting through conversion to a "charge." Perhaps limited space in the text or voiceover would not allow for the subtlety of a "presumption" and the extra explanation that would have to go with it. Or perhaps the word "charge" fit better in the flow of the story and was thought to be more easily understood. However innocent the motivation, failure to match the words to the proof in this way greatly increases risk.

In 1985, Shana Alexander wrote a book called *Nutcracker* which was a nonfiction account of the widely publicized murder of a multimillionaire by his daughter, Frances, and her son. The book discussed how Frances put herself under the care of a psychiatrist whose unpaid bill at one point reached $3,000 and whose relationship with Frances allegedly went beyond psychiatrist-patient. In the left column below is a passage from the book and in the right column, a transcript of precisely what the writer learned from her two sources. (The emphases are added.)

Marilyn [Frances's sister] remembers the size of one of [Frances's] bills:	*Marilyn*: *So I wondered* if there wasn't *a little hanky-panky* going on.
Frances owed her psychiatrist $3,000.00. "My understanding was that her problem was inability facing reality," says Marilyn.	*Shana*: Between the two of them, a romance you mean?
The huge unpaid bill made [Marilyn] think it might be the psychiatrist who had this problem, not his patient. Later, when [a third party] claimed that "Frances always slept with her shrinks,"	*Marilyn*: Yeah. That was *just a wonder* on my part; and I made that statement before—which I shouldn't have . . .
[Marilyn and her husband] *said they were not at all surprised. They'd suspected "hanky-panky,"* they confessed. *Berenice* [Frances's mother] *has said the same*.	*Berenice*: "*I can't prove anything*, but I've always *felt* that man hypnotized her, *and used her sexually*. . . ."

When the psychiatrist sued, the trial judge was highly critical of the author's conversion of Marilyn's mere "wonder" into "suspected hanky-panky" and her additional comment that Marilyn and her husband were "not at all surprised." The judge also compared Berenice's point of view which was by no means "the same," contrary to the book's characterization. Though the writer and her publisher ultimately prevailed on appeal, the imprecision in the language—particularly with respect to such a serious charge—burdened the book with additional and unnecessary risk.[371]

Failing to quote precisely not only risks defamation of third parties to whom a speaker refers, but also defamation of the speaker. Because quotation marks around a passage usually indicate a verbatim reproduction if a speaker's words and not a paraphrase or other interpretation by the author, latitude in reconstructing quotes is limited. The law recognizes that a full and exact quotation from an interview subject rarely appears in print and that a writer or editor might shorten a speaker's rambling comments, add punctuation, fix grammar or syntax, or even correct an obvious misstatement such as an unconscious substitution of one name for another. This kind of deliberate alteration of the words in a quote does not equate with knowledge of falsity for purposes of the Actual Malice Standard or the Private Person Standard as long as the alteration results in no material change in the meaning conveyed by the statement. On the other hand, if deliberate (or sloppy) reconstruction of a quote alters a speaker's words, presents them out of context, or changes emphasis, and effects a material change in meaning, then the speaker may sue and win if he or she suffers injury to reputation as a result.

Misleading quotations may injure reputation by attributing an untrue factual assertion to the speaker (e.g., a statement which admits criminality or demonstrates lack of knowledge). Sometimes more subtly, erroneous quotations can defame by attributing a negative personal trait which the speaker does not have, or an attitude the speaker does not hold. As a result, a speaker might appear arrogant or unprofessional, or otherwise become the target of contempt, ridicule or ostracism. Quotations which include self-criticism also carry more force than criticism by another, and the reader is likely to give them more weight; they must be reported with commensurate rigor.

In a recent decision of the Supreme Court, *The New Yorker* magazine was told that changing the following quotations on the left into the quotations on the right could be defamatory and, in fact, could support a finding of actual malice. The case was brought by a psychoanalyst who was formerly Projects Director of the Sigmund Freud Archive. He was interviewed for an article about his criticisms of Freudian psychology and of Dr. Kurt Eissler and Dr. Anna Freud who controlled the archive. The quotes on the left were taken directly from transcripts of tape recordings of lengthy interviews and the quotes on the right were attributed to him in the article.

"[Eissler and Freud] felt, in a sense, I was a private asset but a public liability. . . . They liked me when I was alone in their living room and I could talk and chat and tell them the truth about things and they would tell me. But that I was, in a sense, much too junior within the hierarchy of analysis, for these important training analysts to be caught dead with me."

"[Freud's library] is priceless in terms of what it contains: All his books with his annotations in them. . . . It's fascinating." [And earlier in the interview speaking of a meeting with a London analyst:] "I like him. . . . and we got on very well. That was the first time we ever met and you know, it was buddy-buddy, and we were to stay with each other and [laughs] we were going to pass women on to each other, and we were going to have a great time together when I lived [at the building holding the archive]. We'd have great parties there and we were . . . going to live it up."

"[Eissler and Freud] liked me well enough 'in my own room.' They loved to hear from me what creeps and dolts analysts are. I was like an intellectual gigolo—you get your pleasure from him, but you don't take him out in public. . . . "

"[The building holding the archive] was a beautiful house, but it was dark and sombre and dead. Nothing ever went on there. I was the only person who ever came. I would have renovated it, opened it up, brought it to life. [It] would have been a center of scholarship, but it would also have been a place of sex, women, fun. It would have been like the change in 'The Wizard of Oz,' from black-and-white into color."

[Speaking of a paper the psychoanalyst presented in 1981] " . . . [T]hey really couldn't judge the material. And, in fact, until the last sentence I think they were quite fascinated. I think the last sentence was . . . [a] possibly, gratuitously offensive way to end a paper to a group of analysts. . . . I didn't believe anybody would agree with me. . . . But I felt I should say something because the paper's still well within the analytic tradition in a sense. . . . it contains all the material that would allow one to criticize Freud but I didn't really do it. And then I thought, I really must say one thing that I really believe, that's not going to appeal to anybody and that was the very last sentence. Because I really do believe psychoanalysis is entirely sterile. . . ."

[The author of *The New Yorker* article first recounts that she asked the psychoanalyst what happened between the time of the lecture and the present to change him from a Freudian psychoanalyst with "somewhat outre views" into the "bitter and belligerent anti-Freudian he had become." His answer:] "You're right, there was nothing disrespectful of analysis in that paper. . . . The remark about the sterility of psychoanalysis was something I tacked on at the last minute, and it was totally gratuitous. I don't know why I put it in."

The psychoanalyst claimed that he never made the comments on the right which portrayed him in a most unflattering light and injured his reputation. The author of the article said he did make those comments but on occasions other than those when the tape recorder was running. The Supreme Court left the issues of what was defamatory, who said what and when and the ultimate question of actual malice for a jury to decide.[372]

Another mistake is to paraphrase one's source with a sloppy choice of words that enlarges the story's defamatory impact. For purposes of defamation suits, this can be tantamount to throwing a source away.

A reporter interviewed a police sergeant who was severely injured when a bomb he was attempting to disarm exploded. His wife, who filed for divorce several months *prior to* the explosion, reconciled with the sergeant shortly before the accident and then took care of her injured husband for two years. After the sergeant had regained some of his sight, hearing and ability to live independently, his wife obtained an uncontested divorce. When the camera crew visited the sergeant in the family home to film the interview, both his wife and his five children had moved out. The sergeant told the reporter that he regretted never discussing the possibility of an accident with his family and remarked that "I know what it feels like to be deserted." On the evening news, a reporter said of the sergeant that the bomb which injured him "was the last bomb he'll ever work on. It exploded . . . taking all of his right hand, parts of his left hand, most of his eyesight and much of his hearing. In addition, his wife and five children have deserted him since the accident." The sergeant's former wife sued for defamation and won. The court found a gulf between a report that the sergeant *felt* deserted and that he *was* deserted. The use of a term with obvious pejorative connotations, without underlying factual support, is evidence of recklessness especially when the reporter has knowledge that the description is in fact untrue.[373]

In other cases, reporters have similarly increased their miseries by:

• Saying that a judge "barged into" another's home when to say he had "entered" would have been more accurate in light of his being acquitted five months before the article appeared on charges of trespass in connection with the same event.[374]

• Reporting that a man had been charged with sexual assault when in fact he was merely apprehended and jailed before release on his own recognizance and another person was subsequently charged with the offense. The court emphasized the big difference between an arrest and a formal indictment which never occurred.[375]

• Describing the sound made by audio speakers as wandering "about the room" when, in fact, the author actually heard the sound moving "along the wall"; the published statement was sufficiently inaccurate to disparage the speakers and potentially expose the author to liability, according to the U.S. Supreme Court.[376]

Reporting allegations as facts is never a good idea. In fact, any interpretation of a source's allegation in a more damaging way than the source allows is a grave mistake.

"Repatriation and Deportation"

A magazine published by Jack Anderson included an article describing the doings of Liberty Lobby, a not-for-profit corporation with a very conservative reputation. The article asserted that

Willis Carto, Liberty Lobby's founder and treasurer, "organized and promoted [a] Joint Council for Repatriation." The article noted that what Carto "meant by 'repatriation' was the forced deportation of all blacks to Africa." When Carto sued, the defendants produced published sources which supported the assertion that Carto created this organization and that its purpose was to "send American blacks back to Africa."

What's wrong here?

"Repatriation and Deportation"
(Answer)

The writer made the mistake of embellishing the statements in the published sources in a way that introduced additional defamatory impact for which there was no proof.

The sources did not establish that Carto's proposal envisioned "*forced* deportation," and in his defamation suit, Carto asserted that he only sought "*voluntary*" repatriation. While the court recognized that Carto's racist scheme was repugnant even with this limitation, the article as published contained "an additional and quite distinct" defamation because "it is possible to be a racist without being guilty of the quite separate fault of advocating the forced deportation of United States citizens."[377]

Another substantial source of risk is the related error of permitting *implications* in a story, a headline, a photocaption or a voiceover to drift beyond the boundaries of what the proof will support.[378] Recall the case of "For Whom Charges Loom" (pages 16–17 above). The reporters could prove that possible incidents of forgery or false swearing were under investigation respecting a petition to force a public referendum. The reporters could also prove that some signatures being investigated were associated with one Lawrence and one Simpson. The eight-column headline of the resulting news article said: "FORGERY CHARGES MAY LOOM FOR LAWRENCE, SIMPSON." When Lawrence and Simpson sued, the court agreed that saying they "may be" charged with criminal conduct was little different from an assertion that charges were forthcoming. As a result, the headline was found to be false and defamatory. A slightly different, but rigorous, report that an investigation was underway might have avoided the lawsuit completely.[379]

Another example of journalistic leaps to unsupported implications involved charges of arson and murder. A local television news program accurately reported that a funeral director admitted to charging survivors of welfare recipients more than the authorized amounts, and to filing false certifications to receive reimbursements from public funds. The following month, the home of a woman employed to dispense reimbursements to funeral directors for the burial of destitute veterans, blew up and killed her. A relative allegedly told arson investigators that the accident victim had remarked, after watching the earlier news report, "If my house ever blows up you'll know who did it," referring to the funeral director.

After police and arson investigators came to the TV station to review videotapes of that earlier story, the station again took to the air waves saying "[t]here may be a connection between a fatal fire . . . and our investigation into funeral fraud." On camera, a detective confirmed that he had received information regarding threats placed on the woman's life which were under investigation. The new report quoted what the deceased woman's relative had told arson investigators and concluded with the following: "There was suspicion that old cellulose nitrate film, which is highly explosive, may have caused the explosions and fatal fire. That theory has not been thrown out but the fact that [the deceased woman] had been threatened while an investigation into funeral fraud is going on has become very suspicious."

The funeral director sued the reporter and the station for their implication that he committed homicide by arson and was a police suspect in the death of the woman. The court refused to reject the plaintiff's contention that the defendants demonstrated actual malice. Among other reasons, there was too large a gap between the detective's confirmation and the story's implication.[380]

"A Game of Golf"

A newspaper columnist obtained the accurate information that a county council member had been socializing with a developer who was interested in converting a country club into a shopping center. The columnist wrote that the politician had "enjoyed a golf outing with [the] developer," and afterwards "seemed more understanding" of the developer's plans. The council member sued, objecting to the implication that he was guilty of profiteering and of receiving unlawful gratuities, both of which were crimes.

Assume that the comment was true to the extent that the council member *did* find new value in the project after a friendly outing. Who would win the lawsuit?

"A Game of Golf"
(Answer)

The columnist would prevail because the column accurately presented the facts without implying that the council member received any unlawful benefit from the developer. Rather, the common meaning of the challenged language simply conveyed the truth.[381]

Another risky detour from precision is to suggest that a source has more knowledge or authority or weight than it actually has. Just as sources must be accurately quoted or paraphrased, their credibility must be accurately and rigorously described. Take, for example, the suit brought by General Westmoreland against CBS. The trial judge found that the editing of segments about the general to imply falsely that an intelligence officer was a member of the general's staff, and thereby give his statements more credibility than they deserved, could establish actual malice. The same applied to use of an answer to a hypothetical question which had been edited to appear as a statement of fact. The judge observed that even when a "reporter may have sufficient evidence of his charge to foreclose any material issue of [actual malice] . . . he may nonetheless make himself liable if he knowingly or recklessly misstates that evidence to make it seem more convincing or condemnatory than it is." As examples, the judge condemned editing statements of witnesses "so they seem to say more than in fact was said" as well as false overstatements of the bases for a witness's accusation.[382] All of these means of presenting information from sources, without also presenting the limitations of those sources, could help justify a jury finding of actual malice or negligence.

When rigor is impossible, or is deliberately avoided, the story should say so and not mislead. If a conversation, a scene, or a characterization is fictional, and not obviously so, it should be labeled as the creation of its author. (This bit of advice applies even when an entire work, such as a docudrama or historical fiction, is known by its viewers or readers to contain some fictionalized elements. If truth cannot be distinguished from fiction, and the fiction is defamatory, a disclaimer or other signpost in the footnotes or credits could very useful in a libel action.) If facts or conversations are based on memory, or faulty sources, or the author's opinion, or are questionably truthful for any other reason, letting the reader or viewer know about it with an appropriate comment or disclaimer is usually prudent.

AVOIDING NAMES AND DISGUISING IDENTITIES

Because statements cannot defame if their subjects cannot reasonably be recognized by those who know them, journalists have another useful means of reducing risk when writing a story. If the identities of real people (or corporations or other business entities) can be completely disguised, liability can be reduced or avoided completely in both non-fiction and fiction based on fact. To succeed at this technique, however, the subject's identity has to be disguised completely by changing so many details that no one can reasonably make an accurate identification.

What details? In addition to names, there are many possibilities: age, place of birth, occupation, names of relatives, number and description of family members, locality of residence, job location, sex, hair color, eye color, race, height, weight, educational background, ethnic group, marital status, personality traits, and so forth. Of course, some details cannot be changed without doing damage to the basic integrity or sense of the story. For example, it would not do, in a story about Greek families, to name one of them Jones. Also, when too many details are changed in some stories, the audience might receive a distorted impression of the characteristics of the subject which gave rise to the conduct or event in question. For example, it would make no sense to disguise the economic status of adolescents found in a story about ghetto youth. So, a balance must be struck between reporting the story in an accurate and sensible way, and disguising the subject so that readers or viewers will not identify the person portrayed. To do this effectively requires close attention.

"The Boy in St. Swithin's"

Gathering research for a series of articles on child abuse, a reporter interviewed a police sergeant about several cases that were being investigated. Without giving any names, the sergeant told the reporter that a nine-month-old brought in June to St.

Swithin's Hospital had died from head injuries, including a skull fracture, which his parents attributed to a fall from bed. The sergeant mentioned that the child's injuries were not consistent with a normal fall and that the incident was being investigated as a homicide.

The reporter wrote a story which included the following:

> Early in June, nine-month-old Mark (not his real name) fought for his short life after receiving head injuries in what police believe was a homicide. Mark lost his fight. . . . Denied the joys of childhood, nine-month-old Mark received a fractured skull during the first week of June and was taken to St. Swithin's Hospital where he died two days later. . . .

Assume everything the sergeant said was correct. What, if anything, did the reporter do wrong?

"The Boy in St. Swithin's"
(Answer)

The reporter's principal fault was that he took the sergeant's report of suspicions and treated them as facts, not checking for later developments. In this case, the police investigation ultimately showed that the child's injury occurred when he fell off a bed after his mother left the room momentarily to help her husband prepare a cake.

The reporter's other fault was that he did not sufficiently change biographical details to avoid letting the parents' friends and neighbors know exactly to whom the erroneous, and defamatory, statements pertained. The child's sex and age, the nature of his injuries, when he died, how he died, the hospital where he died, and how long he lived after sustaining the injuries, all implicated the parents.

In a similar case, the parents alleged that they had been embarrassed and humiliated by the report and presented evidence that neighbors had shunned them. The highest court of the state concluded that a reasonably prudent editor should have been alerted to defamatory potential by the contents of the article (which fit within the particularly risky category of accusation of a crime). The newspaper was found guilty of negligence and paid substantial damages.[383]

As this example also calls to mind, laudable and civic-minded goals— such as publicizing child abuse to deter other abusers—makes no difference to the outcome of a case.

When names and other characteristics are fictionalized, the story should explicitly say so. Giving the reader or viewer notice of this kind is advisable not only for journalistic integrity, but also to help avoid the other trap of changing names and biographical details: defaming someone completely unknown who fits the fictionalized name and description. For example, if a journalist writes a story about schizophrenics in a mental hospital and names one of them Ann Peterson without knowing any Ann Peterson: if a woman by that name lived in the same locality and the details of the article reasonably pointed in her direction, she could have a claim.

In such an instance, the similarity would have to be more than an amusing coincidence; reasonable identification would have to be established. Making such connections, however, is not unheard of. In an actual case, a "sex-crazed" Swinger of the Month in *Club Magazine* was identified as "Marian, Taxi Driver, New Albany, Mississippi," and the accompanying photo caption noted her professed pleasure in "coming on" to her "fares." Mary Raines Phyfer, who actually did drive a taxi in New Albany, Mississippi, sued for defamation, even though the photograph was not hers and the name was not exactly hers either. In fact, the Swinger was entirely fictional. The woman depicted in the photo was a model, and the caption was written by a London-based employee of the magazine who invented the name "Marian" and chose New Albany, Mississippi, at random "from an atlas, map, or almanac." Yet a federal judge refused to dismiss the case and left for a jury the question of whether "a reasonable person could reasonably believe" that the Swinger was Ms. Phyfer.[384]

In another case, a suit brought by the only Manhattan psychiatrist with the surname of Allen *was* dismissed though the portrayal of a "Dr. Allen," with a Manhattan office in a nonfiction book allegedly defamed him. The court noted that the "Allen" name had been chosen at random by the book's author, that the book's "Dr. Allen" had a different office address, that the Allen name was "commonly used," and that no first name and no physical description appeared in the book (other than that

"Dr. Allen" had an "angular face"). Furthermore, a disclaimer at the front of the book gave notice that the name of "Dr. Allen," among others, was fictional.[385]

Courts do recognize that the burden of checking and clearing names must be kept within reason; as one New York judge allowed, no one could be expected "to scan thousands of telephone directories and business indices, to comb voting lists and city rosters, to rake the census roles and myriad listings of names, individual, trade and corporate." The same judge recognized that the wide variety of national origins in our population results in names of "infinite variety" and exacerbates the problem: to disguise a name like Jones by spelling it backwards "would be little protection, for somewhere in this wondrous land there must be someone named Senoj."[386]

However, in addition to stating openly when names are fictionalized, reasonable precautions are required to avoid injuring the unintended and unknown. At the very least, if a story is said to take place in a particular locality, a local telephone directory should be checked for persons bearing the fictionalized name. (This procedure would not have uncovered the taxi driver, however.) The same considerations apply to fictional works. A completely invented story reasonably could be interpreted to defame persons unknown to the writer, and the same precautions should be employed.

An even greater risk lies in the creation of fictional stories based upon real people and real events which have been embellished with fictional activities like rape, murder, incest and fraud to enhance the narrative. Characteristically, stories of this kind do not employ the real names of the persons who "inspired" them. However, just as in the case of non-fiction works, the reasonable reader or viewer should not be allowed to conclude that fictional events in the story, which if true would harm the reputations of real people, actually occurred. (This advice is particularly pertinent when the writer, like most new fiction writers, is using real events and friends and relatives as springboards for the story.) And just as with nonfiction works, the disguise should not be limited to names alone.

"Jed's Story"

A made-for-television mini-series will be aired next week. As usual, this one concerns the intimate lives of the rich and powerful. The story is set in the thick of today's high stakes cable television industry. The principal character is a yacht-loving executive named Jed Terner. During the course of four installments, he takes over an unprepossessing local broadcast station in the deep South and through sheer power of will expands his holdings to 18 national cable networks. Along the way, he enters into five adulterous affairs, ruins the careers of eight corporate rivals, attends three cocaine parties, writes a best-selling book, and becomes a regular feature of publications like *People* magazine. He is also shown embezzling $9 million without getting caught (his faithful secretary shreds incriminating documents just before the last commercial break). The credits bear a disclaimer: "Any resemblance to any actual person living or dead is completely coincidental."

Assume for purposes of argument that there exists in reality a yacht-loving magnate of the cable industry, living in the deep South, who has a similar name and is well known to readers of *People* magazine. Assume that everything else described above, including the name, is fictional. What's wrong with this picture?

"Jed's Story"
(Answer)

Even if the objective of the creator of this story was to write a parody or satire, he or she did not go far enough. Having made the connection with the real-life counterpart, the reasonable viewer would not necessarily recognize that *all* of the fictional—and defamatory—elements are false.[387]

Note how the likelihood of that conclusion could be reduced by changing the locale from the South to Minneapolis, or by giving the central character an ethnic surname, or by changing his hobby to car racing and the industry from cable television to magazine publishing. The more changes, the less reasonable a connection between the living person and the literary invention. Note also in this example, how many of the defamatory statements fit into particularly risky categories, with criminal activity and adultery prominent among them.

Accurate labeling is another important precaution. In nonfiction works, a reader or viewer should be notified that "the names of all persons described in this story, as well as biographical details, have been changed." In fictional works (as demonstrated in the roll of credits at the end of many motion pictures), the disclaimer typically says: "All characters in this work are fictitious, and any resemblance to real persons, living or dead, is purely coincidental." Labels like these will help make identification of the subject less likely or "reasonable," as they did in the case of the psychiatrist Dr. Allen (pp. 125–126 above). But they will not carry the day without corresponding changes in identifying details.

WHEN SOURCES MUST BE NAMED

Good journalistic practice usually requires attribution of sources in the absence of compelling reasons to the contrary, like promises of confidentiality. Source attributions give readers and viewers an indication of the source's quality and a means to assess the severity of a charge. Attributions may also discourage potential plaintiffs who recognize that the Actual Malice and Private Person Standards pose significant obstacles—even when a statement is false—if the journalist relied on trustworthy sources. And when a report concerns the workings of governmental proceedings, or official government reports, or accusations by prominent people against other prominent people, the reasons to cite sources are even more compelling.

As discussed in Section I, the general rule is that a journalist who repeats a false defamatory statement by a third person is subject to liability, just as if the journalist originated the statement. The defamation is treated as though it were "adopted" by the repetition.[388] This rule, which can have a profound effect on the outcome of a libel suit, ordinarily applies whether or not the journalist attributes the statement to the original source.

When reports are in certain specified categories, however, two special privileges offer the media a gaping exception to the general rule. The public records privilege will often permit liability-free reporting on the workings of governmental proceedings and on the contents of official government reports. The doctrine of neutral reportage sometimes does the same for reports of accusations by prominent people against prominent people. Both privileges have certain requirements, including attribution of the source. They also have another characteristic in common: they are recognized to widely varying degrees in different jurisdictions.

When they do apply, these privileges will short-circuit any inquiry into truth or falsity, and avoid completely the tortuous workings of the Actual Malice and Public Person Standards. In their place will stand the journalist's unfettered right to publish fair and balanced reports on matters of public concern. Without attribution of sources, however, both privileges are lost. This does not mean that an unattributed accusation from an official proceeding or document, or from a prominent source, becomes valueless in the absence of attribution. The source will simply take its place among others in the weighing and balancing required by the Actual Malice and Private Person Standards. But by failing to attribute sources, the reporter will have traded the certainty and reduced expense of quick dismissal for the risks of determining truth or falsity, public or private status of the plaintiff, and the presence or absence of actual malice or negligence.

The Public Records Privilege

For many years, the law has provided a public records privilege which applies only to the content of governmental proceedings and official reports.

Under the public records privilege, in many (*but not all*) jurisdictions, the media may repeat defamatory material without liability if:

1. media report describes official activity in judicial, legislative or other official proceedings or the contents of publicly filed reports by officers or agencies of the government.

2. The media report is fair and true (i.e., it is balanced).

3. The source of the statement is noted in the media report.

This public records privilege (also called the "fair reports" privilege) is based on the rationale that keeping the citizenry informed of its government's workings is more important than avoiding occasional damage to individual reputations.[389] This common law privilege is not to be confused with the First Amendment right to publish *truthful* information contained in official court records, open to public inspection.[390] The public records privilege is better; under the right circumstances, it permits a media defendant to avoid liability *without regard* to the truth or falsity of a statement, and—even when a statement proves false—without ever reaching the Actual Malice or Private Person Standards.[391]

Though the scope of the privilege varies considerably from state to state,[392] certain proceedings and documents will almost always be covered, such as court hearings open to the public and judicial documents kept in a court's open file. However, closed hearings, and sealed records and documents may not be covered.[393] Moreover, a number of jurisdictions require that "judicial action" first occur before even openly filed judicial documents (like the complaint and answer which commence a civil suit) become subject to the public records privilege.[394] Otherwise, courts reason, scurrilous charges might be filed without basis just to have them reported as litigation-free libel.

On the criminal side, the privilege will apply to indictments, trials, and hearings, but it may be limited to *public* proceedings.[395] Moreover, a police investigation or the filing of charges might not be covered before a warrant is issued, and arrests might not be covered until formal arraignment takes place.[396] On the other hand, in certain jurisdictions the privilege has been applied to charges made before a grand jury (notwithstanding the secret nature of the proceedings),[397] to a prosecutor's affidavit of probable cause,[398] and to mere arrests.[399]

Reports and affidavits by the FBI can be subject to the privilege particularly when they relate to judicial action, such as an application for a search warrant.[400] Confidential FBI reports which are leaked to the press,[401] however, and police investigation files, are usually not subject to the privilege.[402] Commentary by police about a pending matter, and other observations by law enforcement officers, witnesses, lawyers, or the complainant to a criminal action, which are outside the hearings held or documents filed in a criminal action, are usually beyond the pale.[403] On the other hand, a publicized statement by the head of the New York office of the FBI about the execution of a warrant was held to be within the scope of the privilege.[404]

The public records privilege may also apply to legislative proceedings such as debate in the course of legislative sessions, and reports from the legislative branch. For example, the privilege has been found to include an "intelligence report" released by the House Subcommittee on International Relations investigating Korean-American affairs, which linked the Unification Church to the Korean Central Intelligency Agency.[405] Health department reports, internal police investigations,[406] and other administrative proceedings and reports will often qualify.

Remember, however, that pertinence to the appropriate sort of governmental activity is only part of the criteria which govern application of the privilege. In addition, the report must also be "fair and true" to qualify. By "fair" is meant that a report must be balanced. Even an accurate report may be misleading if information is omitted or presented in such a manner as to convey an erroneous impression.[407] By "true" is meant substantially accurate; a report must be in substance, a truthful recounting of what it purports to describe. This does not require, however, a complete recitation of what occurred at a proceeding or the entire contents of a document. A report can still fit within the privilege if it describes only portions of a proceeding or document which are pertinent to a story. For example, publishing that a witness at a trial, or a state crime commission report, identified someone as a cocaine dealer would be privileged without listing all the other cocaine dealers irrelevant to the story who were also identified.

To say that certain individuals who were merely detained by police had been arrested however would not be a privileged report for lack of accuracy. To say that a construction company's name "appeared several times" in FBI files about the disappearance of Jimmy Hoffa, without noting that there was no accusation of criminality or association with organized crime, is not fair enough to be privileged.[408] Reporting defamatory charges made in a civil action without also reporting the other side's denial and response might also be deemed unfair.[409] Reporting a woman's conviction for depriving others of their civil rights would not be fair and true if it omitted that she was re-tried and acquitted on all counts.[410]

Dramatizations based on official proceedings present special problems when weighed on the scales of fairness and truthfulness. A docudrama based on the famous rape trials of the Scottsboro boys portrayed a community gripped by racial prejudice and intent on vengeance against nine blacks accused of raping two white women. One of those women, thought to be dead when the film aired, was not only alive but voiced strong objections to her depiction as a perjurer and a "loose woman." Because the script was based on an historical book which in turn was based in major part on the judge's findings at the 1933 trial, the defendants asserted the public records privilege as a defense. The court rejected it, however, because the film was not a "completely accurate report of the trial"; witnesses who corroborated the plaintiff's version of the facts were omitted and portions of the trial which portrayed her as a perjurer and a promiscuous woman were emphasized. The court concluded that the "element of balance and neutrality [was] missing."[411]

However, in another case arising from a docudrama portraying a trial, the public records defense succeeded, notwithstanding that the script deviated from the trial transcript. Though testimony was truncated, it was still held to be fairly presented, and the omission of certain details (which, according to the plaintiff, falsified, exaggerated and distorted his role) also presented no obstacle. The court held that editorial judgments, which focused on the evidence presented against the plaintiff, were protected expressions of opinion based on the jury verdict against him.[412]

Other judicial decisions contain special caveats respecting use of the public records privilege. For example, in some jurisdictions actual malice (that is, knowledge of falsity or substantial doubt as to truth) can defeat the privilege.[413] Similarly, in many jurisdictions the privilege can be lost if the press acts for the sole purpose of harming the person defamed or otherwise in bad faith.[414]

All these variables and exclusions might be daunting if they did not collectively point toward a single practical conclusion: the precise scope of the privilege in a given jurisdiction should not trouble journalists on a day-to-day basis. Instead, the essential point is that if any potentially defamatory report can be supported in whole or in part by any source which *might* fit within the privilege of a fair and true report of a judicial, legislative or other official proceeding or document, that source should not be overlooked. And, moreover, once found, it should be cited in the story (and in the headline in some jurisdictions if the defamation appears there too) as the source of the statement.

"The Alleged Cousin"

The Associated Press alleged that an attorney was related to a mobster and had Mafia ties. The reporter based his allegations on conversations with two other reporters, and on a telephone call to a pair of confidential sources at the Pennsylvania Crime Commission who told him that the attorney was related to a known Mafia leader. A third confidential source at the Commission told the reporter that the attorney had represented individuals suspected of having connections with organized crime.

Other sources which supported the statement were discovered after publication: an FBI memorandum identified the attorney as a cousin of a mobster and both a U.S. Senate report and testimony in deportation proceedings established a family relationship between the attorney's father, his uncle, and the Mafia leader (hence by inference showing a connection between the attorney and the mobster).

After the attorney sued for libel, the AP defended itself by pointing to the sources described above and to additional official records, like depositions generated by the lawsuit itself, and real estate filings and records of other judicial proceedings, all of which demonstrated financial, family and social ties between the attorney and persons identified by state and federal officials as participants in organized crime.

The AP moved for summary judgment on the basis of the public records privilege. Did it work?

"The Alleged Cousin"
(Answer)

It did not. An appellate court denied the AP's motion because the sources on which the public records privilege might have been based were discovered too late and the AP failed to make proper attribution in the article. The only arguably "official" source on which the AP relied *before* publishing were the statements by *confidential* Crime Commission personnel. This presented the court with a problem: while reports of official statements or records made or released by public agencies would be protected in the state under the public records privilege, statements by lower level employees would not. Without knowing the identities of the confidential sources, the court found it impossible to say whether their statements constituted official action or not, and refused to say they were privileged.

The other sources of information were no help; the court refused to let the privilege "protect unattributed, defamatory statements supported after-the-fact through a frantic search of official records," because if the media does not directly or indirectly rely upon official records at the time of publication, "the policy underlying the privilege is inapplicable and the privilege itself should not be applied."[415]

When reviewing a story, writers and editors must therefore ask themselves if any official source relied upon in the story's preparation has not

been cited; whether official sources which *are* mentioned have been identified with absolute clarity as the defamation's origin;[416] and whether any
official source which can support a defamatory statement may have been
overlooked.

The Neutral Reportage Privilege

In 1977, a New York federal case recognized a constitutional privilege
for the press to republish other persons' accusations without regard to
whether the reporter writing the story believed the charge to be true or
false or whether the reporter independently verified the charges.[417] This
doctrine, entitled "neutral reportage," corresponds with what many journalists incorrectly think is a universal entitlement: the right to repeat what
other people say without being held responsible, as long as the remarks
are properly attributed. However, the U.S. Supreme Court has not yet
interpreted the Constitution to include this privilege,[418] relatively few
lower courts have adopted it,[419] and even those which have embraced it,
limit its application to narrowly defined circumstances. And, just as with
the public records privilege, if the source of an accusation is not named,
neutral reportage will be of no benefit at all.

Where adopted, the neutral reportage doctrine is usually circumscribed by four limiting factors, the precise contours of which
vary from place to place:

1.   The report must convey a serious charge of such importance
that the accusation is newsworthy simply because it was made.[420]
Some courts have interpreted this criterion to require a pre-existing controversy.[421]

2.   In some formulations of the doctrine, the privilege covers
reports of serious charges from anyone at all without regard to
the source's trustworthiness,[422] the idea being that the public can
serve as the final arbiter of the trustworthiness of the source.[423]
In other jurisdictions, however, the accusation reported must
come from a responsible, prominent organization[424] or from a
responsible prominent person.[425]

3.   The target of the accusation must be a public official or
public figure.[426] (The same uncertainties in identifying public figures and officials, as discussed in the context of the Actual Malice
Standard, ostensibly apply. See pages 42–74 above.)

4. The reporting must be both neutral and accurate.[427] This usually means not only that the report must describe the charges without taking sides and without error, but also that both sides of a controversy must be reported (generally including a reply by the target of the charge)[428] and any limitations to the credibility of source must be disclosed.[429] Generally speaking, neutrality also requires that the report neither espouse nor concur in the charges.[430] However, at least one federal appellate court has adopted a relatively expansive conception of the doctrine which permits its application even when the author makes clear his or her "general disposition" toward the reported matter.[431]

The decision which first recognized the privilege involved a controversy over the effects of DDT on bird life. Some scientists argued that the increasing number of birds recorded in the annual count of the National Audubon Society showed that DDT was not harming the birds. The National Audubon Society, however, asserted that the increase in the count meant there were more and better birdwatchers and not more birds. The editor of *American Birds*, a publication of the society, wrote that any scientist who relies on the bird counts to show that the birds had increased in number was "someone who is being paid to lie, or is parroting something he knows little about." A *New York Times* reporter telephoned the editor to obtain the names of those whom the society considered to be "paid liars," and the editor furnished a list of five prominent scientists. (It was disputed, however, whether he made clear that the scientists on the list misinterpreted the bird counts rather than that they were "paid liars.") Before publishing the list of "paid liars," the reporter tried to obtain comments from the five scientists and succeeded in reaching three who denied the charges vigorously. The court's decision praised the reporter's efforts as an "exemplar of fair and dispassionate reporting of an unfortunate but newsworthy contretemps" and held the defamatory list to be privileged by the neutral reportage doctrine.[432]

Until the U.S. Supreme Court decides whether "neutral reportage" is a constitutionally protected right under the First Amendment, the doctrine's spotty recognition and its wavy outlines are likely to cause continuing confusion in the courts. In the meanwhile, in order to take advantage of the privilege where it *does* exist, journalists need not be unduly concerned with much else than the following two points:

---

1. When accusations are leveled against public officials or
public figures, the sources must be cited.
2. Both sides of the story must be sought out and presented
neutrally.

Without prominent sources, properly attributed charges, and a fair and
accurate presentation of both sides of the story, the doctrine's underlying
premise usually will not apply: namely, to allow the public to assess
charges from responsible parties and make up its own mind.

OPINION AS A SAFE HAVEN

An opinion is either a belief, conclusion or judgment not substantiated
by positive knowledge or proof, or an evaluation based on facts.[433] Either
way, pure opinion is a personal belief or idea and not a statement of fact.
Because only assertions of fact can constitute actionable defamation—
and only false or unprivileged facts at that (at least where the media and
matters of public concern are involved)[434]—opinion is a safe haven for
the media. Expressing critical or pejorative or negative views—the kind
of views that can injure reputation—in the form of pure opinions can
reduce or eliminate risk.

It must be noted, however, that while opinion cannot be defamatory,
any *facts* on which the opinion rests, either expressly stated or implied,
can still defame. Furthermore, expressing an opinion requires some attention; statements which purport to be opinions are sometimes statements
of fact and some statements expressed as fact are really opinions. Merely
labeling a statement an opinion does not make it so if an assertion of fact
is either expressed or implied.[435]

For example, if a speaker says, "In my opinion, Elmo is a liar" the
speaker implies a knowledge of facts which lead to the conclusion that
Elmo does not speak the truth. Even if the speaker gives the facts on
which the opinion is based, and those facts are either incorrect or incom-
plete, or the speaker makes an error in assessing the facts, the statement
may still imply a false assertion of fact and be the proper subject of a
defamation action. Inserting the words "in my opinion" or "I think" in
front of "Elmo is a liar" can cause as much damage to Elmo's reputation
as those four words standing by themselves.[436] This applies whether the

"opinion" appears in an editorial, in a letter to the editor, in a column, or on a sports page. Any statement of "opinion" which is freighted with an expressed or implied defamatory fact will not avoid a defamation suit.

In many instances, separating fact from opinion is simple. Statements which are pure speculation ("Martians will land next Tuesday") are pure opinion. So are evaluative statements reflecting the author's political, moral or aesthetic views,[437] without reference to any verifiable underlying fact ("Watching baseball is more fun than watching football" or "Mr. Chips shows his abysmal ignorance by listening to the Grateful Dead"). Other statements (like "the temperature is 45 degrees" or "Elmo is a convicted rapist") are statements of fact which no one would confuse with opinion.

In many other contexts, separating pure opinion from stated or implied facts is not so easy. Though courts have been struggling to distinguish the two for many years, no dependable, precise and universally accepted means of separating fact from opinion in all instances has yet been devised.[438] The operative question is always whether reasonable readers would actually interpret a statement as expressing or implying defamatory facts,[439] but knowing this does not give the writer much of a predictive measure. And statements which do not fit easily into either of the fact or opinion categories "are the stuff of which litigation is made."[440]

"A Few Seconds with Andy Rooney"

Andy Rooney offers a weekly commentary on the long-running CBS television program "60 Minutes." The national sales manager of Unelko Corp. sent Mr. Rooney a sample of "Rain-X," its "one-step wipe-on automotive glass coating that repels rain, sleet and snow on contact and takes up where windshield wipers leave off!" An accompanying letter invited Mr. Rooney to "personally test and evaluate" the performance of the product.

During a subsequent broadcast of "60 Minutes," Mr. Rooney commented on "junk" he had received in the mail, and part of his commentary indeed evaluated "Rain-X":

> People send me things. I get an awful lot of junk that I don't want that just seems too interesting to throw away. Some people send me stuff because they're friendly. Others, of course, send it because they're looking for a plug on the air.

> I get a lot of caps, and a lot of cups. . . .
>
> I get a lot of music sent to me. . . .
>
> Here's the sort of thing I get a lot of. I don't know why they sent me this. It's a piece of a door. I guess they were pushing some new kind of material.
>
> Here's something for the windshield of your car called Rain-X. The fellow who makes this sent me a whole case of it. He's very proud of it. I actually spent an hour one Saturday putting it on the windshield of my car. I suppose he'd like a commercial or a testimonial. You know how they hold the product up like this? It didn't work.

Other "junk" mentioned in the segment were books, an ashtray in the shape of a human lung, giant paperclips, and an orange peeler.

When Unelko sued over the comment "It didn't work," Rooney's lawyers cited the jocular context and invoked the opinion defense. What happened?

"A Few Seconds with Andy Rooney"
(Answer)

A federal court of appeals found the statement "It didn't work" to be one of fact. By producing the impression that the product failed to perform as guaranteed, it implied an assertion of objective fact; and it was based on a factual observation to such an extent that unlike pure opinion, it was objectively verifiable.[441] The humorous effect of the segment as a whole as well as its presentation as commentary had no bearing on the court's determination that the statement was fact.

In 1990, the Supreme Court turned its attention to the facts-opinion dichotomy and to the degree of protection offered opinions by the U.S. Constitution. The Court concluded (in contrast to a number of lower courts in recent years) that opinion enjoys no special First Amendment privilege just because it is opinion. However, statements of opinion, like all other statements, are entitled to constitutional protection if they cannot be proven false, at least insofar as the media's discussion of matters of public concern is involved.[442] Therefore, opinions in the realm of pure belief and ideas, which cannot be proven false, are constitutionally protected; opinions which assert or imply an objective fact are not.[443]

This returns us to the slippery distinction between pure opinion and express or implied fact.

The Supreme Court specified the following tests to determine whether a purported opinion actually asserts or implies an objective fact[444]:

1. Is the *language* loose, rhetorical, figurative, or hyperbolic— the kind of language *which no one would take as a serious statement of actual fact*? Or does the *general tenor* of the article or broadcast negate the impression that the writer is seriously asserting a fact? If so, the statement is either a pure opinion or parody, satire or humor, and not actionable. (The last three forms of expression are treated separately at pages 149–151.)

2. Is the statement sufficiently factual to be susceptible of being proved true or false? That is, *if the statement is not made on a core of objective evidence and is not an articulation of an objectively verifiable event, it must be opinion.*[445] In this category, one finds statements like "the man is a fascist" (because the word has no clear definition)[446] and "the inside of the meat was undercooked when served" (there being no objective standard of "doneness").

These categories are not necessarily mutually exclusive. The term "fascist" could be considered both "loose" or "hyperbolic" as well as insufficiently factual to be proved true or false.

If a statement proves to be fact instead of opinion it will not receive the special treatment afforded opinion: the Actual Malice Standard will apply when public persons bring suit and the Private Person Standard will apply to suits by private persons. If the statement qualifies as pure opinion, which neither asserts nor implies objective fact, or cannot be proved true or false, or both, then no defamation action can be based on it (at least where the media and matters of public concern are involved).[447]

"The Wrestling Coach Who Went to the Mat"

At a high school wrestling match, the Maple Heights team was involved in an "altercation" with the opposing team from Mentor in which several people were injured. In response to the incident, the state athletic association held a hearing at which the Maple Heights coach testified, among others. The athletic association then placed the Maple Heights team on probation for a year and declared it ineligible for the state tournament. The association also censured the coach for his actions during the incident. Several Maple Heights parents and wrestlers then sued the athletic association claiming denial of due process. In the ensuing court proceeding, the coach and others testified again and persuaded the court to overturn the probation and ineligibility orders of the athletic association.

The next day, the *News-Herald* ran a column by a writer with the initials "T.D." in the sports pages under the title "T.D. Says." (It was accompanied by T.D.'s full name and photograph.) The column's heading stated that "Maple beat the law with the 'big lie,' " and on the jump page, the headline read "[T.D.] says Maple told a lie." In the column, T.D. said that the wrestlers learned an unhappy lesson, namely "[i]f you get in a jam, lie your way out," referring to the coach and the former superintendent of schools who also testified at the hearing. The column also said "[a]nyone who attended the meet, whether he be from Maple Heights, Mentor, or impartial observer, knows in his heart that [the coach] . . . lied at the hearing after . . . having given his solemn oath to tell the truth."

The coach sued. The newspaper argued that the statement was privileged opinion and not actionable. After nearly 15 years of litigation, the case reached the U.S. Supreme Court. What happened?

"The Wrestling Coach Who Went to the Mat"
(Answer)

The Court ruled that T.D.'s statements contained a sufficiently factual connotation to be actionable as defamation, notwithstanding the fact that they appeared in a column in the sports pages and notwithstanding that they may have been intended as an expression of opinion. The Court concluded that a reasonable judge or jury could conclude that the statements implied an assertion that the coach perjured himself in the judicial proceeding.

The language was not loose, figurative, or hyperbolic, and neither it nor the general tenor of the column negated the impression that the writer was seriously maintaining that the coach committed perjury. Furthermore, the connotation that the coach committed a crime was sufficiently factual to be susceptible of being proved true or false, based as it was on a core of objective evidence; the accusation was therefore objectively verifiable and not mere opinion.[448]

As a general rule, accusations of criminal conduct or personal dishonesty (like lying) are not recognized as forms of opinion.[449] In the case of the coach, the accusation not only alleged dishonesty but also the crime of perjury.

The media's goal, therefore, is to find the best means of expressing critical or other reputation-injuring statements to maximize the likelihood of their being interpreted as protected opinion. Obviously, opinions cannot be limited to the favored categories of rhetorical flourishes, hyperbole, loose language, humorous settings and the airy sphere of ideas and beliefs untethered to provable facts. For opinions which are based on facts, the best means of reducing risk is to (1) disclose the facts on which an opinion is based; and (2) measure those facts against the same standards of proof which apply to any other potentially defamatory statement: the Actual Malice Standard or as appropriate, the Private Person Standard (both discussed in Section II above). Disclosure of facts underlying an opinion will deter viewers or readers from inferring other factual underpinnings which the writer either did not intend or cannot prove. With its underlying facts exposed, the opinion is more likely to be interpreted by the reasonable recipient as "pure" opinion—that is, the personal view or belief of its author which cannot be verified as true or false.[450]

Some contexts, like editorial cartoons, may contain too little space to lay out all the premises for the opinion expressed. If the underlying facts are close by in the same edition, or are undisputably common knowledge, failing to repeat them may not pose a problem.[451] The safer course, however, is to lay out the premises whenever space permits.

A few examples will be helpful. The statement "I think Phoebe must be an alcoholic" is potentially libelous. Notwithstanding the "I think," it might cause a jury to find an implication that the speaker was aware of undisclosed facts which justified the statement. Compare the following: "Phoebe moved in 6 months ago. She works downtown and I have seen her only twice during that period in her backyard around 4:30 seated in a deck chair with a portable radio listening to a news broadcast, and with a drink in her hand. I think she must be an alcoholic.'' The disclosure of the comment's factual predicate elevates the statement ''I think she must be an alcoholic'' to the realm of pure opinion which cannot be the basis of a defamation suit.[452] With the underlying basis—which is not defamatory—fully disclosed, reasonable people could not interpret the statement ''I think he must be an alcoholic'' to imply defamatory facts.

Statements made upon disclosed facts were found to be protected expressions of opinion in all of the following cases:[453]

• A statement in *Time* magazine that a lawyer was one of his profession's ''shadier practitioners'' was supported by the following substantially true facts in the same article: ''Thanks to painfully slow bar discipline, a northern California lawyer named Jerome Lewis is still practicing law despite a $100,000 malpractice judgment against him in 1970 and a $60,000 judgment including punitive damages in 1974 for defrauding clients of money. . . .''[454]

• The characterization in a *Chicago Sun-Times* editorial of a nudist camp's ''Mr. and Miss Nude Teeny Bopper'' pageant as pornography was put like this: ''When people run around naked in the privacy of a nudist camp, it's their business. But when someone arranges for children ages 6 to 16 to parade naked and has fully clothed people pay to watch and photograph them, it's pornography.''[455]

• A newspaper's description of a 150-story Manhattan skyscraper proposed to be built by Donald Trump, as ''[o]ne of the silliest things anyone could inflict on New York'' was protected opinion. The same article included the size of the building, its cost, and other facts on which the opinion was based.[456]

• A newspaper editorial in the *Tulsa Tribune* accompanied by a cartoon with similar content, declared that a gubernatorial candidate had descended to ''sewer politics'' and strongly suggested that the candidate was unqualified, was based on the true fact that the candidate had asked the front-runner whether he was a homosexual or bisexual with no evidence of either proclivity.[457]

Remember, this means of expressing opinions will be useful only if the underlying facts cannot be proven false.[458]

To sum up: Journalists can reduce their risk by expressing potentially defamatory statements in the form of opinions if:

1. The opinion relates to a matter of public concern.

2. The statement lies either in the realm of belief or idea without asserting or implying any fact; or the statement exists in the realm of loose, figurative or hyperbolic speech or in a context which otherwise negates the impression that a serious statement of actual fact is being made.

3. In the alternative, if a statement either asserts or implies the existence of verifiable facts, those facts should be examined with care and proved in accordance with the Actual Malice Standard, or, better yet, the Private Person Standard (see Section II above).

4. And the factual predicate of an opinion must always be clearly stated, to preclude readers and viewers from drawing implications of facts which can be proved false.

5. Charges of criminal activity or personally dishonest behavior, such as lying, should be avoided even in the form of opinions.

WRITING WITH FLAIR ENCOURAGED

Notwithstanding the rules, caveats, signposts and other directives in this book toward the straight and narrow, reports with a tendency to injure reputation need not be dry and lifeless—especially when personal expression, comment, opinion or heated debate provides the context. In fact, writing with some flair, provided the writing is channeled into certain favored categories like loose, figurative or hyperbolic language, jokes, satire and epithets can actually *reduce* risk.

However, reasonable readers and viewers have to interpret such statements in the way they were intended for these privileges to work. The job of the writer and editor is to make clear when a statement is not intended to be taken literally. Sometimes it even makes sense to change a literal statement with defamatory impact into something outrageous, unbelievable and therefore unactionable. As with separating fact from opinion, the pivotal question is the effect of the statement on its audience. A half-way effort will not reduce risk.

"Loose" language (which is not susceptible to precise definition), figurative speech (such as figures of speech or other representations by analogy or resemblance) and hyperbole (rhetorical exaggeration) generally enjoy First Amendment protection as undefamatory expressions of ideas rather than facts. In many instances, such literary devices are means of expressing pure opinion—the kind that cannot be proven true or false. But even statements of fact do not become actionable when expressed through literary devices that magnify and distort to a degree which would injure reputation if taken seriously—*just as long as no one reasonably can take them seriously.*

As one court has observed, "[t]o deny to the press the right to use hyperbole . . . would condemn the press to an arid, desiccated recital of bare facts."[459] The law recognizes and encourages the author's right to use "[m]ere exaggeration, slight irony or wit, or all those delightful touches of style which go to make an article readable. . . . Facts do not cease to be facts because they are mixed with the flair and expectant comment of the story teller, who adds to the recital a little touch by his piquant pen."[460]

The law's assurance "that public debate will not suffer for lack of 'imaginative expression' or the 'rhetorical hyperbole' which has traditionally added much to the discourse of our Nation,"[461] also extends to humor, parody and satire. Intent to injure, resultant hurt feelings and even reduced esteem in the eyes of others do not dent this protection in the arena of public debate about public officials and public figures[462] where even "slashing and one-sided" expressions full of scorn and ridicule—like political cartoons and their literary equivalents—enjoy the same protection.[463] The law's coverage also includes name-calling and garden variety vituperation, especially in heated debates where "lusty and imaginative expression" is encouraged.[464] This wide range of possibilities is bounded only by the audience's reasonable interpretation: protection applies only to statements that cannot reasonably be understood as describing actual facts or actual events.[465]

The lines separating loose, figurative language, rhetorical hyperbole, humor, satire and vituperative epithets are not sharply defined, but this is of small moment for the writer. It is enough to choose language from one of these favored categories without identifying precisely which.

Loose or Figurative Language

In most contexts, "statements that are 'loosely definable' or 'variously interpretable' cannot support an action for defamation."[466] Language in this category has included:

- "Fascist" when applied to William F. Buckley. (The word's meaning was deemed "so debatable, loose and varying that [it is] insusceptible to proof of truth or falsity," and any search for a "precisely articulable meaning" to the ordinary reader could be "an arbitrary one.")[467]

- "Little Amazons" used by *Penthouse* magazine to describe young girls who spent their schoolyard recesses beating up the boys. (The word denotes one of a race of female warriors, or a female warrior, or a strong, tall, masculine woman, or even a sexually aggressive and insatiable female and therefore lacks "a single precise meaning.")[468]

- "Scam" to describe an effort to sell interests in a time-share condominium by enticing potential purchasers with promises of a lobster dinner, which might be forgotten if the purchasers did not respond to the sales pitch. (The word lacks a precise meaning, connotes different things to different people, lacks a single usage in common phraseology, and has so little precision that it is incapable of being proved true or false.)[469]

- "Sleaze-bag" who "slimed up from the bayou" used to describe an agent for professional football players. (Though they "do not rank as descriptive words one would prefer to have in letters of recommendation," their meanings in this context were too imprecise to be considered assertions of fact. "While it may not be a compliment to be called a 'sleaze-bag agent,' or 'sleaze-bag journalist,' or 'sleaze-bag coach' or whatever kind of sleaze-bag one may happen to be, the mere absence of complimentary affect does not render a statement defamatory.")[470]

Although it cannot be guaranteed that every court would find these words to be lacking in precise meaning, it seems fair to say that in similar contexts, most would.

Rhetorical Hyperbole

The following descriptions were exaggerated sufficiently to find protection under the First Amendment's umbrella for rhetorical hyperbole:

- "Filthiest stunt" to describe a senatorial candidate's role in disseminating allegations that his opponent was a homosexual.[471]

- "Animal from Alabama," "caveman incarnate," and "more bestial than academic" to describe a college football player known for his rough play.[472]

- "Near-Neanderthal" to describe a newspaper publisher;[473]

• Characterization of a newspaper as being published "by paranoids for paranoids."[474]

Restaurant reviews (like aesthetic criticism) seem to generate hyperbole of particular piquancy. For example, a food critic declared that the "green peppers . . . remained still frozen on the plate," the rice was "soaking . . . in oil" and the pancakes were "the thickness of a finger" in a review of a Chinese restaurant. Though the restaurant owner had no tolerance for literary license and sued for defamation, the judge applauded the critic's "attempt to interject style into the review rather than . . . convey with technical precision literal facts about the restaurant." The judge refused to limit the author and others like him to pedestrian observations like "the peppers were too cold, the rice was too oily and the pancakes were too thick," and also observed that the statements were incapable of being proved false: "What is too oily for one person may be perfect for some other person. The same can be said for the temperature of vegetables, [and] the thickness of pancakes."[475] In another review, a sauce was described as "yellow death on duck" and the poached trout renamed "trout ala green plague." For essentially the same reasons, these statements too were deemed hyperbolic expressions of pure opinion and not statements of fact.[476] (Contrast these statements with a remark like, "the sauce was so bad, the kitchen must have been unsanitary," which *is* capable of corroboration, implies serious defamatory facts, and would *not* enjoy any protection.)[477]

As the restaurant cases and most of the other examples suggest, the *context* of a statement will often influence whether the reasonable reader or viewer will interpret a statement to be fact or hyperbole. In the following cases, the context of statements proved to be most significant in assessments of their literal believability:

• A journalist's statement during a televised panel discussion that a well-known civil rights activist had "put a contract out" on the journalist in response to a story unwelcomed by the activist, was held to be nondefamatory hyperbole. (In context, "[n]o one listening to the discussion as a whole could have formed a reasonable belief that [the activist] had hired someone to kill [the journalist]."[478]

• In a satirical and cynical first-person account of a reception at a private home for Democratic presidential primary candidate Walter Mondale, the following observation was held not to defame the host of the party: "Maybe it is the bizarre acoustics of the setup, or maybe there was a mickie in the

Canadian Club. I don't know. But sometime during the weird . . . debacle I snap my binder, blow my bung, lose my handle.'' (Given the article's ''format'' and tongue-in-cheek style, the court concluded that only ''supersensitive persons, with morbid imaginations'' could understand the comment about the mickie to accuse the host of illegally drugging his guests' drinks.)[479]

• In the same article, the description of the host as ''a fat version of Dustin Hoffman's 'Ratso' in 'Midnight Cowboy' '' was also considered protected hyperbole. (In context, the observation connoted only the author's opinion about the host's physical appearance which was permissible; had the context suggested that the comparison was meant to suggest a *dishonest character*, it would have defamed.)[480]

• A newsletter article likening employees who had not joined a union to Judas, Benedict Arnold and other ''traitors,'' was approved as a ''lusty and imaginative expression of the contempt felt by union members toward those who refused to join.'' (The Supreme Court found it ''impossible to believe'' that any reader would have understood the newsletter to charge the criminal offense of treason.)[481]

• In a report about a heated public meeting at which a developer's refusal to accept the Board if Education's price for a plot of land until the city endorsed his request for higher density rezoning of two other tracts, the quoted observation, ''It seems that this is a slight case of blackmail,'' was not defamatory. (No reader could have thought that either the speaker at the meeting or the newspaper article reporting the words was charging the commission of a criminal offense and, in fact, there was no proof that anyone in the city had thought so.)[482]

• A remark that a television sports reporter was ''the only newscaster in town who is enrolled in a course for remedial speaking'' was clearly ''metaphorical, exaggerated or even fantastic'' and therefore protected. (The context was an article describing the best and worst sports personalities in a series of ''one-liners.'')[483]

This analysis is unvarying no matter where rhetorical hyperbole appears, be it in the letters to the editor, the editorial column, or cartoons. The core question is always the effect on the reasonable reader or viewer.

"Two Cartoons"

Two editorial cartoons published at different times depicted Governor King in an unflattering way. The first cartoon entitled

"King Signs School Prayer Bill" showed the governor at a desk signing what could reasonably be regarded as the legislation mentioned. He was flanked by two symbolic figures labeled "Patronage" and "Cronyism." The first symbolic figure carried a satchel bearing the caption "pay raise" and the second figure, surrounded by packets of dollar bills, held the Governor's arm as he signed the bill. The caption beneath said "So Let Us Prey!"

The second cartoon depicted the governor in a pin-stripe suit wearing a black shirt and a white tie on which the words "Can Do" appear. He was holding a hat with a pinwheel and was handcuffed to a police officer who was reading to a desk sergeant a list of the governor's controversial political appointments who had experienced forced resignations.

The governor sued for libel claiming that the first cartoon falsely implied that he signed the school prayer bill in exchange for cash payments. He also asserted that the second cartoon conveyed that he was a criminal or had the mental state of a criminal when he appointed individuals knowing of their criminal or unethical conduct.

Who won?

"Two Cartoons"
(Answer)

Both cartoons were found to be undefamatory expressions of "artistic rhetorical hyperbole." The court found that no one could reasonably interpret the first cartoon to state "facts"; rather, at most, it expressed the undefamatory opinion that the governor was motivated to sign the school prayer bill by his interest in attracting legislative support for the pay raise bill which, in the cartoonist's view, constituted "preying" on the public. Questioning and impugning the motives of public officials in this manner is protected under the First Amendment.

In the court's view, the average reasonable reader would also find it impossible to interpret the second cartoon as a factual report that the governor had been arrested, handcuffed and charged, or was a criminal, or knew of his appointees' criminal or unethical conduct before their selection. Instead, the cartoon expressed the artist's protected opinion that the governor was responsible for "several ill-advised appointments."[484]

Humor and Satire

As some of these examples suggest, humor and satire are also covered by the same First Amendment protection as long as their content is not reasonably subject to interpretation as an expression of fact, either express or implied. Judges are fond of quoting a nineteenth-century Irish opinion which observed: "The principle is clear that a person shall not be allowed to murder another's reputation in jest."[485] But when context demonstrates that a statement "otherwise libelous" is a jest, unambiguously jocular, and to be regarded by all as good natured fun, then the reputation of the person mentioned cannot be "so undermined as to support a cause of action for libel."[486] The test, then, is not so much what the author intends but rather how an assertion is likely to be interpreted. Too much subtlety can be risky, but too much subtlety is usually not funny, either.

Humor does not have to be high-minded to be protected. On the contrary, in its more outrageous, vehement and tasteless forms, humor is less likely to be taken literally and is therefore more clearly protected. Moreover, judges do not consider it their job to exclude humor from protection simply because of its offensiveness. "To hold otherwise would run afoul of the First Amendment and chill the free speech rights of all comedy performers and humorists, to the genuine detriment of our society."[487] A good number of opportunities have allowed judges to reconsider and re-embrace this principle:

• The producer of Rege Wines took offense at a cable television program and record album in which the comedian Robin Williams demanded to know why there were no black wines: "Whoa—White Wine. This is a little wine here. If it's not wine it's been through somebody already. Oh.— There are White wines, there are Red wines, but why are there no Black wines like REGGAE, a MOTHERF***ER. It goes with fish, meat, any damn thing it wants to. I like my wine like I like my women, ready to pass out." The winemaker's case was dismissed.[488]

• The comedienne Martha Raye sued the comedian David Letterman after he parodied a widely broadcast product advertisement in which she was introduced, "Here is Martha Raye, actress, denture-wearer." Letterman said, "I saw the most terrifying commercial on television last night, featuring Martha Raye, actress, condom user." Ms. Raye's action was also dismissed.[489]

• The nationally known minister, Jerry Falwell, who has been active as a commentator on politics and public affairs, objected to a *Hustler* magazine parody of advertisements for Campari Liqueur which contained his name and picture and bore the caption, "Jerry Falwell talks about his first time." The actual Campari advertisements included interviews with various celebrities about their first times tasting the liqueur, playing on the sexual double entendre of "first times." In the parody, Reverend Falwell was depicted as saying that his "first time" was during a drunken incestuous rendevous with his mother in an outhouse. Small print at the bottom of the page noted "ad parody—not to be taken seriously." A jury rejected the Reverend's claim of defamation, and the Supreme Court rejected his second claim, based on infliction of emotional distress.[490]

• *Hustler* magazine also lampooned an opponent of pornography with a cartoon depicting two women engaged in a lesbian act of oral sex with the caption "You remind me so much of [the plaintiff], Edna. It's a dog-eat-dog world." In subsequent months, more graphic sexual commentary appeared in the magazine which even the judge described as "disgusting and distasteful abuse" of the pornography foe. But in view of the "spirited debate" on pornography, and the judge's reluctance to limit opinion to "high-minded discourse," the judge granted summary judgment to the magazine because the statements were obviously not of a factual nature. Said the judge, "We have little doubt that the outrageous and the outlandish will be recognized for what they are."[491]

It is worth noting that the most vehement and offensive examples above were set in the context of vigorous public debate over pornography, politics, and public positions. Expressions with this degree of nastiness and intentional malice might be less acceptable in the absence of public issues and public figures.[492] Milder forms of humor, however, do not depend on a context of public debate or public figures to qualify for protection. For example, a suit brought by an accountant named Maurice Frank against NBC was dismissed notwithstanding his private person status. His complaint pertained to a skit on Saturday Night Live in which a tax consultant with the same name gave tax advice which was "ludicrously inappropriate." The skit's "Fast Frank" advised tax write-offs like the following: "Got a horrible acne?... use a lotta *Clearasil*...

that's an Oil Depletion Allowance. . . . Got a rotten tomato in your frige? Frost ruined your crops—that's a farm loss. Your tree gets Dutch Elm Disease . . . Sick leave—take a deduction. Did you take a trip to the bathroom tonight? If you *took* a trip . . . and you did *business*—you can write it off.'' The court found that the skit could not give rise to an impression that Mr. Frank truly gave such advice, observing further that the statements were ''neither a malicious nor vicious personal attack.''[493]

Epithets and Name-Calling

By and large, the law accepts that words of general abuse, even if crude, uncouth and vexatious, are not defamatory when they cannot be taken literally. Often the context in which statements are made, like a public debate or a labor dispute, will lead an audience to anticipate epithets, fiery rhetoric or hyperbole rather than actual accusations.[494] In heated, spirited exchanges of viewpoints, name-calling is expected and belittling a position by vilifying its advocate is ungrudgingly permitted.[495] Again, the theory holds that name-calling will be interpreted as expressions of rage or outrage, and not as literal facts.

Protected epithets uttered in the course of vigorous expressions of opinion have included the following:

Idiots[496]

Tightassed housewife

Frustrated

Fanatic

Crackpot

Deluded busybody[497]

Fat ass[498]

Gutless bastard

Black son-of-a-bitch[499]

Commie

Not traveling with a full set of luggage[500]

Scoundrel

Hatchet man[501]

Raving idiot

Raving maniac[502]

Asshole of the month

Wacko

Bizarre paranoia

Pus-bloated [503]

Slum bums[504]

From this list it might seem impossible to defame someone by epithet, but it is not. As soon as name-calling (like hyperbole and humor) crosses the line toward a descriptive territory that might be interpreted as actual or implied fact, the courts come down hard. As with other statements of opinion, two categories which are so "laden with factual content" that they are more likely to be interpreted as fact, are accusations of criminal conduct and charges of personal dishonesty which may or may not be criminal.[505] The courts refused to rule out defamatory effect in response to accusations of lying (even in a newspaper editorial),[506] thievery (e.g., alleged against automobile salesmen),[507] con-artistry,[508] probable corruption (e.g., against a judge),[509] perjury (even in a column on a sports page),[510] and the intent to "pick off" a mayoral candidate with a rifle,[511] notwithstanding the arguably figurative or hyperbolic or humorous contexts in which these statements appeared. Even literary dishonesty is difficult to assert with impunity; a judge refused to accept as nonactionable opinion the observation by Mary McCarthy about the memoir-writing author, Lillian Hellman that "every word she writes is a lie, including 'and' and 'the.' "[512]

As several examples cited on page 147 demonstrate, allegations of criminal activity like treason, blackmail and "taking out a contract" on another's life are not impossible to fit within the First Amendment's protection in the proper context. Proving that a statement could not be interpreted as a literal assertion of fact, however, can be considerably more difficult when accusations of criminal conduct and dishonesty are put in issue.

SECTION SUMMARY

After identifying defamation and obtaining the necessary quantum of factual support, the writer must confirm that the words of the defamatory statement are chosen precisely to reflect the proof. Jumping to a conclusion not directly supported, or reporting allegations as facts, or otherwise failing to reflect exactly what can be proved, frequently leads to regret.

Another mistake is to allow the implications in a story to stretch beyond the limits of proof or to paraphrase a source with a sloppy choice of words that enlarges the story's defamatory sting. Stretching a source's credibility by attributing more knowledge or authority or weight than it actually has should also be avoided. Any limits to a source's credibility should be reflected in a story.

Avoiding the use of actual names and otherwise disguising identities, is a useful tool for avoiding lawsuits as long as the disguise is complete. Care should be exercised, however, in the invention of fictitious names; reasonable precautions must be taken to avoid identifying a real person by mistake. And a writer should always specify when the names and events have been invented—particularly when they are *based on* real people and real events. When reports are based on governmental proceedings or records, or they relate to a serious charge by a responsible person against a public official or public figure in a controversy of public concern, they can be entitled to special media privileges. When researching a story, a writer must not overlook these sources; and when used, they must be named whenever possible. Care should also be taken to make the story both fair and accurate.

Expressions of opinion cannot be defamatory unless they include express or implied factual statements. Loose rhetorical language which is not based on a core of objective evidence, and unlikely to be taken seriously, is more likely to be accepted as opinion. The factual predicate of an opinion must always be clearly stated and based on proof.

The law acknowledges and endorses the press's need to express itself and the thoughts of others in language which demonstrates flair, style, wit and sometimes rage, just as long as the reasonable reader or viewer is highly unlikely to accept as literal fact statements which—if they were facts—would be defamatory. Writers and editors must take care to leave no room for reasonable doubt. Loose, figurative, hyperbolic language, jokes, satire, and vitriolic epithets are not meant to be literally interpreted. When public debates concerning public figures are involved, even intentionally malicious, grossly offensive and tasteless remarks fit under the First Amendment's protective umbrella as long as they cannot be interpreted as actual fact. Allegations of criminal or dishonest intent or actions, however, no matter how fanciful they may appear to the writer, should be treated with special care because they are more likely to be interpreted as assertions of fact.

Epilogue

What's to be done when despite your best efforts, a claim letter or a telephone call or a personal visit from a potential plaintiff (or worse, an attorney), threatens you with a defamation action over one of your stories and demands a retraction? Unless you have an expert on staff who can write retractions to conform strictly with the applicable state law's requirements, the answer is simple: consult a lawyer with expertise in defamation law.

If your report is false and defamatory, issuing a retraction (sometimes called a "correction") is usually the best response. Although your error may be privileged if you published the statement with the requisite amount of care, it could take years of litigation to resolve that issue; a retraction might satisfy the potential plaintiff and avoid a lawsuit completely. As also noted above, refusing to issue a retraction in the face of a demonstrably false statement can be cited as circumstantial evidence of intentional falsehood when other factors point in that direction. Adding further incentive, some states limit a plaintiff's claim for damages when a publisher or broadcaster complies promptly with a demand for a retraction. And of course, a retraction can always be commended out of consideration for the person whose reputation was erroneously injured.

However, writing retractions is not a simple job, particularly when the defamation is a serious one. For example, admitting in a retraction that a defamatory statement is false, or wording a retraction to suggest that little or no evidence existed in the first place, could cripple a legal defense if the person defamed still decides to sue. Framing the retraction in a way that further damages the plaintiff's reputation is another common error. There are means of writing retractions to avoid these pitfalls, but special expertise is often necessary for the purpose. Also, the laws of some states which limit a plaintiff's recovery when retractions are issued, contain specific requirements for their form, location, and content. Skill is required to meet these requirements with precision.

So much for retractions. Having read this book from beginning to end, you're in a much better position than you ever were to avoid legal trouble. By now, the drill for minimizing and avoiding the risk of libel litigation should be difficult to forget: first, identify all potential defamation and publish only what's necessary; second, use common sense to determine the necessary quantum of proof (commensurate with the potential damage of the defamation); and third, write the story to make the most of the law's special privileges.

That's it. May you never be a defendant.

Appendixes

17 Do's and Don'ts

*How to Be Sure to Meet the Necessary
Standard of Care in Publishing Defamation*

1. Have trustworthy sources—in quality and number—commensurate with the weight of the defamation; use no anonymous sources—at least *you* must know their names.

2. Be sure to understand the story; when relying on legal documents and the like, make sure you understand them and their terminology, and cite the documents accurately (e.g., don't confuse *charges* with *findings*).

3. Evaluate each source: form an opinion regarding his or her veracity. Does the source have a reputation as a liar? A criminal? Any animosity toward the subject? Any motive or self-interest in lying?

4. Ask the person who is the subject of the statement, whenever possible, whether the statement is true. A reporter is not required to accept denials of wrongdoing as conclusive, or to prefer them over "apparently creditable accusations," but it pays to give the subject an opportunity to offer evidence in support of a denial.

5. If there is more than one party to a particular event, ask more than one party what happened. More generally, interview the people who obviously are most likely to know the truth.

6. If the interviewees have documents, ask for them and look at them (even notes). Compare the writings carefully to what the interviewees say.

7. If there are limitations on the credibility of sources, state them in the report (don't make sources appear more credible than they are). Never report allegations as facts.

8.   If a publication is not "hot news," investigation must be more thorough, commensurate with the additional time you have to do it.

9.   Employ a system of editorial review by knowledgeable editors. Establish internal policies and follow them.

10.   Bring an attitude of open-mindedness to your work; avoid muckraking with preconceived conclusions.

11.   If you're an employer, use reputable reporters.

12.   Be sure to ask sources the "key questions"; do not fail to ask a question when you expect an answer that is inconsistent with your idea of where the story is headed.

13.   Don't rely on memory; and take good notes or record the interview (with permission) and review carefully these notes and other materials before writing a story.

14.   Be sure to attribute defamatory charges made (a) by prominent persons or organizations and (b) in the records of judicial, legislative or administrative proceedings. Use these sources whenever possible.

15.   Be rigorous in your choice of language. Say no more than you can directly support. Avoid conclusions, inferences or interpretations that lack direct support.

16.   Try to avoid defamatory statements which do not pertain to matters of legitimate public concern.

17.   Don't ever publish a potentially defamatory statement if you doubt its truth.

Quick Questions and Short Answers

For more information, see the text of this book at the page numbers following each of the Short Answers.

I. THE BASIC ELEMENTS

1. What is defamation? Is it the same as libel?

2. Can the dead be defamed?

3. What categories of defamation are particularly clear-cut and therefore especially sensitive?

4. Does libel have to be intentional to be the subject of a lawsuit?

5. Is truth an absolute defense to a libel suit?

6. Does someone have to be mentioned by name in order to be defamed?

7. Can implied facts, which are not directly stated, defame?

8. If a defamatory statement is shown to be false, will the media defendant always be liable for damages?

9. What level of proof is required of media defendants for defamatory statements about public officials and public figures, to avoid liability when a statement is shown to be false?

10. What level of proof is required of media defendants for defamatory statements about private figures to avoid liability when a statement is shown to be false?

11. Who is a "public official"?

12. Who is a "public figure"?

13. Who is a private person?

14. Are corporations and other business entities private or public figures?

15. What is the advantage of applying the Private Person Standard to everyone?

16. In order to demonstrate that a defamatory statement was not negligently published or broadcast even if it is later shown to be false, what factors should be balanced to assess the level of proof needed to support the statement?

17. What are the disadvantages of poor journalistic practices like relying on memory, taking poor notes, and misinterpreting legal documents?

II.   PARTICULARIZED QUESTIONS

1. Must the information received from all sources be verified?

2. How many sources are necessary for corroboration?

3. Are there any special privileges for reporting "hot news" without verifying information from sources?

4. Are there any special privileges for reporting call-in comments in live radio or television or for letters to the editor?

5. If a show is taped for later broadcast, and contains defamatory statements, must it be edited before broadcast?

6. When must the subjects of defamatory statements be asked for their responses?

7. Must denials of the truth by the subjects of defamatory statements and broadcasts be accepted as true?

8. What are the disadvantages of using unattributed sources?

9. Can prior published sources and broadcasts be relied upon as verification?

10. Must any special precautions be taken with defamatory material sent in by members of the public?

11. Why is rigorous limitation to source material so important?

12. Will avoiding names and disguising identities be of any help in avoiding liability for defamation?

13. What is the advantage of using official proceedings and reports as sources?

14. What is the neutral reportage privilege?

15. What types of statements can express rage or criticism without being defamatory?

16. How should opinion be presented to make the most of legal privileges?

17. Are there any special risks in publishing defamatory statements which are not about matters of legitimate public concern?

ANSWERS TO THE BASIC ELEMENTS

1. **What is defamation? Is it the same as libel?**

The definition of a defamatory statement usually contains four elements: (1) it is a statement of fact; (2) it has a tendency to injure reputation or diminish the esteem, respect, good will or confidence in which the subject is held by at least a substantial and respectable minority; (3) it is made about a living person, corporate entity or other business unit, without its subject's consent; (4) it is "of and concerning" someone—that is, the subject must be identifiable to a legally significant group even if not explicitly named. Libel is written defamation (as opposed to slander which is oral defamation). [pp. 3–8]

2. **Can the dead be defamed?**

No—but a statement about the dead (e.g., that a deceased child was born out of wedlock or died of neglect) can defame the living. [pp. 3–4, 30]

3. **What categories of defamation are particularly clear-cut and therefore especially sensitive?**

There are at least eight clear-cut categories of defamation. They are statements which: (1) impute to another a loathsome disease (like leprosy, VD or AIDS); (2) accuse another of serious sexual misconduct; (3) impugn another's honesty or integrity; (4) accuse another of committing a crime, or of being arrested or indicted; (5) allege racial, ethnic or religious bigotry; (6) impugn another's financial health or creditworthiness; (7) accuse another of associating with criminals or other unsavory characters; (8) assert incompetence or lack of ability in one's trade, business, profession or office. [pp. 8–13]

4. **Does libel have to be intentional to be the subject of a lawsuit?**

No. A media defendant acting without fault will often be excused but the defense of "I didn't mean it" or "I didn't see it" generally offers no easy escape. [pp. 5–6, 27–29]

5. **Is truth an absolute defense to a libel suit?**

At least when matters of public concern are involved, truth is an absolute defense in a libel action against a media defendant and the media will usually escape liability when a report is not shown to be false. Yet truth is often elusive. [pp. 4–5]

6. **Does someone have to be mentioned by name in order to be defamed?**

No. Information contained in a statement which allows people to identify an unnamed person can defame; so can unidentified photos set in defamatory contexts; also, individual members of a group can be defamed by disparaging the entire group, without ever naming individuals. [pp. 3–4, 29–33]

7. **Can implied facts, which are not directly stated, defame?**

Yes. The interpretation which the reasonable recipient may be expected to give a statement can be defamatory even if the statement itself is not literally so. Dual meanings and implications derived from juxtapositions with defamatory effect should be avoided. [pp. 15–27]

8. **If a defamatory statement is shown to be false, will the media defendant always be liable for damages?**

No. The media will not be held liable for defamatory statements which are proved to be false as long as the defendant exercised a requisite amount of care before publishing or broadcasting the defamatory statement and believed the statement to be true at the time of publication or broadcast. The requisite level of care is higher for statements made about private persons and lower for statements made about public officials and public figures. The most important component of the standard of care is the level of proof obtained by the media defendant before publishing or broadcasting the defamatory statement. [pp. 39–111]

9. **What level of proof is required of media defendants for defamatory**

statements about public officials and public figures to avoid liability when a statement is shown to be false?

When public officials and public figures are plaintiffs, the media can be held liable only if they deliberately or recklessly falsified the truth. This standard is called the Actual Malice Standard in this book. [pp. 40–42, 74–91]

10. **What level of proof is required of media defendants for defamatory statements about private persons to avoid liability when a statement is shown to be false?**

Where private persons are concerned, the media can only be held liable if they acted with a lack of care amounting at least to negligence. Depending on the jurisdiction, negligence is determined by measuring what the media did against what a "reasonable person" would do or against what established standards of professional journalistic conduct would require. This standard is called the Private Person Standard in this book. [pp. 40–42, 92–106]

11. **Who is a "public official?"**

The public official designation applies to those among the hierarchy of government who (1) at the very least have or appear to the public to have substantial responsibility for, or control over, the conduct of governmental affairs; and (2) hold a position which has such apparent importance that the public has an independent interest in the qualifications and performance of the person who holds it, beyond the general public interest in the qualifications and performance of all government employees; and (3) hold a position which would invite public scrutiny and discussion of the person holding it entirely apart from the scrutiny and discussion occasioned by the particular charges in controversy. (Moreover, for the "public official" designation to apply in a libel suit, the false defamatory statement at issue must relate to the employee's official conduct or fitness for office and usually the employee's official position must be named in the story.) Identifying public officials for libel purposes is not always a simple matter. [pp. 42–49]

12. **Who is a "public figure?"**

Public figures are distinguished by two principal characteristics: (1) they have voluntarily exposed themselves to increased risk, for the most part by assuming roles of special prominence in the affairs of society through prominence in the affairs of society through purposeful action of their own; and (2) they usually enjoy pre-existing access to the media and therefore have a more realistic opportunity to counteract false statements than do private individuals. There are two subcategories of public figures: (1) *general public figures* who occupy positions of persuasive power and influence and attain pervasive fame or notoriety and achieve pervasive involvement in the affairs of society by shaping events in the areas of concern to society at large; and (2) *limited public figures* who have thrust themselves or are voluntarily drawn into the forefront of a particular public controversy in order to influence the resolution of the issues involved, thereby becoming public figures only for the limited range of public issues with which they become involved. Identifying public figures for libel purposes is not always a simple matter either. [pp. 49–74]

13. **Who is a "private person?"**

Private persons include everyone who is neither a public official nor a public figure. For purposes of libel law, this category embraces not only individuals who usually relish their privacy and lead ordinary lives, but also everyone else who has fallen through the cracks of the "public person" definitions. [pp. 91–92]

14. **Are corporations and other business entities private or public figures?**

Corporations and other business entities can be public figures but are not necessarily so. They are often found to be private figures. [pp. 55, 73–74]

15. **What is the advantage of applying the Private Person Standard to everyone?**

The standard of care described by the Private Person Standard is the least common denominator of journalistic conduct: it applies to stories about public *and* private persons and avoids the risks inherent in distinguishing public figures from private persons, as well as other ambiguities of the Actual Malice Standard. [pp. 107–111]

16. **In order to demonstrate that a defamatory statement was not negligently published or broadcast, even if it is later shown to be false, what factors should be balanced to assess the level of proof needed to support the statement?**

There are five factors to be balanced: (1) the extent or lack of real time pressure; without "hot news," the law expects that time be taken for more thorough investigation; (2) the importance of the disclosure; newsworthy reports in the public interest receive more protection; (3) the severity of the defamation and the extent of damage of the subject should the statement prove to be false; more potential damage requires more proof; (4) the trustworthiness of the sources relied upon; past performance is important; (5) the availability of other sources to offer further corroboration; obvious sources, including the subject of the defamation, should not be overlooked. Furthermore, confidential sources must be used with care; if they cannot be named, they may be useless in a litigation. [pp. 93–102, 106–7]

17. **What are the disadvantages of poor journalistic practices like relying solely on memory, taking poor notes, and misinterpreting legal documents?**

Avoiding negligence requires not only good research and investigation but also basic care on the part of the media. Avoiding mistakes through mis-recollection, poor notes, and misinterpretation of legal documents, are basic elements of due care. Even actual malice can be imputed in cases of extreme journalistic sloppiness. [pp. 78–79, 102–4]

ANSWERS TO PARTICULARIZED QUESTIONS

1. **Must the information received from all sources be verified?**

Theoretically, a single unimpeachable source can be sufficient under the Actual Malice Standard (applicable to public officials and public figures) and even under the Private Person Standard and its factor-balancing test; see the answer to question 16 above. However, in most instances, reliance on unverified sources poses a substantial risk that the requisite standard of care will not be met and a media defendant will be held responsible for a false defamatory statement. [pp. 40–42, 74–91, 92–106]

2. **How many sources are necessary for corroboration?**

Generally speaking, the answer to this question requires an exercise in common sense and a balancing of factors described in the answer to question 16 above. In assessing the number of sources necessary, the trustworthiness of sources relied upon and the availability of other sources for further corroboration are especially important. A dozen unreliable sources will never be as good as one that is unimpeachable; moreover, in the absence of an unimpeachable source, other sources—particularly the obvious ones—should not be overlooked. [pp. 107–111]

3. **Are there any special privileges for reporting "hot news" without verifying information from sources?**

There are no special privileges for reporting "hot news" without verification. Under the Actual Malice Standard, a defamatory statement published with knowledge of falsity or reckless disregard of truth or falsity would be actionable if proven false, whether or not it is "hot news." Under the Private Person Standard, the topicality of a report is but one factor among five to be balanced. Publishing even "hot news" without sufficient verification, measured in the balance of all five factors, may still demonstrate negligence. (See the answer to question 16 above.) [pp. 87, 94–95]

4. **Are there any special privileges for letters to the editor or for call-in comments on live radio or television?**

Generally speaking, there are no special privileges for defamatory statements in these contexts. This is why a seven-second delay and screening procedures are prudent for broadcasts; and why the same care given to reports by reporters should be applied to letters to the editor. [pp. 87, 103–4, 110, 137, 147]

5. **If a show is taped for later broadcast, and contains defamatory statements, must it be edited before broadcast?**

The same rule applies in this context as elsewhere: if the defamatory statement is shown to be false, and was broadcast without meeting the applicable standard of care, those responsible may be held liable. Therefore, in the case of a taped program, if the applicable standard of care has not been met, defamatory statements should be deleted before broadcast. [pp. 40–42, 74–91, 92–106]

6. **When must the subjects of defamatory statements be asked for their responses?**

Generally speaking, all obvious sources with knowledge of the pertinent facts should be interviewed and this generally includes the subject of defamatory statements. There are exceptions—for example, if other sources are exceptionally conclusive, or if the subject is unavailable—provided the applicable standard of care (described above) is otherwise met. [pp. 86–87, 99–100]

7. **Must denials of truth by the subjects of defamatory statements be accepted as true?**

A reporter does not necessarily have to accept the subject's point of view, particularly when denials are unspecific or patently unpersuasive. On the other hand, when the subject of a defamatory statement provides convincing, detailed reasons to question the truthfulness of the statement, proceeding with publication would be a mistake without substantial support to the contrary. [pp. 86–87, 99–100]

8. **What are the disadvantages of using unattributed sources?**

Even when disclosure of a confidential source cannot be compelled, refusing to reveal the source is likely to influence how a judge and jury weigh other factors in an actual malice or negligence test. It may be more difficult to dispose of the suit prior to trial, and at trial the media defendant may be precluded from making any mention whatsoever of the confidential source. (See also the answers to questions 13 and 14 below.) [pp. 106–107]

9. **Can prior published sources and broadcasts be relied upon as verification?**

Prior publications and broadcasts are often good sources of verification, particularly if the subjects of the defamatory statements have failed to complain. Some sources, like reputable wire services, are particularly favored. However, most prior published and broadcast sources usually must be assessed for trustworthiness in the same manner as other sources. [pp. 89, 98]

10. **Must any special precautions be taken with defamatory material sent in by members of the public?**

Screening procedures must be set up to flag potentially defamatory statements requiring verification in all editorial content including material sent in by members of the public. Particularly damaging statements—such as a person's sexual preferences—should be verified with special care to be certain that the person who purports to be the supplier of the information is truthfully identifying himself or herself. [pp. 87, 103–4, 110]

11. **Why is rigorous limitation to source material so important?**

If the words of the defamatory statement are not rigorously chosen to reflect precisely the underlying factual support, the effects may be a complete lack of proof, and liability for the media defendant.

Moreover, any interpretation of a source's allegation in a more damaging way than the source allows, or giving a source more credibility than it deserves, can be a grave mistake. [pp. 114–123]

12. **Will avoiding names and disguising identities be of any help in avoiding liability for defamation?**

Yes. Because statements cannot defame if their subjects cannot reasonably be recognized by those who know them, avoiding names and disguising identities can be helpful as long as the subject's identity is disguised completely. [pp. 4, 31, 123–128]

13. **What is the advantage of using official proceedings and reports as sources?**

The public records privilege permits a media defendant to avoid liability without regard to the truth or falsity of the statement and— even while a statement proves false—without ever applying the Actual Malice or Private Person Standards. However, the scope of the privilege varies considerably from state to state and the source of the information must always be specified. Also, the report must be fair and accurate for the privilege to apply. [pp. 128–134]

14. **What is the neutral reportage privilege?**

Some jurisdictions recognize a constitutional privilege for the press to republish another person's accusations without regard to whether the reporter writing the story believes the charge to be true or false or whether the reporter independently verified the charges. However, even where adopted, the privilege is circumscribed by limiting factors: e.g., the report must convey a serious charge which is newsworthy simply because it was made; the accusation may have to come from a responsible prominent organization or person; the target of the accusation must be a public official or public figure; and the reporting must be both neutral and accurate. Moreover, if the source of the accusation is not named, the privilege will not apply. [pp. 128–129, 134–135]

15. **What types of statements can express rage or criticism without being defamatory?**

Loose, figurative language, rhetorical hyperbole, humor, satire and vituperative epithets can express rage and criticism without being defamatory. One must be careful, however, to express statements in a way which no one would take seriously as literal statements of fact; allegations of criminal or dishonest intent or actions, which are more likely to be interpreted as assertions of fact, should be avoided. [pp. 143–152]

16. **How should opinion be presented to make the most of legal privileges?**

Expressions of opinion cannot be defamatory unless they include express or implied factual statements. Loose rhetorical language which is not based on a core of objective evidence, and unlikely to be taken seriously, is more likely to be accepted as opinion. When an opinion is based on facts, the factual predicate must be clearly stated and based on proof. Charges of criminal activity or dishonest behavior should be avoided, even in the form of an opinion. [pp. 136–143]

17. **Are there any special risks in publishing defamatory statements which are not about matters of legitimate public concern?**

The Supreme Court has dropped broad hints that constitutional protections soon may only apply when stories report matters of public concern. Even now, statements about public officials must pertain to official duties or fitness for office and statements about limited public figures must pertain to public controversies. If the Court eliminates constitutional protection for matters not of public concern, media defendants would find it more difficult to avoid liability when defamatory statements about private matters are shown to be false. [pp. 55–56, 92]

Notes

Full case citations can be found in the Table of Cases. Parallel citations for state decisions are made to Media Law Reporter (B.N.A.).

1. U.S. Const. amend. I.

2. Time Inc. v. Hill, 385 U.S. 374, 388, 389 (1967) (quoting Thornhill v. Alabama, 310 U.S. 88, 102 (1940)).

3. Bose Corp. v. Consumer's Union of United States, Inc., 466 U.S. 485, 503, 504 (1984), *quoted in* Hustler Magazine Inc. v. Falwell, 485 U.S. 46, 50, 51 (1988).

4. New York Times Co. v. Sullivan, 376 U.S. 254, 270 (1964).

5. St. Amant v. Thompson, 390 U.S. 727, 732 (1968).

6. Gertz v. Robert Welch Inc., 418 U.S. 323, 340 (1974).

7. NAACP v. Button, 371 U.S. 415, 433 (1963), *quoted in* New York Times v. Sullivan, 376 U.S. at 271, 272 (1974).

8. *See* Lovell, *The "Reception" of Defamation by the Common Law*, 15 Vand. L. Rev. 1051, 1053 (1962) (citing a passage from the laws of Alfred the Great, compiled in approximately A.D. 880: "If anyone is guilty of public slander, and it is proved against him, it is to be compensated with no lighter penalty than the cutting off of his tongue"; *also cited in* R. Smolla, Law of Defamation §1.02[1], at 1-4 (1990)).

9. W. Shakespeare, Othello, Act III, Sc. iii, *quoted* (among many other places) *in* Milkovich v. Lorain Journal, _____ U.S. _____, 110 S.Ct. 2695, 2702 (1990).

10. Rosenblatt v. Baer, 383 U.S. 75, 92 (1966), concurring opinion of Justice Stewart *quoted* (among many other places) *in* Gertz v. Robert Welch Inc., 418 U.S. at 341, and Philadelphia Newspapers Inc. v. Hepps, 475 U.S. 766, 781 (1986) (dissenting opinion of Justice Stevens).

11. Gertz v. Robert Welch Inc., 418 U.S. at 341. *See also* Curtis Publishing Co. v. Butts, 388 U.S. 130, 150 (1967).

12. Gertz v. Robert Welch Inc., 418 U.S. at 325.

13. Gertz v. Robert Welch Inc., 418 U.S. at 343-344.

14. M. Garbus, *The Many Costs of Libel*, Publisher's Weekly, Sept. 5, 1986, at 34 (quoting Ann Havner, Assistant Vice President at Johnson & Higgins, an insurance broker in New York). *See also*, *The Cost of Libel: Economic and Policy Implications*, at 3 (1986), a conference report published by the Gannett Center for Media Studies.

15. M. Garbus, *Cost of Libel–How Lawyers Can Best Represent Publishers*, N.Y. Law Journal, October 27, 1986, at 6. Other sources, such as the American Society of Newspaper Editors, put the average cost of defending a libel case at $95,000. *The Cost of Libel*, *supra* note 14, at 3.

16. H. Lottman, *Media Won 40% of Libel Cases in Past Two Years*, Publisher's Weekly, Sept. 8, 1989, at 10 (citing a study by the Libel Defense Resource Center (LDRC) for the years 1987-1988). The article further notes that, according to the LDRC, the 40% success rate (unfortunately) is a record high for the media, and that damage awards averaged $431,730 in 1987-1988 compared with an average of $1,167,189 during the previous two-year period.

17. According to *The Cost of Libel*, *supra* note 14, at 2, the LDRC estimated an average award of $2 million in 1986.

18. H. Lottman, *supra* note 16.

19. L. Levine & D. Perry, *No Way to Celebrate the Bill of Rights*, Colum. Journ. Rev., July-Aug. 1990, at 38.

20. Sprague v. Philadelphia Newspapers, Inc., Pa. Ct. Com. Pls., Philadelphia County, April Term, 1973, No. 3644, May 3, 1990, *cited in* 17 Media L. Rep., *News Notes*, May 15, 1990.

21. Srivastava v. Harte-Hanks Television, Inc., Tex. Dist. Ct. No. 85-CI-15150, April 15, 1990, *cited in* 17 Media L. Rep., *News Notes*, May 29, 1990.

22. H. Lottman, *supra* note 16, citing a report by the LDRC. Between 1980-1985, about two thirds of the awards challenged by the media were reversed or modified in favor of defendants and the average affirmed award was decreased by half to under $100,000 between 1980 and 1985. H. Kaufman, *Libel 1980-85: Promises and Realities*, 90 Dick. L. Rev., 545, 556, 557 (1986).

23. M. Garbus, *supra* note 14, at 34.

24. Green v. Alton Telegraph Printing Co., 107 Ill. App. 3d 755, 8 Media L. Rep. 1345 (Ill. App. Ct. 1982). The *Telegraph* later settled for $1.4 million, which enabled it to reorganize from bankruptcy, following which the owners sold the paper. S. Shapiro, *Libel Lawyers as Risk Counselors: Pre-Publication and Pre-Broadcast Review and the Social Construction of News,* 11 Law & Policy (No. 3, 1989), republished in Libel Litigation 1990, Practicing Law Institute, 345, 365 n.15 (1990).

25. Lyle Denniston, Supreme Court reporter for the *Baltimore Sun*, quoted in *News Notes*, 16 Media L. Rep., Nov. 28, 1989, from remarks made at a conference sponsored by the Practising Law Institute in New York City, November 9-10, 1989. *See also*, M. Garbus, *supra* note 15, who quotes a question posed by William Rehnquist, now Chief Judge of the Supreme Court, at a libel argument in 1984: "Why, he asked, should the law be any different whether a person is damaged by a libelous statement or by a defective train?" As Mr. Garbus observed, this query does not indicate a strong attachment to journalistic privileges.

26. Lerman v. Flynt Distributing, Co., 745 F.2d 123, 141 (2d Cir. 1984).

27. After a lawsuit has been commenced, *see* "Other Sources" on page 209 for treatises intended for use in litigation.

28. Restatement (Second) of Torts §568A (1977).

29. Kimmerle v. New York Evening Journal, 262 N.Y. 99, 102 (1933).

30. Isaksen v. Vermont Castings, Inc., 825 F.2d 1158, 1165, 1166 (7th Cir. 1987), *cert. denied*, 486 U.S. 1005 (1988).

31. Davis v. Costa-Gavras, 619 F. Supp. 1372, 1375 (S.D.N.Y. 1985).

32. M. Franklin & D. Bussel, *The Plaintiff's Burden in Defamation Awareness and Falsity*, 25 Wm. & Mary L. Rev. 825, 830 n.14 (1984) (citing Ben-Oliel v. Press Publishing Co., 251 N.Y. 250, 254, 255 (1929)). In that case, a newspaper attributed to the plaintiff, a professional lecturer, writer and teacher, descriptions of social customs in Palestine which "[e]verybody acquainted with life in Palestine" would recognize as inaccurate. By making the plaintiff appear an "ignorant impostor," even to this audience, the defendant would libel her.

33. Peck v. Tribune Co., 214 U.S. 185, 189, 190 (1909) Holmes, J.; Restatement (Second) of Torts §559 comment e (1977).

34. R. Smolla, Law of Defamation §4.11[1][a] at 4-53 (1990); Restatement (Second) of Torts §560 comment a (1977).

35. R. Sack, Libel, Slander and Related Problems §V.2.7 (1980).

36. Milkovich v. Lorain Journal Co., _____ U.S. _____ , 110 S. Ct. 2695, 2706, 2707 (1990); Philadelphia Newspapers Inc. v. Hepps, 475 U.S. 767, 775, 776 (1986). It is not clear that truth is an absolute defense under the Constitution for a nonmedia defendant who defames a private plaintiff, especially when the defendant acts with intentional ill-will. *Milkovich*, at n. 6; M. Franklin & D. Bussell, *supra* note 32, at 851-54, and n.107. *See also* R. Smolla, Law of Defamation §5.03 (1990). The burden of proving falsity, moreover, rests on the plaintiff if he or she is a public official or public figure, or even a private figure if the subject matter of the report is a matter of public concern. Philadelphia Newspapers Inc. v. Hepps, 475 U.S. at 775-778 and cases cited. This constitutes a great advantage for the media when a statement cannot easily be proved false.

37. Hellman v. McCarthy, 10 Media L. Rep. 1789 (N.Y. Sup. Ct. 1984). On the defendants' motion for summary judgment, only Dick Cavett in his personal capacity was dismissed from the action because, unlike the production company, he had no affirmative responsibility to edit the program and no actual malice or negligence on his part could be shown. (The case against the other defendants was discontinued after Ms. Hellman's death and never went to trial.)

38. Anderson v. Avco Embassy Pictures, Corp., No. 82-0752-K (U.S.D.C. Mass. 1982).

39. Liberty Lobby Inc. v. Anderson, 746 F.2d 1563, 1568, 1576, 1578 (D.C. Cir. 1984), *vacated on other grounds*, 477 U.S. 242 (1986).

40. Macon Telegraph v. Elliot, 165 Ga. App. 719, 9 Media L. Rep. 2252 (Ga. Ct. App. 1983), *cert. denied*, 466 U.S. 971 (1984).

41. Dostert v. Washington Post Co., 531 F. Supp. 165, 168 (N.D. W.Va. 1982).

42. The legal term for a statement which is defamatory on its face is "libel per se." A statement which is not defamatory on its face but becomes so with extrinsic facts is called "libel per quod."

43. Guccione v. Hustler Magazine, Inc., 632 F. Supp 313, 317 (S.D.N.Y. 1986), *rev'd*, 800 F.2d 298, *cert. denied*, 479 U.S. 1091 (1987).

44. McDowell v. Paiewonsky, 769 F.2d 942, 947 (3d Cir. 1985).

45. Mahoney v. Adirondack Pub. Co., 71 N.Y.2d 31, 38, 39, 14 Media L. Rep. 2200 (1987) (The newspaper won the case on appeal because the coach failed to show actual malice).

46. Buller v. Pulitzer Publishing, Inc., 684 S.W.2d 473, 11 Media L. Rep. 1289 (Mo. Ct. App. 1984).

47. Reeves v. American Broadcasting Cos., 580 F. Supp. 84, 90 (S.D.N.Y.), *aff'd*, 719 F.2d 602 (2d Cir. 1983).

48. McBride v. Merrell Dow, 717 F.2d 1460, 1465 (1983), *adhered to*, 800 F.2d 1208, 1210 (D.C. Cir. 1986).

49. Grass v. News Group Publications, Inc., 570 F. Supp. 178 (S.D.N.Y. 1983).

50. Gertz v. Robert Welch, Inc., 418 U.S. 323, 347, 348 (1974).

51. For example, In Charlottesville Newspapers Inc. v. Matthews, 229 Va. 1, 11 Media L. Rep. 1609 (1985), a report that a "Miss Matthews" was pregnant at the time she was allegedly raped, was not only defamatory (since she was married at the time), but the court considered its potential danger to reputation apparent to a reasonably prudent editor and the newspaper defendant was held liable for $25,000 in compensatory damages.

52. This example is based on Quartana v. Utterback, 789 F.2d 1297 (8th Cir. 1986), in which the plaintiff was a salesperson for Company A, whose customers included Company B. Company C was a high-volume purchaser of Company A's products, and the plaintiff persuaded Company C to permit Company B to bill its purchases from A through C so that B could receive a discount. When B failed to keep up with its payments to C, the head of C wrote a letter to the head of A which claimed the plaintiff had told him that Company B had a $5,000 credit rating and that plaintiff would "personally see that they pay their bills." Company A had a policy against its sales persons guaranteeing payment of bills in this manner and the plaintiff lost her job as a result. The plaintiff claimed she never made any such statement about B's credit or any guarantee. The court sustained the plaintiff's claim for libel both on the basis that extrinsic evidence of the company policy combined with the statement against her did defame her as did the implication in the statement that she had lied to Company B about the credit rating and the guarantee.

53. In some jurisdictions, a defamatory implication against a public official or public figure will not be actionable when the underlying facts are true. (See note 378 below.) Even in those instances, however, truth can be elusive, and the focus of this Section I is the identification of *potentially* defamatory statements to permit the writer to eliminate them or treat them with the care they deserve.

54. One state, Illinois, will exculpate a media defendant if, among multiple meanings, one of them is "innocent." No other state, however, offers this defense and it is therefore of limited use to the bulk of writings and reports. Ollman v. Evans, 750 F.2d 970, 980 n.18 (D.C. Cir. 1984), *cert. denied*, 471 U.S. 1127 (1985).

55. Williams v. First Federal Savings Bank of Puerto Rico, 14 Media L. Rep. 1033, 1037 (U.S. D. V.I. 1987).

56. Silvester v. American Broadcasting Cos., 650 F. Supp. 766, 771 (S.D. Fla. 1986), *aff'd*, 839 F.2d 1491 (11th Cir. 1988). The appellate court accepted "arguendo" that the statements were "susceptible of defamatory interpretations" before affirming summary judgment to the defendants on the ground that the plaintiffs, as limited public figures, failed to demonstrate actual malice.

57. Lawrence v. Bauer Publishing & Printing, Ltd., 89 N.J. 451, 455, 456, 459, 460, 8 Media L. Rep. 1536, *cert. denied*, 459 U.S. 999 (1982).

58. Adams v. Daily Telegraph Printing Co., 292 S.C. 273, 279, 280, 13 Media L. Rep. 2034 (1986), *modified*, 295 S.C. 218, 15 Media L. Rep. 1672 (1988).

59. Saenz v. Playboy Enterprises, Inc., 841 F.2d 1309, 1315 (7th Cir. 1988). Notwithstanding the court's holding that the statement was susceptible of defamatory interpretation, the public official lost his case on summary judgment because the defendants did not act with actual malice (a concept discussed in Section II of this book).

60. Heymann v. Dodd Mead & Co., 260 App. Div. 573, 574 (N.Y. App. Div. 1940), *appeal denied*, 261 A.D. 1, 803 (N.Y. App. Div. 1941).

61. Wilhoit v. WCSC, Inc., 293 S.C. 34, 13 Media L. Rep. 2156 (Ct. App. 1987).

62. *See* Metzger v. Dell Publishing, 207 Misc. 182, 136 N.Y.S.2d 888 (N.Y. Sup. Ct. 1955), which was based on the same set of facts except that no caption was reported in the decision. In *Metzger*, a jury found for the plaintiffs and imposed punitive damages, reduced by the trial court.

63. Morrell v. Forbes, Inc., 603 F. Supp. 1305, 1307 (D. Mass. 1985) (summary judgment for both parties was denied).

64. Duncan v. WJLA-TV, Inc., 10 Media L. Rep. 1395 (U.S. D.D.C. 1982).

65. Clark v. American Broadcasting Cos, 684 F.2d. 1208 (6th Cir. 1982), *cert. denied*, 460 U.S. 1040 (1983).

66. Theoretically, a fictional story could defame real people totally unknown to the author of the fictional work if the fictional characters are reasonably interpreted to represent real people. *See, e.g.*, Brafman v. Houghton Mifflin, Co., 11 Media L. Rep. 1354 (N.Y. Sup. Ct. 1984), and other examples at pages 125–127 of this book. However, the plaintiff would still have to show some degree of fault on the part of a media defendant in order to prevail; for example, a writer's failure to check a local telephone book before selecting the names of villainous characters set in a real location, might be fault enough.

67. Corrigan v. Bobbs-Merrill Co., 228 N.Y. 58, 63-64 (1920). (A "supposedly fictitious narrative" was still actionable even if published without intent to defame, as long as the plaintiff "connects himself with the publication, at least, in the absence of some special reason for a positive belief that no one existed to whom the description answered").

68. Fetler v. Houghton Mifflin Co., 364 F.2d 650, 651 (2d Cir. 1966), citing Miller v. Maxwell, 16 Wend 9, 18 (N.Y. Sup. Ct. 1836), which in turn quoted older authority.

69. Triangle Publications v. Chumley, 253 Ga. 179, 10 Media L. Rep. 2076 (1984).

70. Hamilton v. United Press International, Inc., 9 Media L. Rep. 2453 (U.S. S.D. Iowa 1983).

71. Dion v. Kiev, 566 F. Supp. 1387, 1389 (E.D. Pa. 1983).

72. Ortiz v. Valdescastilla, 102 A.D. 2d 513, 516, 517, 10 Media L. Rep. 2193 (N.Y. App. Div. 1984).

73. Kennedy v. Ministries, Inc., 10 Media L. Rep. 2459 (U.S. E.D. Pa. 1984).

74. Ogren v. Employers' Reinsurance Corporation, 119 Wis.2d 379, 10 Media L. Rep. 2043 (Wis. Ct. App. 1984).

75. This example is based on Brewer v. Memphis Publishing Co., 626 F.2d 1238, 1244 (5th Cir. 1980), *cert. denied*, 452 U.S. 962 (1981), which is different principally because the husband was identified by name and the wife *and* husband were public figures. Though they established they had been defamed, the Brewers ultimately lost the war. Following a third trial, which resulted in a $150,000 award to Anita and $60,000 to John, the appellate court found that because the newspaper had relied on the report of a reliable sales clerk, no actual malice was established.

76. Khalid Abdullah Tariq Al Mansour Faissal Fahd Al Talal v. Fanning, 506 F. Supp. 186, 187 (N.D. Cal. 1980).

77. R. Sack, Libel, Slander, and Related Problems §II.8.3., at 117 (1980) citing Restatement (Second) of Torts §564A comment b (1977); and W. Prosser, The Law of Torts §112, at 750, 751 (4th ed. 1971). Both Sack and cases citing these authorities note that the rule has exceptions. *See, e.g.*, Brady v. Ottaway Newspapers, 84 A.D. 2d 226, 236, 8 Media L. Rep. 1671 (N.Y. App. Div. 1981), in which the court favored an "intensity of suspicion" test in which size of the group was but one factor along with definiteness in number and composition of the group, its "degree of organization," and its prominence.

78. Fawcett Publications, Inc. v. Morris, 377 P.2d 42, 47, 48 (Okla. 1962), *cert. denied* and *appeal dismissed*, 376 U.S. 513 (1964).

79. Brady v. Ottaway Newspapers, Inc., 84 A.D. 2d 226 (N.Y. App. Div. 1981). (*See* note 77 above.)

80. *Id*. at 229.

81. *See, e.g.*, Golden Palace Inc. v. National Broadcasting Co., Inc., 386 F. Supp. 107, 109 (D.D.C. 1984), *aff'd mem.*, 530 F.2d 1094 (D.C. Cir. 1976); Coronado Credit Union v. KOAT Television, Inc., 99 N.M. 233, 9 Media L. Rep. 1031 (N.M. Ct. App. 1982); R. Smolla, Law of Defamation §4.11[3], at 4-55 (1990).

82. *See, e.g.*, Isaksen v. Vermont Castings, Inc., 825 F.2d 1158, 1166 (7th Cir. 1987), *cert. denied*, 486 U.S. 1005 (1988) (*citing* Converters Equipment Corp. v. Condes Corp., 80 Wis.2d 257, 262, 263 (1977)).

83. Restatement (Second) of Torts §561(a) (1977); Trans World Accounts, Inc. v. Associated Press, 425 F. Supp. 814, 818 (N.D. Cal. 1977).

84. Brown & Williamson Tobacco Corp. v. Jacobson, 644 F. Supp. 1240 (N.D. Ill. 1986), *aff'd in part* and *rev'd in part*, 827 F.2d 1119 (7th Cir. 1987).

85. Golden Bear Distributing Systems, Inc. v. Chase Revel, Inc., 708 F.2d 944 (5th Cir. 1983). The jury also found—and the appellate court affirmed—that the error was published with actual malice (a concept discussed in detail in Section II).

86. In cases of product disparagement, unlike defamation, some courts require proof of actual pecuniary loss. Menefee v. Columbia Broadcasting System Inc., 458 Pa. 46, 53 (1974); R. Sack, Libel, Slander and Related Problems §IX.8.6.3, at 459 (1980). Some courts also require intent to harm. R. Sack, *supra*, §IX.8.6.2, at 456 citing among other sources, Restatement (Second) of Torts §623A comment d (1977). *Compare with* Charles Atlas Ltd. v. Time-Life Books, Inc., 570 F. Supp. 150, 154 (S.D.N.Y. 1983). ("It is extremely questionable whether the plaintiff must show common law malice to state a claim for product disparagement").

87. Bose Corporation v. Consumers Union of the United States, Inc., 466 U.S. 485, 488-491 (1984). Bose lost the case, however, because it was a "public figure" and Consumers Union had not made its disparaging comment with actual malice; that is, with knowledge at the time of its inaccuracy or with reckless disregard of the truth.

88. Charles Atlas, Ltd. v. Time-Life Books, Inc., 570 F. Supp. 150 (S.D.N.Y. 1983).

89. S. Shapiro, *Libel Lawyers as Risk Counselors: Pre-Publication and Pre-Broadcast Review and the Social Construction of News*, 11 Law & Policy (No. 3, 1989), republished in Libel Litigation 1990, Practicing Law Institute, at 345 (1990); based on empirical study, Shapiro concluded that lawyers often believe that the inadvertent targets, on whom "no one is focusing," often bring suit.

90. The Actual Malice Standard (see page 41) is generally thought to be applicable to nonmedia defendants as well as media defendants, in defamation actions brought by public officials and public figures. The Supreme Court so indicated in New York Times v. Sullivan, 376 U.S. 254 (1964), and St. Amant v. Thompson, 390 U.S. 727 (1968), but later "reserved judgment" on the issue in Hutchinson v. Proxmire, 443 U.S. 111, 133 n.16 (1979) and then in Philadelphia Newspapers Inc. v. Hepps, 475 U.S. 766, 776, 777, 779 n.4 (1986) pointedly applied the Actual Malice Standard to a media defendant as if different treatment might apply to others. Still, the better bet is that identical levels of care will be expected from media and nonmedia defendants responsible for making defamatory statements about public persons which prove to be false. R. Smolla, Law of Defamation §3.02(2), at 3-11 (1990). There may be occasional exceptions, however, such as advertisements. *See* U.S. Healthcare Inc. v. Blue Cross of Greater Philadelphia, 898 F.2d 914, 927-929, 937 (3d Cir.), *cert. denied*, _____ U.S. _____ , 111 S.Ct. 58 (1990). ("[C]ommercial speech does not warrant heightened constitutional protection.") As for assessment of damages, media and nonmedia defendants may receive like treatment. In a recent case involving a private plaintiff and a nonmedia defendant, the Court's plurality opinion made no distinction between media and nonmedia defendants in finding a plaintiff eligible for presumed or punitive damages in the absence of actual malice. Dun & Bradstreet, Inc. v. Greenmoss Builders, Inc., 472 U.S. 749 (1985). Other distinctions have been recognized, however, and will probably continue to apply in cases against nonmedia defendants. Respecting the burden of proving falsity, the Supreme Court has held that at least statements about matters of public concern must be proved false by all plaintiffs before media defendants can be held liable. But the Court reserved judgment respecting cases involving matters of private concern or nonmedia defendants. Philadelphia Newspapers Inc. v. Hepps, 475 U.S. at 779 n.4. *See also* Milkovich v. Lorain Journal Co., _____ U.S. _____ , 110 S.Ct. 2695, 2706 n.6 (1990).

91. S. Shapiro, *Libel Lawyers as Risk Counselors: Pre-Publication and Pre-Broadcast Review and the Social Construction of News*, 11 Law and Policy (No. 3, 1989), republished in Libel Litigation 1990, Practicing Law Institute, at 356, 357, and 367 n.31. According to Shapiro, prepublication reviewers "evaluate who the story is about and try to make a ballpark guess about whether the subjects are likely to be treated by the court as public or private figures." However, most lawyers "indicate that such guesses are notoriously unreliable and conduct their review as if subjects are private figures and entitled to the weakest standard of fault."

92. New York Times Co. v. Sullivan, 376 U.S. 254, 256-259 (1964).

93. Commissioner Sullivan objected to a full-page advertisement run in *The New York Times* on March 29, 1960, in support of nonviolent demonstrations by "Southern Negro students" who, the ad stated, were "being met by an unprecedented wave of terror." Sullivan complained that, while not specifically naming him, the advertisement suggested he was responsible for intimidating students with "truckloads of police armed with shotguns and tear-gas," for padlocking their dining hall "in an attempt to starve them into submission," and even for attempting to intimidate and harass Dr. Martin Luther King by bombing his home, arresting him for minor offenses and charging him with perjury. The advertisement contained a number of false statements (for example, the dining room was never padlocked) but because neither *The New York Times* nor the individuals who sponsored the advertisement acted with "actual malice," the $500,000 jury award rendered against the defendants was dismissed. The Supreme Court also held

that the Commissioner's evidence was constitutionally insufficient to support a finding that the statements referred to him.

94. Curtis Publishing Co. v. Butts, 388 U.S. 130 (1967).

95. Rosenbloom v. Metromedia Inc., 403 U.S. 29, 43, 44 (1971) (opinion of Brennan, J.).

96. Gertz v. Robert Welch, Inc., 418 U.S. 323 (1974).

97. New York Times Co. v. Sullivan, 376 U.S. 254 (1964).

98. St. Amant v. Thompson, 390 U.S. 727, 730 (1968).

99. Garrison v. Louisiana, 379 U.S. 64, 74 (1967).

100. St. Amant v. Thompson, 390 U.S. 727, 731 (1968).

101. *Id.* at 732.

102. Gertz v. Robert Welch., Inc., 418 U.S. 323, 347, 348 (1974).

103. Rosenblatt v. Baer, 383 U.S. 75, 85, 86 n.13 (1966).

104. New York Times Co. v. Sullivan, 376 U.S. 254, 279, 280 (1964).

105. Garrison v. Louisiana, 379 U.S. 64, 77 (1964).

106. In most states which have considered the issue, the employee's official position must be described in the story to invoke the Actual Malice Standard, and failure to do so can forfeit the privilege. For example, a federal court of appeals in New York held that an appointed Borough Solicitor in a small Pennsylvania town who advised the Borough Council on a part-time basis could not be considered a public official simply because the article which defamed him failed to mention his public position. Conceding that the Supreme Court has not ruled upon the significance of a news report's failure to identify a public office holder as such, the court nevertheless based its decision on an underlying principle: that the reduced standard of liability applicable to public officials was intended to encourage discussion of official conduct. The privilege should not apply, the court reasoned, where the media's statements do not directly or impliedly identify the plaintiff as a public official and there is no showing that his name is otherwise immediately recognized as one in the community (as the President or governor might). Bufalino v. Associated Press, 692 F.2d 266 (2d Cir. 1982), *cert. denied*, 462 U.S. 1111 (1983). The court cited other decisions in Texas and Florida which reached the same conclusion and rejected decisions to the contrary from Delaware and Massachusetts.

107. *See* Restatement (Second) of Torts §580B (1977).

108. Hutchinson v. Proxmire, 443 U.S. 111, 119 n.8 (1979).

109. New York Times Co. v. Sullivan, 376 U.S. 254, 283 n.23 (1964).

110. Hutchinson v. Proxmire, 443 U.S. 111, 119 n.8 (1979).

111. R. Smolla, Law of Defamation §2.26[2], at 2-91 (1990); S. Metcalf, R. Bierstedt & E. Bildner, Rights and Liabilities of Publishers, Broadcasters and Reporters §1.51, at 1-111 (1989).

112. R. Smolla, *supra* note 111, §2.26[3], at 2-91 (1990).

113. R. Smolla, *supra* note 111, §2.26[1], at 2-89, 2-90 (1990).

114. There have been occasional exceptions to the general rule that police officers qualify as public officials. In Nash v. Keene Pub. Corp., 127 N.Y. 214, 221, 222, 12 Media L. Rep. 1025 (1985) (Souter, J.) the court refused to designate a police officer as a public official and reserved the issue for a jury (see pages 47–48). In Himango v. Primetime Broadcasting, 37 Wash. App. 259, 262, 263, 10 Media L. Rep. 1724, 1726 (Wash. Ct. App., 1984) the court found that the plaintiff patrolman did not exercise a general influence on government affairs sufficient to qualify as a public official.

115. Metcalf et al., *supra* note 111, §1.50, at 1-109 (1989).

116. *Compare with* Jones v. Palmer Communications, Inc., 440 N.W.2d 884, 895, 16 Media L. Rep. 2137 (Iowa 1989), which rejects this "expansive view" as "being inconsistent with the plain meaning of the standards articulated in *Rosenblatt* and *Hutchinson.*"

117. *See* R. Smolla, *supra* note 111, §2.25[1], at 2-87, 2-88 (1990).

118. Sewell v. Brookbank, 119 Ariz. 422, 4 Media L. Rep. 1475 (Ariz. Ct. App. 1978). A number of other decisions have unaccountably found public school teachers to be public officials. *See generally* R. Smolla, Law of Defamation, §2.26[4], at 2-92 (1990); and S. Metcalf, R. Bierstedt & E. Bildner, Rights and Liabilities of Publishers, Broadcasters and Reporters, §1.53, at 1-117, 118 (1989).

119. Auvil v. Times Journal Company, 10 Media L. Rep. 2302 (U.S. E.D. Va. 1984).

120. Green v. Northern Publishing Co., 655 P.2d 736, 740, 741, 8 Media L. Rep. 2515 (Ala. 1982), *cert. denied*, 463 U.S. 1208 (1983).

121. Press Inc. v. Verran, 569 S.W.2d 435, 441, 4 Media L. Rep. 1229 (Tenn. 1978).

122. Wilkinson v. Florida Adult Care Association, 450 So.2d 1168, 1172, 1173, 10 Media L. Rep. 2246 (Fla. Dist. Ct. App. 1984), *review denied*, 461 So.2d 114 (Fla. 1985).

123. Brown v. K. N. D. Corp., 7 Conn. App. 418, 12 Media L. Rep. 2201 (Conn. App. Ct. 1986), *rev'd on other grounds*, 205 Conn. 8, 14 Media L. Rep. 1757 (1987).

124. Rosenblatt v. Baer, 383 U.S. 75, 77-79, 87, 88 (1966).

125. Press, Inc. v. Verran, 569 S.W.2d 435, 437, 443, 4 Media L. Rep. 1229 (Tenn. 1978).

126. Smith v. Copley Press, Inc., 140 Ill. App. 3d 613, 617, 12 Media L. Rep. 1775 (Ill. App. Ct. 1986), *cert. denied*, 479 U.S. 916 (1986).

127. *E.g.*, Gertz v. Robert Welch, Inc., 418 U.S. 323, 344, 345 (1974) (emphasis added); *cited in* Dun & Bradstreet, Inc. v. Greenmoss Builders, Inc., 472 U.S. 749, 756 (1985) (plurality opinion by Justice Powell); Milkovich v. Lorain Journal, _____ U.S. _____, 110 S.Ct. 2695, 2704 (1990).

128. Nash v. Keene Publishing, 127 N.H. 214, 220-222, 12 Media L. Rep. 1025 (1985), citing for the "access to media" underlying assumption, Gertz v. Robert Welch, Inc., 418 U.S. at 344; and for the "risk of injury" assumption, Time, Inc. v. Firestone, 424 U.S. 448, 456 (1976), which in turn was quoting Gertz v. Robert Welch, Inc., 418 U.S. at 344.

129. *See also* Kassel v. Gannett Co., 875 F.2d 935, 940, 941 (1st Cir. 1989), involving a clinical psychologist at a Veterans' Administration Hospital who counseled veterans and their families, treated emergency cases, performed psychological evaluations and led group therapy sessions. The court also emphasized the same two additional underlying principles of media access and the assumed risk of diminished privacy and rejected public official status. (The court also decided that the three standard criteria did not apply to the psychologist, either.).

130. Gertz v. Robert Welch Inc., 418 U.S. 323, 344, 345 (1974), Garrison v. Louisiana, 379 U.S. 64, 77 (1964). *See also* Restatement (Second) of Torts §580A comment b (1977).

131. Himango v. Prime Time Broadcasting, Inc., 37 Wash. App. 259, 262, 263, 10 Media L. Rep. 1724 (Wash. Ct. App. 1984), *review denied*, 102 Wash.2d 1004 (1984).

132. R. Smolla, Law of Defamation §2.26 [3], at 2-89 (1990).

133. Rosenblatt v. Baer, 383 U.S. 75, 87 n.14 (1966).

134. Finkel v. Sun Tattler Co., 348 So.2d 51 (Fla. Dist. Ct. App. 1977) *cert. denied*, 358 So.2d 135 (Fla. 1978).

135. Rinaldi v. Viking Penguin, Inc., 101 Misc.2d 1928, 5 Media L. Rep. 1295 (N.Y. Sup. Ct. 1979), *modified*, 73 A.D. 2d 43, 5 Media L. Rep. 2506 (N.Y. App. Div. 1980), *aff'd*, 52 N.Y.2d 422, 7 Media L. Rep. 1202 (1981).

136. Zerangue v. TSP Newspapers, 814 F.2d 1066, 1069, 1070 (5th Cir. 1987).

137. Hart v. Playboy Enterprises Inc., 5 Media L. Rep. 1811, 1813 (U.S. D. Kan. 1979).

138. Rosenblatt v. Baer, 383 U.S. 75, 87 n.14 (1966).

139. Gertz v. Robert Welch, Inc., 418 U.S. 323, 343, 344 (1974).

140. This colorful marine metaphor first appeared in Rosanova v. Playboy Enterprises, Inc., 411 F.Supp. 440, 443 (S.D. Ga. 1976), *aff'd*, 580 F.2d 859 (5th Cir. 1978), to describe the task of distinguishing public and private figures. It has been frequently quoted: *e.g.*, Marcone v. Penthouse, 754 F.2d 1072, 1082 (3d Cir.), *cert. denied*, 474 U.S. 864 (1985); Rosanova v. Playboy Enterprises, Inc., 580 F.2d 859, 861 n.2 (5th Cir. 1978); Jacobson v. Rochester Communications Corp., 410 N.W.2d 830, 833, 14 Media L. Rep. 1786 (Minn. 1987); Dombey v. Phoenix Newspapers, Inc., 150 Ariz. 476, 483, 13 Media L. Rep. 1282 (1986).

141. Rosanova v. Playboy Enterprises, Inc., 580 F.2d 859, 861 (5th Cir. 1978), quoting Mr. Justice Stewart's famous observation about obscenity in Jacobellis v. Ohio, 378 U.S. 184, 197 (1964) (concurring opinion).

142. Gertz v. Robert Welch, Inc., 418 U.S. at 344, 345, 351, 352. *See also* Waldbaum v. Fairchild Publications, Inc., 627 F.2d 1287, 1292 (D.C. Cir. 1980), *cert. denied*, 449 U.S. 898 (1980).

143. Waldbaum v. Fairchild Publications, Inc., 627 F.2d at 1292.

144. *See* Gertz v. Robert Welch, Inc., 418 U.S. at 352.

145. Waldbaum v. Fairchild Publications, Inc., 627 F.2d at 1294.

146. Gertz v. Robert Welch, Inc., 418 U.S. at 345.

147. This distinguishes the general public figure from the public official who is required to demonstrate ''actual malice'' only when the defamatory statement concerns his or her official conduct or fitness for office; and from the limited public figure who theoretically must prove ''actual malice'' only when the defamatory statement pertains to a public controversy in which the limited public figure is involved. At least for the present, the general public person is deemed to have thrust his or her personality so far into the public domain for all purposes and all contexts, that the Actual Malice Standard applies to all defamatory statements which may be broadcast or published. (The Supreme Court has indicated, however, that constitutional privileges may apply only to matters of public concern. *See* pages 55–56, 92.)

148. Waldbaum v. Fairchild Publications, Inc., 627 F.2d 1287, 1295 n.20 (D.C. Cir. 1980), *cert. denied*, 449 U.S. 898 (1980).

149. Gertz v. Robert Welch, Inc., 418 U.S. 323, 352 (1974).

150. *Id*.

151. Waldbaum v. Fairchild Publications, Inc., 627 F.2d at 1295.

152. Waldbaum v. Fairchild Publications, Inc., 627 F.2d at 1294 n.15, 1295.

153. Waldbaum v. Fairchild Publications, Inc., 627 F.2d at 1292.

154. Carson v. Allied News Co., 529 F.2d 206, 209, 210 (7th Cir. 1976).

155. Newton v. National Broadcasting Co., 913 F.2d 652, 18 Media L. Rep. 1001 (9th Cir. 1990), *amended by* 930 F.2d 662 (9th Cir. 1991).

156. G. Ashdown, *Of Public Figures and Public Interest—The Libel Law Conundrum,* 25 Wm. & Mary L. Rev. 937, 942 (1984).

157. Buckley v. Littell, 539 F.2d 882, 886 (2d Cir. 1976), *cert. denied,* 429 U.S. 1062 (1977).

158. Ratner v. Young, 465 F. Supp. 386, 399 (D.V.I.1979).

159. *See* Nader v. De Toledeano, 408 A.2d. 31, 34 n.1, 5 Media L. Rep. 1550 (D.C. 1979), *cert. denied,* 444 U.S. 1078 (1980). Nader conceded public figure status without specifying which type, though general public figure status would doubtless apply.

160. Gertz v. Robert Welch, Inc., 418 U.S. 323, 352 (1974).

161. Waldbaum v. Fairchild Publications, Inc., 627 F.2d 1287, 1295, 1296 n.22 (D.C. Cir. 1980).

162. Williams v. Pasma, 202 Mont. 66, 74, 9 Media L. Rep. 1004 (1982), *cert. denied,* 461 U.S. 945 (1983).

163. Adams v. Frontier Broadcasting Co., 555 P.2d 556, 559, 560, 562, 2 Media L. Rep. 1166 (Wyo. 1976).

164. Steere v. Cupp, 226 Kan. 566, 573, 5 Media L. Rep. 2046 (1979).

165. Gertz v. Robert Welch, Inc., 418 U.S. 323, 351, 352 (1974); *see also* Wolston v. Reader's Digest Asso., Inc., 443 U.S. 157, 167 (1979).

166. Dalitz v. Penthouse International, Ltd., 11 Media L. Rep. 2153, 2158, 2159 (Cal. Ct. App. 1985).

167. Burnett v. National Enquirer, Inc., 144 Cal. App. 3d 991, 9 Media L. Rep. 1921 (Cal. Ct. App. 1983), *appeal dismissed,* 465 U.S. 1014 (1984).

168. Reliance Insurance Co. v. Barron's, 442 F. Supp. 1341, 1348 (S.D.N.Y. 1977).

169. Holy Spirit Asso. for Unification of World Christianity v. Sequoia Elsevier Publishing Co., 75 A.D. 2d 523, 6 Media L. Rep. 1191 (N.Y. App. Div. 1980). The church's public figure status was conceded.

170. Gertz v. Robert Welch, Inc., 418 U.S. 323, 345 (1974).

171. Wolston v. Reader's Digest Assoc., Inc., 443 U.S. 157, 166 n.7 (1979).

172. *See generally* R. Smolla Law of Defamation §2.19[4] (1990).

173. Waldbaum v. Fairchild Publications, Inc., 627 F.2d 1287, 1295 n.18 (D.C. Cir.), *cert. denied,* 449 U.S. 898 (1980).

174. Justice Brennan, who retired from the Supreme Court in the summer of 1990, was universally regarded as a champion of media rights. He wrote the seminal decision in New York Times Co. v. Sullivan. He has also written, however, that "some aspects of the lives of even the most public men fall outside the area of matters of public or general concern." Rosenbloom v. Metromedia, 403 U.S. 29, 48 (1971). More recently, and more ominously, the Supreme Court made a point of emphasizing that "matters of public concern" are entitled to greater first amendment protection, thereby justifying an award of presumed or punitive damages absent a showing of actual malice when matters of *private* concern are in issue. Dun & Bradstreet v. Greenmoss Builders, 472 U.S. 749, 761 (1985). And in Philadelphia Newspapers v. Hepps, 475 U.S. 767 (1986), the Court required private plaintiffs to bear the burden of proving the falsity of defamatory statements, as long as the statement is of public concern, but pointedly contrasted the lesser constitutional weight to be given matters of private concern. Finally, in Milkovich v. Lorain Journal Co., _____ U.S. _____, 110 S.Ct. 2695 (1990), Chief Justice Rehnquist's

majority opinion reviewed the privileges afforded the media by the Constitution and in dicta made *repeated* references to "matters of public concern" as if their presence were prerequisites for the invocation of those privileges. *Compare with* Dworkin v. Hustler Magazine, Inc., 867 F.2d 1188, 1195, 1196 (9th Cir.), *cert. denied,* _____ U.S. _____, 110 S.Ct. 59 (1989) (the court refused to accept that "private concern speech" about public figures is unprotected by the First Amendment).

175. Private concern, as opposed to matters of public concern, have been characterized by the Supreme Court as "solely in the individual interest of the speaker and its . . . audience." Dun & Bradstreet, 472 U.S. 749, 762 (1985). Otherwise, the Supreme Court has done little to define the phrase "matters of public concern." Smolla, Law of Defamation §3.03[1], at 3-14 (1990). However, some state courts, like New York's, have included most everything newsworthy within the "public concern" criterion of its "grossly irresponsible" test. *See* pages 104–106 above.

176. Smolla further opines that even strict liability would "arguably" apply, though this seems doubtful. R. Smolla, Law of Defamation 3.04, at 3-16, 3-17 (1990).

177. Gertz v. Robert Welch Inc., 418 U.S. 323, 342(1974).

178. *Id.* and at 344, 345.

179. In the plurality opinion in Rosenbloom v. Metromedia Inc., 403 U.S. 29 (1971), less than a majority of the Supreme Court concluded that the Actual Malice Standard should apply to defamatory falsehoods about private persons if the statements concern matters of general or public interest. This would have obviated the distinction between public persons on the one hand and private individuals on the other, focusing the test instead on society's interest in learning about newsworthy issues. *See* Gertz v. Robert Welch Inc., 418 U.S. 323, 337 (1974). Three years later, in *Gertz*, a majority of the Supreme Court decided that a status-based approach was more effective in balancing the rights of individuals against those of the press.

180. Gertz v. Robert Welch, Inc., 418 U.S. at 352.

181. Time Inc. v. Firestone, 424 U.S. 448 (1976).

182. *Id.* at 454 n.3.

183. Mrs. Firestone won a $100,000 judgment affirmed by the Florida Supreme Court; the Supreme Court remanded the case, however, for a determination of whether the defendant showed the requisite degree of fault.

184. Wolston v. Reader's Digest Assoc., Inc., 443 U.S. 157 (1979).

185. Hutchinson v. Proxmire, 443 U.S. 111 (1979).

186. Waldbaum v. Fairchild Publications, Inc., 627 F.2d 1287, 1296 (D.C. Cir.), *cert. denied*, 449 U.S. 898 (1980).

187. Warford v. Lexington Herald-Leader, 789 S.W.2d 758, 676, 768, 17 Media L. Rep. 1785 (Ky. 1990) *cert. denied*, _____U.S._____, 111 S. Ct. 754 (1991) (citing *Hutchinson*).

188. Blake v. Gannett Co., 529 So.2d 595, 601, 602, 15 Media L. Rep. 1561 (Miss. 1988) (citing *Hutchinson*).

189. Blue Ridge Bank v. Veribanc, Inc., 866 F.2d 681, 687, 688 (4th Cir. 1989) (citing *Gertz, Firestone* and *Hutchinson*).

190. Healey v. New England Newspapers, Inc., 555 A.2d 321, 325, 16 Media L. Rep. 1753 (R.I.), *cert. denied,* _____U.S. _____, 110 S.Ct. 63 (1989) (citing *Wolston*).

191. Jadwin v. Minneapolis Star & Tribune Co., 367 N.W.2d 476, 485, 486, 11 Media L. Rep. 1905 (Minn. 1985) (citing *Firestone, Wolston,* and *Hutchinson*).

192. Fairley v. Peekskill Star Corp., 83 A.D. 2d 294, 8 Media L. Rep. 1427 (N.Y. App. Div. 1981) (citing *Firestone* among other cases).

193. Davis v. Keystone Printing Service, Inc., 111 Ill.App.3d 427, 9 Media L. Rep. 1712 (Ill. App. Ct. 1982) (citing *Gertz, Firestone* and other cases).

194. Georgia Soc. of Plastic Surgeons Inc. v. Anderson, 257 Ga. 710, 711, 712, 14 Media L. Rep. 2065, 2067 (1987) (relying on *Gertz* for the "definitive test").

195. McBride v. Merrell Dow & Pharmaceuticals, Inc., 800 F.2d 1208, 1211 (D.C. Cir. 1986).

196. Bagley v. Iowa Beef Processors, Inc., 797 F.2d 632, 645 (8th Cir. 1986), *cert. denied*, 479 U.S. 1088 (1987).

197. Marcone v. Penthouse International Magazine for Men, 754 F.2d 1072, 1083 (3d Cir.), *cert. denied*, 474 U.S. 864 (1985).

198. *Id.* at 1085 n. 8.

199. Ruebke v. Globe Communications Corp., 241 Kan. 595, 601, 14 Media L. Rep. 1193, 1196 (1987).

200. Rosanova v. Playboy Enterprises Inc., 411 F. Supp. 440, 445 (S.D. Ga. 1976), *aff'd*, 580 F.2d 859, 861 (5th Cir. 1978).

201. Chuy v. Philadelphia Eagles Football Club, 431 F. Supp. 254, 267 (E.D. Pa. 1977), *aff'd*, 595 F.2d 1265 (3d Cir. 1979), cited approvingly in *Marcone*. (Note that *Chuy* antedated *Wolston* and *Hutchinson*.) *See also* Holt v. Cox Enterprises, 590 F. Supp. 408, 412 (N.D. Ga. 1984). (A member of the University of Alabama football team, who "voluntarily played that sport before thousands," both enjoyed access to the media and assumed the risk "that these persons would comment on the manner in which he performed"; he was therefore a public figure.)

202. Gertz v. Robert Welch, Inc., 418 U.S. 323, 345 (1974).

203. Hutchinson v. Proxmire, 443 U.S. 111, 135, 136 (1979), Wolston v. Reader's Digest Asso., Inc., 443 U.S. 157, 168 (1979), Time Inc. v. Firestone, 424 U.S. 448 (1976).

204. The *Wolston* decision made it appear that the door to involuntary public figures had been "closed and would only be reopened in unusual circumstances." S. Metcalf, R. Bierstedt and E. Bildner, 1 Rights and Liabilities of Publishers, Broadcasters and Reporters §1.58 at 1-127 (1989).

205. McBride v. Merrell Dow & Pharmaceuticals, Inc., 800 F.2d 1208, 1211 (D.C. Cir. 1986).

206. Capuano v. Outlet Co., 579 A.2d 469, 18 Media L. Rep. 1030 (R.I. 1990).

207. Bagley v. Iowa Beef Processors, Inc., 797 F.2d 632, 646 (8th Cir. 1986), *cert. denied*, 479 U.S. 1088 (1987).

208. Blake v. Gannett Co., 529 So.2d 595, 601, 602, 606, 15 Media L. Rep. 1561 (Miss. 1988).

209. Dalitz v. Penthouse International, Ltd., 11 Media L. Rep. 2153, 2159, 2160 (Cal. Ct. App. 1985).

210. Plotkin v. Van Nuys Publishing Co., Cal. Super. Ct., Los Angeles County, February 25, 1986.

211. Jacobson v. Rochester Communications Corp., 410 N.W.2d 830, 835, 14 Media L. Rep. 1786 (Minn. 1987).

212. Pesta v. CBS, Inc., 686 F. Supp. 166, 169, 170 (E.D. Mich. 1988).

213. In some instances, judicial yearning for a simple, less rigorous standard for media

reports about matters of public concern—even when private persons are involved—has expressed itself in the creation of a standard other than negligence, applicable to private persons involved in matters of public concern, instead of a distortion of the criteria for limited public figure status. New Jersey, for example, applies the Actual Malice Standard to reports involving private persons if they relate to matters of public concern, and New York created a distinct "grossly irresponsible" test for private person cases which is less demanding of the media, but limited to stories in the "sphere of legitimate public concern" (discussed further at pages 104–106). Sisler v. Gannett Co. Inc., 104 N.J. 256, 262-270, 13 Media L. Rep. 1577 (1986); Chapadeau v. Utica Observer-Dispatch, Inc., 38 N.Y.2d 196, 1 Media L. Rep. 1693 (1975).

214. Waldbaum v. Fairchild Publications, Inc., 627 F.2d 1287, 1299, 1300 (D.C. Cir. 1980), *cert. denied*, 449 U.S. 898 (1980).

215. Clyburn v. News World Communications, Inc., 903 F.2d 29, 31-33 (D.C. Cir. 1990).

216. Marcone v. Penthouse International Magazine for Men, 754 F.2d 1072, 1086 (3d Cir.), *cert. denied*, 474 U.S. 864 (1985).

217. Rosanova v. Playboy Enterprises Inc., 411 F. Supp. 440, 445 (S.D. Ga. 1976), *aff'd*, 580 F.2d 859, 861, 4 Media L. Rep. 1550 (5th Cir. 1978).

218. Dombey v. Phoenix Newspapers, Inc., 150 Ariz. 476, 483, 484, 13 Media L. Rep. 1282 (1986).

219. Ruebke v. Globe Communications Corp., 241 Kan. 595, 601, 602, 14 Media L. Rep. 1193 (1987). The court noted the U.S. Supreme Court's reasoning in *Wolston* that a person who engages in criminal conduct does not automatically become a "public figure"—but excepted "an event of great concern to the public" like a triple murder. The plaintiff's defamation claim was also weakened, of course, by his conviction of the crime.

220. Wolston v. Reader's Digest Assoc., Inc., 443 U.S. 157, 167-168 (1979), Time Inc. v. Firestone, 424 U.S. 448, 454 (1976).

221. Hutchinson v. Proxmire, 443 U.S. 111, 135 (1979).

222. Pesta v. CBS Inc., 686 F. Supp. 166, 170 (E.D. Mich. 1988).

223. Dalitz v. Penthouse International, Ltd., 11 Media L. Rep. 2153, 2159 (Cal. Ct. App. 1985).

224. Gertz v. Robert Welch Inc., 418 U.S. 323, 351 (1974) (" . . . an individual . . . becomes a public figure for a limited range of issues"); Waldbaum v. Fairchild Publications, Inc., 627 F.2d 1287, 1298 (D.C. Cir.), *cert. denied*, 449 U.S. 898 (1980).

225. Bagley v. Iowa Beef Processors Inc., 797 F.2d 632, 636, 646 (8th Cir. 1986), *cert. denied*, 479 U.S. 1088 (1987).

226. McBride v. Merrell Dow & Pharmaceuticals, Inc., 800 F.2d 1208, 1211 (D.C. Cir. 1986).

227. Gertz v. Robert Welch Inc., 418 U.S. at 352.

228. Wolston v. Reader's Digest Assoc., Inc., 443 U.S. 157, 167 (1979).

229. Hutchinson v. Proxmire, 443 U.S. 111, 136 (1979).

230. Gertz v. Robert Welch, Inc., 418 U.S. at 344; Waldbaum v. Fairchild Publications, Inc., 627 F.2d at 1287.

231. Warford v. Lexington Herald-Leader Co., 789 S.W.2d 758, 771, 17 Media L. Rep. 1785 (Ky. 1990), *cert. denied*, _____U.S. _____, 111 S. Ct. 754 (1991).

232. Pesta v. CBS, Inc., 686 F. Supp. 166, 170 (E.D. Mich. 1988).

233. Re v. Gannett, 480 A.2d 662, 666, 10 Media L. Rep. 2267 (Del. Super. Ct. 1984), *aff'd*, 496 A.2d 553, 11 Media L. Rep. 2327 (Del. 1985).

234. Jadwin v. Minneapolis Star & Tribune Co., 367 N.W.2d 476, 478, 479, 486, 11 Media L. Rep. 1905 (Minn. 1985).

235. *See* Waldbaum v. Fairchild Publications, Inc., 627 F.2d at 1300.

236. The question of whether a press conference, or series of press conferences, occurring prior to the defamation constitute sufficient media access, did arise in the celebrated Supreme Court case involving the divorce proceeding between Mary Alice Firestone and Russell Firestone. (*See* pages 58–59.) The Supreme Court noted that Ms. Firestone "may have held a few press conferences during the divorce proceedings in an attempt to satisfy inquiring reporters." It was unclear, however, whether this fact satisfied the media access requirement because the Court failed to find a public controversy and addressed the press conferences only in the context of their not constituting a voluntary intention to affect the outcome of a controversy. Time Inc. v. Firestone, 424 U.S. 448, 454 n.3 (1976).

237. Gertz v. Robert Welch, Inc., 418 U.S. 323, 344 n. 9 (1974),for example, *in* Waldbaum v. Fairchild Publications, Inc., 627 F.2d 1287, 1291 n.8 (D.C. Cir.), *cert. denied*, 449 U.S. 898 (1980). *See also* Wolston v. Reader's Digest Assoc. Inc., 443 U.S. 157, 164 (1979), and Marcone v. Penthouse, 754 F.2d 1072, 1081 (3d Cir.), *cert. denied*, 474 U.S. 864 (1985) (characterize assumption of risk as more important). *Compare* Milkovich v. Lorain Journal, Co., _____U.S. _____, 110 S.Ct. 2695, 2704 (1990), which in dicta, treats both assumption of risk and access to media without distinguishing their relative importance.

238. Clyburn v. News World Communications, Inc., 903 F.2d 29, 32 n.2 (D.C. Cir. 1990).

239. *See, e.g.*, Marcone v. Penthouse 754 F.2d at 1086; Ruebke v. Globe Communications, 241 Kan. 595, 14 Media L. Rep. 1193 (Kan. 1987).

240. Though a minority of jurisdictions will confer public figure status on corporations when the defamatory material concerns a matter of legitimate public interest, most courts apply the same Supreme Court criteria applicable to individuals. *See* R. Smolla, Law of Defamation §2.24 [5] and [6] (1990).

241. Waldbaum v. Fairchild Publications, Inc., 627 F.2d at 1299. *See also* Sisler v. Gannett, 104 N.J. 256, 13 Media L. Rep. 1577 (1986).

242. Blue Ridge Bank v. Veribanc, Inc., 886 F.2d 681, 687, 688 n.10 (4th Cir. 1989).

243. *See* R. Smolla, *supra* note 240, §2.24 [6], at 2-87.

244. Wolston v. Reader's Digest Assoc., Inc., 443 U.S. 157, 166 n.7 (1979).

245. *See, for example*, Holt v. Cox Enterprises, 590 F. Supp. 408, 412 (N.D. Ga. 1984) in which a former college football player who employed rough tactics was still a limited public figure 18 years later; Hartnett v. CBS, 12 Media L. Rep. 1824, 1829 (N.Y. Sup. Ct. 1986) (a plaintiff who would have qualified as a limited public figure during the debate over Communist sympathizers in the 1950's, remained a public figure for purposes of a docudrama about those events broadcast 19 years later); Street v. National Broadcasting Co., 645 F.2d 1227, 1235, *cert. dismissed*, 454 U.S. 1095 (1981) (the court noted "once a person becomes a public figure in connection with a particular controversy, that person remains a public figure thereafter for purposes of later commentary or treatment of *that controversy*." Emphasis original.). *See also* Dameron v. Washington Magazine, Inc., 779 F.2d 736, 743 (D.C. Cir. 1985), *cert. denied*, 476 U.S.

1141 (1986) (the court did not find it necessary to address the issue of whether the plaintiff had lost public figure status over the course of 8 years in connection with an air crash because the plaintiff admitted that he was still "known to the public in connection with the . . . crash and would be immediately recognized as the target" of the defamatory statement which did not use his name).

246. As noted above, the Supreme Court specifically rejected the newsworthy standard for public figure status in *Gertz* contrary to the earlier position taken by the plurality decision in Rosenbloom v. Metromedia Inc., 403 U.S. 29 (1971). Yet the natural tendency of most people, including members of the media, lawyers, and judges, is to apply public figure status to people who are involved in legitimate matters of public concern. The Supreme Court of New Jersey resolved the problem by interpreting its state constitution to require application of the Actual Malice Standard whenever a person has voluntarily and knowingly risked exposure on a matter of legitimate public concern. For example, by taking an executive job in a government-regulated industry like banking which would invite close scrutiny and could attract attention with the accompanying risk of inaccurate or false statements, one becomes a public figure. In cases such as this, the court reasoned, the press's investigation into matters of legitimate public concern would not be "wholly unexpected or aberrational, and indeed, is to be encouraged." Therefore a person can become a limited public figure in New Jersey without a public controversy (in the Supreme Court's sense) and without any voluntary thrust into the vortex of a controversy when one exists. Sisler v. Gannett Co., Inc., 104 N.J. 256, 275, 279, 13 Media L. Rep. 1577 (N.J. 1986). (*See also* note 213 above.)

247. New York Times Co. v. Sullivan, 376 U.S. 254 (1964) (public officials must show actual malice to collect any damages at all); Gertz v. Robert Welch Inc., 418 U.S. 323, 349 (1974) (neither public nor private plaintiffs may recover presumed or punitive damages without showing actual malice); Dun & Bradstreet Inc. v. Greenmoss Builders, Inc., 472 U.S. 749 (1985) (for defamatory statements of private concern, not relevant to a matter of public concern, presumed and punitive damages are available without a showing of actual malice).

248. As Justice White bluntly put it, the press is "permitted to err and misinform the public as long as they act unknowingly and without recklessness." Dun & Bradstreet, Inc. v. Greenmoss Builders, Inc., 472 U.S. 749, 770 (1985) (Justice White concurring). As Justice White's characterization implies, he does not favor the Actual Malice Standard.

249. Harte-Hanks Communications, Inc. v. Connaughton, _____ U.S. _____ , 109 S.Ct. 2678, 2685 n.7 (1989).

250. *Id.* at 2685.

251. *Id.* at 2684, 2685.

252. *Id.* at 2685, 2686.

253. St. Amant v. Thompson, 390 U.S. 727, 731 (1968).

254. Garrison v. Louisiana, 379 U.S. 64, 79 (1964).

255. *E.g.*, Newton v. National Broadcasting Co., 913 F.2d. 652, 18 Media L. Rep. 1001 (9th Cir. 1990), *amended by* 930 F.2d. 662 (9th Cir. 1991).

256. Harte-Hanks Communications, Inc. v. Connaughton, _____U.S. _____, 109 S.Ct. 2678, 2686 (1989).

257. *Id.* The Supreme Court also noted, however, that courts must be careful not to place too much reliance on factors such as circumstantial evidence. *Id. See also* Herbert v. Lando, 441 U.S. 153, 160 (1979), *cited in Harte-Hanks*.

258. *See* Gertz v. Robert Welch, 680 F.2d 527, 537-539 (7th Cir. 1982), *cert. denied*, 459 U.S. 1226 (1983).. This decision followed a remand from the Supreme Court and resulted in affirmance of a jury award for the plaintiff of $100,000 compensatory damages and $300,000 punitive damages.

259. *See*, *e.g.*, Buckley v. Littell, 539 F.2d 882, 896 (2d Cir. 1976).

260. St. Amant v. Thompson, 390 U.S. 727, 732 (1968).

261. Herbert v. Lando, 441 U.S. 153, 157 n.2 (1979).

262. Curtis Publishing Co. v. Butts, 388 U.S. 130, 169, 170 (1967) (Chief Justice Warren, concurring).

263. Liberty Lobby, Inc. v. Anderson, 746 F.2d 1563, 1574 (D.C. Cir. 1984), *vacated on other grounds*, 477 U.S. 242 (1986).

264. St. Amant v. Thompson, 390 U.S. 727, 732 (1968).

265. Nevada Independent Broadcasting Corp. v. Allen, 99 Nev. 404, 9 Media L. Rep. 1769 (1983).

266. Healey v. New England Newspapers, Inc., 555 A.2d 321, 16 Media L. Rep. 1753 (R.I.), *cert. denied*, ____U.S. ____, 110 S.Ct. 63 (1989).

267. Zerangue v. TSP Newspapers, Inc., 814 F.2d 1066, 13 Media L. Rep. 2438 (5th Cir. 1987). *See also* Dombey v. Phoenix Newspapers, Inc., 150 Ariz. 476, 488-490, 13 Media L. Rep. 1282 (1986). In that decision, seven mistaken reports accusing a county insurance agent of irregularities were forgivable under the Actual Malice Standard, notwithstanding "failure to investigate, sloppy investigation, [or] poor reporting practice." But subsequent articles in the same series repeated old errors and introduced new ones notwithstanding rebuttals by the agent which the newspaper failed to investigate. In one instance, a writer who was reassigned to the series several weeks into it, based his report on the newspaper's file which contained incorrect allegations and not the most recent stories which contradicted them. Though the newspaper received detailed demands for a retraction, it published new mistakes instead. All this sloppiness surpassed mere "bad journalism" in the view of the court and combined to support a finding of actual malice with convincing clarity. *Compare with* New York Times Co. v. Sullivan, 376 U.S. 254, 287 (1964). The New York Times accepted a political advertisement which contained defamatory information inconsistent with stories in the New York Times's own files. This did not establish knowledge of falsity, however, because the prior stories were not "brought home" to the person in the organization "having responsibility for the publication of the advertisement."

268. Deloach v. Beaufort Gazette, 281 S.C. 474, 10 Media L. Rep. 1733, *cert. denied*, 469 U.S. 981 (1984).

269. Gertz v. Robert Welsh, Inc., 418 U.S. 323, 332 (1974); St. Amant v. Thompson, 390 U.S. at 729, 730, 732, 733 (a candidate for public office could legitimately rely on a sworn affidavit from a union member, with no reputation for veracity or lack of it, accusing a deputy sheriff of criminal conduct, without further verification).

270. Fitzgerald v. Penthouse International, Ltd., 691 F.2d 666, 670 (4th Cir. 1982), *cert. denied*, 460 U.S. 1024 (1983); Ryan v. Brooks, 634 F.2d 726, 734 (4th Cir. 1980).

271. Harte-Hanks Communications, Inc. v. Connaughton, ____ U.S. ____ , 109 S.Ct. 2678, 2698, 2699 (1989).

272. Warford v. Lexington Herald-Leader Co., 789 S.W.2d 758, 772, 17 Media L. Rep. 1785 (Ky. 1990), *cert. denied*, ____ U.S. ____, 111 S. Ct. 754 (1991). Stickney v. Chester County Communications, Ltd., 361 Pa. Super. 166, 172, 13 Media L. Rep. 2192 (Pa. Super. Ct.), *appeal denied*, 516 Pa. 643, 533 A.2d 713 (1987).

273. Stickney v. Chester County Communications, Ltd., 361 Pa. Super. 166, 170, 172, 13 Media L. Rep. 2192 (Pa. Super. Ct.), *appeal denied*, 516 Pa. 643 (1987). The two officers were awarded a total of $150,000 against the newspaper, its publisher and the reporter.

274. Curtis Publishing Co. v. Butts, 388 U.S. 130 (1967).

275. Warford v. Lexington Herald-Leader, Co., 789 S.W.2d 758, 773, 17 Media L. Rep. 1785 (Ky. 1990), *cert. denied*, ____U.S. ____, 111 S.Ct. 754 (1991). Whether actual malice was in fact present was left for a jury to decide.

276. Loeb v. New Times Communications Corp., 497 F. Supp. 85, 92 (S.D.N.Y. 1980).

277. Clyburn v. News World Communications, Inc., 903 F.2d 29, 34 (D.C. Cir. 1990).

278. Harte-Hanks Communications, Inc. v. Connaughton, ____U.S. ____, 109 S.Ct. 2678 (1989).

279. Loeb v. The New Times Communications Corp., 497 F. Supp. 85, 93 (S.D.N.Y. 1980).

280. *E.g.*, Gertz v. Robert Welch Inc., 680 F.2d 527, 539 n.19 (7th Cir. 1982), *cert. denied*, 459 U.S. 1226 (1983). The reporter's efforts to research the article were characterized as "slipshod and sketchy" in part because of his failure to contact the plaintiff.

281. Pep v. Newsweek, Inc., 553 F. Supp. 1000, 1002 n.2 (S.D.N.Y. 1983).

282. Liberty Lobby Inc. v. Anderson, 746 F.2d 1563, 1569 (D.C. Cir. 1984), *vacated on other grounds*, 477 U.S. 242 (1986); Dombey v. Phoenix Newspapers, Inc., 150 Ariz. 476, 489, 13 Media L. Rep. 1282 (1986).

283. Remember also that the seminal case of New York Times v. Sullivan involved a political advertisement accepted from third parties. New York Times Co. v. Sullivan, 376 U.S. 254 (1964).

284. Hunt v. Liberty Lobby, 720 F.2d 631, 643 (11th Cir. 1983), citing Vandenburg v. Newsweek, Inc., 441 F.2d 378, 380 (5th Cir.), *cert. denied*, 44 U.S. 864 (1971).

285. *See also e.g.*, Masson v. New Yorker Magazine, Inc., No. 89–1799, ____U.S. ____(June 20, 1991); Gertz v. Robert Welch, Inc., 680 F.2d at 538, 539; Curtis Publishing Co. v. Butts, 388 U.S. 130, 157 (1967). *Compare with* Loeb v. New Times Communications Corp., 497 F. Supp. 85, 93 (S.D.N.Y. 1980); the court rejected the plaintiff's argument that "since the story was not 'hot news,' defendants were required to maintain higher standards of an investigative reporting"; rather, the defendants demonstrated sufficient investigation to avoid actual malice.

286. It has also been suggested that the question of whether or not a communication is "hot news" should not be over-emphasized since no publication is made without time pressure or with the ability to double-check every fact. "Rare, indeed, is the document that is totally error-free, irrespective of the haste with which it was composed." R. Sack, Libel, Slander and Related Problems, §V.5.2.1., at 216 n.175 (1980). *See also* R. Smolla, Law of Defamation, §3.21 [1] at 3-62 (1990).

287. Chang v. Michiana Telecasting Corp., 900 F.2d 1085 (7th Cir. 1990).

288. *E.g.*, Zerangue v. TSP Newspapers, Inc., 814 F.2d 1066, 1071 (5th Cir. 1987).

289. Scacchetti v. Gannett Co., 123 A.D. 2d 497, 13 Media L. Rep. 1396 (N.Y. App. Div. 1986). *See also* Kerwick v. Orange County Publications Div. of Ottaway Newspapers, Inc., 53 N.Y.2d 625, 627, 7 Media L. Rep. 1152 (1981) in which the New York Court of Appeals reached the same conclusion.

290. *See, e.g.,* Marcone v. Penthouse International Magazine For Men, 754 F.2d 1072, 1089 (3d Cir.), *cert. denied,* 474 U.S. 864 (1985) ("Reliance on the professional reputation of [a freelance author] may help to defeat an allegation of actual malice"); Hunt v. Liberty Lobby, 720 F.2d 631, 648, 649 (11th Cir. 1983); Grebner v. Runyon, 132 Mich.App. 327, 333, 334, 10 Media L. Rep. 1719 (Mich. Ct. App. 1984).

291. *See, e.g.,* Liberty Lobby Inc. v. Dow Jones & Co., 838 F.2d 1287, 1297 (D.C. Cir. 1988), *cert. denied,* 488 U.S. 825 (1988) (reliance by the *Wall Street Journal* on previous articles and publications such as the *National Review* helped rebut charges of actual malice); Rosanova v. Playboy Enterprises, Inc., 580 F. 2d 859, 862 (5th Cir. 1978) (the publisher's allegations were supported "by a multitude of previous reports upon which the publisher reasonably relied. . . . [D]efendants will not be forced to defend, nor will a trial judge in a later libel case have to retry, the truthfulness of previous reports made by independent publishers").

292. Mehau v. Gannett Pacific Corp., 66 Haw. 133, 147, 148, 9 Media L. Rep. 1337 (1983) (a newspaper was entitled to rely on UPI's reputation as a reliable source of news; in the same case, however, the UPI's reliance on a new publication apparently given to "sensationalizing" was insufficient to overcome charges of actual malice). It may not always be possible, however, to be dismissed from a suit solely on the basis of wire service reliance; Bessent v. Times-Herald Printing Co., 709 S.W.2d 635, 12 Media L. Rep. 1622 (Tex. 1986) (the plaintiff was still entitled to discover facts under the control of the newspaper's employees to determine whether knowing or reckless falsity was present).

293. Grebner v. Runyon, 132 Mich. App. 327, 334-337, 10 Media L. Rep. 1719 (Mich Ct. App. 1984).

294. Mehau v. Gannett Pacific Corp., 66 Haw. 133, 147, 9 Media L. Rep. 1337 (1983).

295. Hotchner v. Castillo-Puche, 551 F.2d 910 (2d Cir.), *cert. denied,* 434 U.S. 834 (1977). Some of the facts in the example come from the lower court's decision, 404 F. Supp. 1041 (S.D.N.Y. 1975).

296. *See, e.g.,* the following cases in which the Supreme Court found no actual malice: Time Inc. v. Pape, 401 U.S. 279, 290 (1971) (the reporter made a "rational interpretation" of a report by the U.S. Commission on Civil Rights and reported as fact what was only an allegation); Beckley Newspapers Corp. v. Hanks, 389 U.S. 81, 84 (1967) (an editorial writer relied on his feeling that "there was a possibility" that an opponent of water fluoridation had intimidated a court clerk to join in his positions and reported the "threats" without further proof).

297. *See* pages 42–74 above.

298. Gertz v. Robert Welch, Inc., 418 U.S. 323, 344 (1974).

299. *Id.* at 344, 345.

300. *See* notes 174 and 175 above. *See also* R. Smolla, Law of Defamation, §3.05, at 3-19 (1990).

301. Gertz v. Robert Welch, Inc., 418 U.S. at 347. In permitting states to fashion their own standards of liability provided they do not impose liability without fault, the Supreme Court reserved the right to curb state-made rules if they "purported to condition civil liability on a factual misstatement whose content did not warn a reasonably prudent editor or broadcaster of its defamatory potential." Gertz v. Robert Welch Inc., 418 U.S. at 348.

302. As noted above, the presence of actual malice as a condition for awarding presumed or punitive damages applies even to suits brought by private persons (Gertz v. Robert Welch Inc., 418 U.S. at 349), as long as the subject matter of the defamation is one of public concern (Dun & Bradstreet, Inc. v. Greenmoss Builders, Inc., 472 U.S. 749 (1985)). See note 247 above. As also discussed above, the Supreme Court has hinted that even more restrictive tests for the media may soon apply to statements made about private individuals which are not matters of public concern. *See* pages 55–56, 92 above, and R. Smolla, Law of Defamation, §3.05 (1990).

303. See, R. Smolla, *supra* note 302, at §3.11, for the current state roster, which changes from time to time through both additions and deletions.

304. How can journalists, publishers, editors, and broadcasters who make a false defamatory statement be negligent? The Restatement has suggested five contexts. This section will focus on one of them: paying too little attention to determining whether the statement was true or false, such as by not obtaining sufficient verification. The four others are failing to notice that a particular statement is defamatory—that it has the capacity for injuring reputation because of what it says directly or because of extrinsic facts known to those who read or hear the statement; erring in the content of a statement, for example through a typo or an error in transcription or the wrong choice of words; mistakenly referring to the plaintiff when either another person or a fictitious person is intended; and making a statement public before intending to. Restatement (Second) of Torts §580B comment b (1977).

305. The negligence test fits along a spectrum of journalistic error. Strict liability for a defamatory mistake, without regard to fault, is the most stringent standard for the media and has been outlawed since New York Times v. Sullivan. On the other side of negligence is the Actual Malice Standard, which is the least stringent test of journalistic fault. In the middle lies negligence which logically "subsumes" the higher level of fault required for liability under the Actual Malice Standard. *See*, *e.g.*, Gertz v. Robert Welch, Inc., 680 F.2d 527, 537 n.17, 539, 540 (7th Cir. 1982), *cert. denied*, 459 U.S. 1226 (1983) (the negligence standard "clearly would be subsumed in a finding of actual malice"); Richmond Newspapers, Inc. v. Lipscomb, 234 Va. 277, 14 Media L. Rep. 1953 (1987), *cert. denied*, 486 U.S. 1023 (1988) and cases cited ("the higher standard of New York Times malice subsumed the required negligence standard").

306. Ashby v. Hustler Magazine, Inc., 802 F.2d 856, 858, 13 Media L. Rep. 1416 (6th Cir. 1986) (citing McCall v. Courier - Journal & Louisville Times Co., 323 S.W.2d 882, 886, 7 Media L. Rep. 2118 (Ky. 1981), *cert. denied*, 456 U.S. 975 (1982)); KARK-TV v. Simon, 280 Ark. 228, 232, 10 Media L. Rep. 1049 (1983).

307. Appleby v. Daily Hampshire Gazette, 395 Mass. 32, 36, 11 Media L. Rep. 2372 (1985) (quoting Restatement (Second) of Torts, §580B, comment g (1977)). *See also* Stone v. Banner Publishing Corp., 677 F. Supp. 242, 247, 248 (D. Vt. 1988). The Restatement (Second) of Torts §580B comment g (1977), also frames the negligence standard in terms of whether the defendant had "reasonable grounds for believing that the communication was true."

308. *Compare with* St. Amant v. Thompson, 390 U.S. 727, 731 (1968), which emphasized that recklessness under the Actual Malice Standard "is not measured by whether a reasonably prudent man would have published, or would have investigated before publishing."

309. Restatement (Second) of Torts §299A and §580B comments g and h (1977).

310. *See, e.g.*, Jones v. Palmer Communications Inc., 440 N.W.2d 884, 898, 16 Media L. Rep. 2137 (Iowa 1989); Triangle Publications Inc. v. Chumley, 253 Ga. 179, 181, 182, 10 Media L. Rep. 2076 (1984); Restatement (Second) of Torts §580B comments g and h (1977).

311. *See, e.g.*, Jones v. Palmer Communications Inc., 440 N.W.2d 884, 898, 899, 16 Media L. Rep. 2137 (Iowa 1989); and Triangle Publications Inc. v. Chumley, 253 Ga. 179, 181, 10 Media L. Rep. 2076 (1984). *See also* Kassel v. Gannett Co. Inc., 875 F.2d 935, 943 (1st Cir. 1989).

312. Both the reasonable person test and the reasonable professional test are recognized to have serious flaws for the assessment of journalistic conduct. As applied to journalists, the reasonable person test is somewhat stricter than the test for liability which applies in lawsuits against members of other trades and professions (like plumbers, accountants, architects, hairdressers, lawyers) who do not even enjoy the same advantages under the First Amendment. Such other negligence tests only hold professionals up to the prevailing standards of their own professions and trades, which may be less demanding than what the layman might think appropriate after the fact. *See, e.g.*, Re v. Gannett, 480 A.2d 662, 666, 10 Media L. Rep. 2267 (Del. Super. Ct. 1984), *aff'd*, 496 A.2d 553, 11 Media L. Rep. 2327 (Del. 1985). On the other hand, the problem with a professional standards test for journalists is that unlike plumbers, accountants, architects, hairdressers and lawyers, journalists lack any specialized education, a certification process and a set of universally applicable standards. D. Daniels, *Public Figures Revisited*, 25 Wm. & Mary L. Rev. 957, 959 (1984). And even if "accepted practice" in the media is still negligence to any objective viewer, it is unlikely to be accepted as a standard of performance. *See, e.g.*, Kassel v. Gannett Co., Inc., 875 F.2d 935, 943 (1st Cir. 1989), and the authorities cited. Moreover, journalism is different from most trades and professions for other reasons; the unique facts which surround each story will not permit an accurate comparison of conduct necessary to establish a standard, and different journalists perceive things differently. D. Daniels, *supra* at 960, 961. Virginia's Supreme Court has also noted the profit motive of newspapers in publishing startling sensational stories as a further reason to adopt a lay person's standard instead of the standard of care in the journalistic community. Richmond Newspapers Inc. v. Lipscomb, 234 Va. 277, 14 Media L. Rep. 1953 (1987), *cert. denied*, 486 U.S. 1023 (1988).

313. *See, e.g.*, Stone v. Banner Publishing Corp., 677 F. Supp. 242, 247 (D. Vt. 1988); Jones v. Taibbi, 400 Mass. 786, 799, 14 Media L. Rep. 1844 (1987); Appleby v. Daily Hampshire Gazette, 395 Mass. 32, 36, 37, 11 Media L. Rep. 2372 (1985). *Stone* and *Jones* appear to adopt a "reasonable belief in the truth or falsity" standard without settling on either the reasonable person test or the prudent professional test; *Appleby* applied a reasonable person test while conceding the relevance of customs and practices within the profession.

314. *See* Jones v. Palmer Communications Inc., 440 N.W.2d 884, 898, 899, 16 Media L. Rep. 2137 (Iowa 1989); Triangle Publications Inc. v. Chumley, 253 Ga. 179, 182, 10 Media L. Rep. 2076 (1984); Restatement (Second) of Torts §580B comment g (1977). *See also* R. Smolla, Law of Defamation §3.28, at 3-73 (1990) ("In general courts appear to apply traditional tort cost/benefit style analysis in assessing the negligence issue. . . . ").

315. *See, e.g.*, Harte-Hanks Communications Inc. v. Connaughton, _____ U.S. _____ 109 S.Ct. 2678 (1989), which addressed this factor in an actual malice analysis.

316. *See* Restatement (Second) of Torts §580B comment h (1977).

317. Stone v. Banner Publishing Corp., 677 F. Supp. 242, 247 (D. Vt. 1988).

318. Kassel v. Gannett Co. Inc., 875 F.2d 935, 944 (1st Cir. 1989).

319. *See*, *e.g.*, Re v. Gannett Co. Inc., 480 A.2d 662, 666, 10 Media L. Rep. 2267 (Del. Super. Ct. 1984), *aff'd*, 496 A.2d 553, 11 Media L. Rep. 2327 (Del. 1985).

320. Re v. Gannett Co. Inc., 480 A.2d at 666, 668. The jury's finding against the defendant was upheld, but the case was remanded because the award of $1,335,000 in damages was not supported by the evidence; the court recognized that "from the standpoint of having produced a useful and competitive vehicle it is doubtful that in the marketplace the invention of an automobile which would only travel 1/4 mile is of substantially greater value than a vehicle which would not start." This was particularly so in view of the limited maximum range of the vehicle.

321. *See* Ashby v. Hustler Magazine, Inc., 802 F.2d 856 (6th Cir. 1986).

322. *See* dicta in Hardin v. Santa Fe Reporter, Inc., 745 F.2d 1323, 1324, 1326, 11 Media L. Rep. 1026 (10th Cir. 1984) (Notwithstanding such negligence found by the trial court, the plaintiff, a public official, failed to show actual malice and his complaint was dismissed).

323. Ashby v. Hustler Magazine, Inc., 802 F.2d at 859, 860.

324. Richmond Newspapers Inc. v. Lipscomb, 234 Va. 277, 14 Media L. Rep. 1953 (1987), *cert. denied*, 486 U.S. 1023 (1988). The $100,000 award of compensatory damages, reduced from $1,000,000 by the trial court, was upheld on appeal.

325. A study of libel lawyers who review news stories prior to publication and broadcast has determined that the answers to these questions are of particular concern in the lawyer's evidentiary review. *See* S. Shapiro, *Libel Lawyers as Risk Counselors: Pre-Publication and Pre-Broadcast Review and the Social Construction of News*, 11 Law & Policy (No. 3 1989) republished in Libel Litigation 1990, Practicing Law Institute, 345, 354, 355 (1990).

326. Appleby v. Daily Hampshire Gazette, 395 Mass. 32, 38-40, 11 Media L. Rep. 2372 (1985). The court noted that other jurisdictions also permit reliance on the accuracy of wire services, at least where the story raises no doubts as to its veracity (citing Mehau v. Gannett Pacific Corp., 66 Haw. 134, 149, 9 Media L. Rep. 1337 (1983), a case involving the actual malice test); Zetes v. Richman, 86 A.D. 2d 746, 747, 8 Media L. Rep. 1588 (N.Y. App. Div. 1982) (a case involving the New York "gross irresponsibility" test); Torres-Silva v. El Mundo, Inc., 3 Media L. Rep. 1508, 1512 (P.R. 1977) (the court in this case also suggested that information in a wire service story which "can be easily corroborated due to special circumstances" ought to be corroborated); Layne v. Tribune Co., 108 Fla. 177, 186 (1933); and others. Agreeing with the court in Layne v. Tribune Co., the Massachusetts court concluded that it would impose an impermissibly time-consuming and expensive obligation on disseminators of news to verify specially every item reported by established news-gathering agencies.

327. Stone v. Banner Publishing Corp., 677 F. Supp. 242 (D. Vt. 1988); *see also* Rouch V. Enquirer & News, 184 Mich. App. 19, 17 Media L. Rep. 2305 (Mich. Ct. App. 1990).

328. KARK-TV v. Simon, 280 Ark. 228, 232, 233, 10 Media L. Rep. 1049 (1983).

329. *See e.g.*, Rouch v. Enquirer & News, 184 Mich., App. 19, 36, 37, 17 Media L. Rep. 2305 (Mich. Ct. App. 1990).

330. Curtis Publishing Co. v. Butts, 388 U.S. 130 (1967).

331. Re v. Gannett, 480 A.2d 662, 666, 10 Media L. Rep. 2267 (Del. Super. Ct. 1984), *aff'd*, 496 A.2d 553, 11 Media L. Rep. 2327 (Del. 1985).

332. *See* Newton v. National Broadcasting Co., 913 F. 2d. 652, 18 Media L. Rep. 1001 (9th Cir. 1990), *amended by* 930 F 2d. 662 (9th Cir. 1991).

333. Gazette, Inc. v. Harris, 229 Va. 1, 11 Media L. Rep. 1609 (1985).

334. Kassel v. Gannett Co., 875 F.2d 935, 938, 943 (1st Cir. 1989). The precise source of the error was never pinpointed, but a likely source noted by the court was misattribution by the reporter in the original interview. (The quotation may also have been garbled in the course of transmission from the reporter to his editor or distorted during later editing.) The court also found that the principal source of negligence was the newspaper's failure to verify the quotation.

335. Zerangue v. TSP Newspapers, Inc., 814 F.2d 1066, 1071 (5th Cir. 1987). Because the Actual Malice Standard applied to the error, however, the newspaper defendant won a dismissal.

336. As noted above (see note 93), the seminal case of New York Times Co. v. Sullivan involved the acceptance by the *Times* of a political advertisement without verifying its contents; the Supreme Court regarded this as negligence though not actual malice. Also remember the *TV Guide* case (see pages 28–29 above) involving the model who gave no permission for use of her picture to advertise a program about teenage pregnancies; the magazine employed a screening procedure but it did not identify the offending ad as "suspect." Triangle Publications, Inc. v. Chumley, 253 Ga. 179, 182, 10 Media L. Rep. 2076 (1984).

337. *See*, *e.g.*, Morrell v. Forbes, 603 F. Supp. 1305, 11 Media L. Rep. 1869 (D.C. Mass. 1985). The court refused to say that a reasonably prudent editor would not have spotted the risk to a fisherman's reputation from a photo caption implying involvement in "Fishy Business" in an article about organized crime (See page 21).

338. Kohn v. West Hawaii Today, Inc., 65 Haw. 584, 588, 589, 9 Media L. Rep. 1238 (1982).

339. However, as the Supreme Court has observed, error-avoiding procedures should not be terminated or stifled "simply because there is liability for culpable error and because the editorial process will itself be examined in the tiny percentage of instances in which error is claimed and litigation ensues." Herbert v. Lando, 441 U.S. 153, 174 (1979). Given the exposure to liability, when the Actual Malice Standard or the Private Person Standard is not met, there is ample reason to resort to prepublication precautions.

340. *See*, *e.g.*, Harte-Hanks Communications, Inc. v. Connaughton, _____U.S. _____, 109 S.Ct. 2678, 2686 (1989), an actual malice case.

341. *Id*. *See also* Curtis Publishing Co. v. Butts, 388 U.S. 130 (1967) in which a magazine's decision to assume a new investigative role was cited as evidence of actual malice.

342. Chapadeau v. Utica Observer Dispatch, Inc., 38 N.Y.2d 196, 199, 1 Media L. Rep. 1693 (1975).

343. Gaeta v. New York News, Inc., 62 N.Y.2d 340, 350 (1984).

344. Hogan v. The Herald Company, 84 A.D. 2d 470, 476, 446 N.Y.S.2d 836, 8 Media L. Rep. 1137 (N.Y. App. Div.), *aff'd mem.*, 58 N.Y.2d 630, 8 Media L. Rep. 2567 (1982).

345. Chapadeau v. Utica Observer-Dispatch, Inc., 38 N.Y.2d 196, 200, 1 Media L. Rep. 1693 (1975).

346. Goldman v. New York Post Corp., 58 A.D. 2d 769, 3 Media L. Rep. 1079 (N.Y. App. Div. 1977).

347. Geiger v. Dell Publishing Co., 719 F.2d 515, 517 (1st Cir. 1983).

348. Ortiz v. Valdescastilla, 102 A.D. 2d 513, 10 Media L. Rep. 2193 (N.Y. App. Div. 1984).

349. Chapadeau v. Utica Observer-Dispatch, Inc., 38 N.Y.2d at 200.

350. Geiger v. Dell Publishing Co., 719 F.2d 515, 517 (1st Cir. 1983); Karaduman v. Newsday, Inc., 51 N.Y.2d 531, 550, 551, 6 Media L. Rep. 2345 (1980). *Geiger* involved the memoirs of the director Federico Fellini which included a description of the plaintiff as a "half-drunk" soldier. The United States publisher of the book was not guilty of "gross irresponsibility" particularly because the objectionable passage had been published on four prior occasions (once in the United States) over a period of years without objection.

351. Ortiz v. Valdescastilla, 102 A.D. 2d 513, 522, 10 Media L. Rep. 2193 (N.Y. App. Div. 1984). This court also reached the questionable conclusion that reliance on an emotionally distraught and embittered woman as a source of the article could not be gross irresponsibility since a "victim of plaintiff's alleged broken promises and a party to the incident described in the article, is a much more reliable source than a third party— no matter how trustworthy in the past—whose information is nonetheless hearsay." The reporter, who did have the opportunity to observe the demeanor of the witness, "could have, not unreasonably, concluded that she was telling the truth. . . . "

352. Zucker v. County of Rockland, 111 A.D. 2d 325, 327, 11 Media L. Rep. 2213 (N.Y. App. Div. 1985).

353. O'Brien v. Troy Pub. Co., 121 A.D. 2d 794, 12 Media L. Rep. 2355 (N.Y. App. Div. 1986).

354. *See* R. Smolla, Law of Defamation §12.06[2][b], at 12-28 (1990).

355. *See* Branzburg v. Hayes, 408 U.S. 665 (1972); S. Metcalf, R. Bierstedt and E. Bildner, Rights and Liabilities of Publishers, Broadcasters and Reporters §§3.02-3.05, 3.08, 3.10 (1990).

356. *See* S. Metcalf, et al., *supra* note 355, §3.11; R. Smolla, *supra* note 354, §12.06[2][b].

357. *See* R. Smolla, *supra* note 354, §12.06[2][b][ii] at 12-30.

358. Capuano v. Outlet Co., _____R.I. _____, 18 Media L. Rep. 1030 (1990).

359. R. Smolla, *supra* note 354, §12.06[2][c].

360. *See, e.g.*, Coronado Credit Union v. KOAT Television, Inc., 99 N.N. 233, 9 Media L. Rep. 1031 (N.M. Ct. App. 1982) ("No fixed rule precluding summary judgment under such circumstances is appropriate and each case must turn on the particular facts which exists therein." The court denied summary judgment).

361. *See e.g.*, Laxalt v. McClatchy, 116 F.R.D. 438, 452, 14 Media L. Rep. 1199 (D. Nev. 1987) (interpreted Nevada's "extremely strong" shield law to bar plaintiff "absolutely" from learning the identities of witnesses and to bar the press from making any mention of them at trial); and Greenberg v. CBS Inc., 49 A.D. 2d 693, 5 Media L. Rep. 1470 (N.Y. App. Div. 1979) (precluded the defendants from any use of confidential sources at trial as evidence of verification or responsibility). *See also* McCoy v. Hearst Corp., 42 Cal.3d 835, 870, 13 Media L. Rep. 2169 (1986), *cert. denied*, 481 U.S. 1041 (1987).

362. Laxalt v. McClatchy, 116 F.R.D. 438, 452, 14 Media L. Rep. 1199 (D. Nev. 1987).

363. Delaney v. National Broadcasting Co., 13 Media L. Rep. 2456 (N.Y. App. Div. 1987).

364. McCoy v. Hearst Corp., 220 Cal. Rptr. 848, 865, 866, 12 Media L. Rep. 1313 (Cal. Ct. App. 1985), *rev'd on other grounds*, 42 Cal.3d 835, 13 Media L. Rep. 2169 (1986), *cert. denied*, 481 U.S. 1041 (1987).

365. Sprague v. Walter, 518 Pa. 425, 436, 437, 15 Media L. Rep. 1625, *appeal dismissed*, 488 U.S. 988 (1988).

366. Restatement (Second) of Torts §580(B) comments g and h (1977).

367. Harte-Hanks Communications Inc. v. Connaughton, _____U.S. _____, 109 S.Ct. 2678 (1989); Curtis Publishing Co. v. Butts, 388 U.S. 130 (1967).

368. Harte-Hanks Communications Inc. v. Connaughton, _____ U.S._____, 109 S.Ct. 2678, 2686 (1989).

369. Herbert v. Lando, 441 U.S. 153, 173, 174 (1979).

370. In a study based on interviews with 53 in-house and outside counsel who regularly review stories for newspapers, television stations, networks, magazines, and other news organizations, most of these lines of inquiry were identified by lawyers as their principal concern in reviewing stories. *See* S. Shapiro, *Libel Lawyers as Risk Counselors: Pre-Publication and Pre-Broadcast Review and the Social Construction of News*, 11 Law & Policy (No. 3 1989) republished in Libel Litigation 1990, Practicing Law Institute, 345, 355 (1990). *See also* 17 Media L. Rep., *News Notes*, "Court Seen Ready to Act on Punitive Damages Issue," June 5, 1990, which described similar advice by Barbara Wartelle, Assistant General Counsel, Gannett Co. Inc., to a seminar on libel litigation sponsored by the Practising Law Institute, May 21, 22, 1990.

371. Weiner v. Doubleday & Company, Inc., 14 Media L. Rep. 2107 (N.Y. Sup. Ct. 1987), *rev'd*, 142 A.D. 2d 100, 15 Media L. Rep. 2441 (N.Y. App. Div. 1988), *aff'd*, 74 N.Y.2d 586, 17 Media L. Rep. 1165 (1989), *cert. denied*, _____U.S. _____, 110 S.Ct. 2168 (1990). The trial judge awarded summary judgment to the plaintiff, but Ms. Alexander won on appeal because reliance on the allegation of the *third* party that Frances "always slept with her shrinks," following corroboration to a degree by Marilyn, Berenice and others, was not considered grossly irresponsible. The New York Court of Appeals also, somewhat inexplicably, decided that "the challenged paragraphs accurately summarize[d] the statements made to Alexander and her researcher." Under different circumstances (and perhaps under another state's negligence test instead of New York's "grossly irresponsible" criteria), the author's failure to reflect the views of interviewees with more precision could have more serious consequences. Even in this case, the plaintiff might not have been encouraged to pursue his claim through two appeals and a petition for certiorari but for the writer's imprecise choice of words.

372. Masson v. New Yorker Magazine, Inc., No. 89–1799, _____ U.S. _____ (June 20, 1991).

373. Burns v. McGraw-Hill Broadcasting Co., 659 P.2d 1351, 9 Media L. Rep. 1257 (Co. 1983).

374. Dostert v. Washington Post Co., 531 F. Supp. 165, 168, 8 Media L. Rep. 1170 (N.D. W.Va. 1982).

375. Rouch v. Enquirer & News, 184 Mich.App. 19, 35, 17 Media L. Rep. 2305 (Mich. Ct. App. 1990).

376. Bose Corporation v. Consumers Union of United States, Inc., 466 U.S. 485 (1984).

377. Liberty Lobby, Inc. v. Anderson, 746 F.2d 1563 (D.C. Cir. 1984), *vacated on other grounds*, 477 U.S. 242 (1986). After the Supreme Court required that the lower court reconsider whether Carto would be able to prove with "clear and convincing evidence" that this defamatory statement was made with actual malice, the claim was dismissed. Still, the illustration demonstrates how a source's true statement, through lack of rigor, can be converted into a false statement and expose the reporter and his newspaper to potential liability. *See also* Stickney v. Chester Communications, Ltd., 361 Pa. Super. 166, 170, 13 Media L. Rep. 2192 (Pa. Super. Ct.), *appeal denied*, 516 Pa. 643 (1987).

378. Some recent cases have refused to recognize "defamation by implication" when the underlying facts cannot be proven false and the target of the implication is a public official or public figure. *See, e.g.*, Diesen v. Hessburg, 17 Media L. Rep. 1849, 1852, 1853 (Minn. 1990), *cert. denied*, _____U.S. _____, 112 L. Ed. 2d. 1177, 111 S. Ct. 1071, 1072 (1991) and cases cited. The Supreme Court, however, has not recognized this position and it is not universally accepted. Moreover, even in jurisdictions where this rule applies, it may be limited to instances in which facts are omitted and not apply when unsupported implications are expressly stated. *See Diesen*, 17 Media L. Rep. at 1851.

379. Lawrence v. Bauer Publishing & Printing, Ltd., 89 N.J. 451, 459, 460, 468, 8 Media L. Rep. 1536, *cert. denied*, 459 U.S. 999 (1982). The defendants in this case were excused from liability because the plaintiffs were public figures and their evidence was not "clear and convincing" that the headline was published with actual malice; the court did, however, characterize the defendants' actions as "careless and perhaps irresponsible."

380. Meadows v. Taft Broadcasting Co., 98 A.D. 2d 959, 10 Media L. Rep. 1363 (N.Y. App. Div. 1983).

381. Based on Riley v. Moyed, 529 A.2d 248, 14 Media L. Rep. 1379 (Del. 1987). In *Riley*, the columnist reported that the council member had gone golfing with developers when actually he had socialized with them in other ways. The court, however, found this to be a distinction without a difference for purposes of defamation because the sting of the columnist's statement would have been no less had it been accurate.

382. Westmoreland v. CBS, Inc., 596 F. Supp. 1170, 1174, 1176, 1177 (S.D.N.Y. 1984).

383. Based on Porter Packet Corp. v. Lewis, *sub nom.*, Gazette v. Harris, 229 Va. 1, 11 Media L. Rep. 1609, *cert. denied*, 473 U.S. 905 (1985). Compensatory damages of $50,000 were awarded against the newspaper and upheld on appeal.

384. Phyfer v. Fiona Press, Inc., 12 Media L. Rep. 2211, 2216 (U.S. N.D. Miss. 1986).

385. Allen v. Gordon, 86 A.D. 2d 514, 8 Media L. Rep. 1124 (N.Y. App. Div. 1982), *aff'd mem.*, 56 N.Y.2d 780 (1982). *See also* Brafman v. Houghton Mifflin Co., 11 Media L. Rep. 1354 (N.Y. Sup. Ct. 1984) which involved a libel claim by four sisters who had the same maiden surname as a fictitiously named grandmother and her fictitiously named siblings in a Pulitzer Prize winning book about the illness and treatment of a schizophrenic. They lost their case because, among other reasons, the book contained an explicit disclaimer that the names had been fictionalized and dissimilarities of characteristics were great enough that no reader knowing the plaintiffs could reasonably understand the book to portray them.

386. Landau v. Columbia Broadcasting System, Inc., 205 Misc. 357, 360-361 (N.Y. Sup. Ct. 1954) *aff'd mem.*, 1 A.D. 2d 660 (N.Y. App. Div. 1955).

387. This illustration is not based on any actual case.

388. *See, e.g.*, Medico v. Time, Inc., 643 F.2d 134, 137 (3d Cir.), *cert. denied*, 454 U.S. 836 (1981) (citing W. Prosser, The Law of Torts, at 798 (4th ed. 1971), and other authorities).

389. Three policies underlie the privilege. First, the media is thought to act as the agent of the citizenry, who have a right to attend a proceeding or examine its results. The media informs them of what they may have seen for themselves. A second rationale is based on a theory of "public supervision": the citizenry should be able to satisfy itself as to the manner in which public duties are discharged. A third rationale has to do with the public's "right to know" insofar as matters of legitimate public interest are concerned. Medico v. Time, Inc., 643 F.2d 134, 141–143 (3d Cir.), *cert. denied*, 454 U.S. 836 (1981). Different judicial decisions emphasize different rationales. In Gertz v. Robert Welch Inc., 680 F.2d 527, 535 n.12, 536 (7th Cir. 1982), *cert. denied*, 459 U.S. 1226 (1983), the court emphasized the third rationale based on the interest in public information which, as the court noted, favors application of the privilege to reports of contemporaneous activities and proceedings as opposed to historical ones.

390. Cox Broadcasting Corp. v. Cohn, 420 U.S. 469 (1975). *Compare with* Time, Inc. v. Firestone, 424 U.S. 448 (1976) in which the Court rejected the magazine's argument that the "New York Times privilege" should extend automatically to all re-ports—both true and false—of judicial proceedings. Instead the Court reiterated its more "confined version" of this argument, as stated in *Cox Broadcasting Corp.*

391. Medico v. Time, Inc., 643 F.2d at 137, 138.

392. The legal source of the privilege also varies. Some states have codified the privilege in statutory form. Most state law, however, derives the privilege from the common law as reflected in the Restatement (Second) of Torts §611 (1977).

393. W. Prosser & W. Keeton, The Law of Torts §115, at 837 (5th ed. 1984).

394. *See id.*, which cites the "prevailing view . . . that a pleading or a deposition filed in a case but not yet acted upon may not be reported under the claim of privilege" (footnotes omitted). *See also* 2 Harper & James, Torts (2d ed. 1986) §5.24, at 205 which agrees. *Compare with* McClain v. Arnold, 275 S.C. 282, 285, 6 Media L. Rep. 1831 (1980) (the common law privilege attaching to reports of judicial proceedings insulates the publisher in a subsequent libel action even when the report is based on a mere summons and complaint against the plaintiff); and Newell v. Field Enterprises, Inc., 91 Ill. App. 735, 747, 6 Media L. Rep. 2450 (Ill. App. Ct. 1980) ("Simply because a suit has proceeded to the point where judicial action of some kind has taken place does not necessarily mean that the suit is less likely to be groundless and brought in bad faith").

395. *See, e.g.*, W. Prosser & W. Keeton, The Law of Torts §115, at 837 (5th ed. 1984) ("sealed records and documents withheld from the public eye under court order may not be so reported," footnotes omitted).

396. *See, e.g.*, Rouch v. Enquirer & News, 427 Mich. 157, 172, 173, 13 Media L. Rep. 2201 (1986) (report of a mere arrest is not covered by the privilege). *Compare with* Restatement (Second) of Torts §611 comment h (1977) (report of a mere arrest *is* covered by the privilege).

397. *See, e.g.*, Reeves v. American Broadcasting Cos., 719 F.2d 602 (2d Cir. 1983) (relying on W. Prosser, The Law of Torts, §114 at 777-779 (4th ed. 1971) among other authorities).

398. Mark v. Seattle Times, 96 Wash.2d 473, 488, 7 Media L. Rep. 2209 (1981), *cert. denied*, 457 U.S. 1124 (1982).

399. Restatement (Second) of Torts §611 comment h (1977).

400. *See, e.g.*, Lavin v. New York News Inc., 757 F.2d 1416, 1419 (3d Cir. 1985) (an FBI agent's affidavit in support of a search warrant was conceded to be covered by the privilege); and Medico v. Time Inc., 643 F.2d 134, 6 Media L. Rep. 2529 (3d Cir.), *cert. denied*, 454 U.S. 836 (1981) (an FBI report on the Philadelphia branch of La Cosa Nostra, and a personal profile report on an alleged member of organized crime were held subject to the privilege because they were compiled by government agents acting in their official capacities, and publication of the material served the public's legitimate interest in learning about organized crime).

401. Schiavone Constr. Co. v. Time Inc., 847 F.2d 1069, 1087 n.28 (3d Cir. 1988).

402. *See* Gertz v. Robert Welch Inc., 680 F.2d 527, 537 n.14 (7th Cir. 1982), *cert. denied*, 459 U.S. 1226 (1983).

403. Jones v. Taibbi, 400 Mass. 786, 796, 14 Media L. Rep. 1844 (1987) ("There is also no privilege to report the unofficial talk of such officials as policemen, as distinct from their official utterances or acts, such as an arrest," quoting W. Prosser & W. Keeton, The Law of Torts §115, at 836, 837 (5th ed. 1984) (footnotes omitted). *See also*, Restatement (Second) of Torts §611 comment b (1977).

404. Foster v. Turner Broadcasting System, Inc., 844 F.2d 955, 960, 961 (2d Cir.), *cert. denied*, 488 U.S. 994 (1988).

405. Holy Spirit Assoc. for Unification of World Christianity v. New York Times Company, 49 N.Y. 63, 67, 5 Media L. Rep. 2219 (1979).

406. White v. Fraternal Order of Police, 909 F.2d 512, 527 (D.C. Cir. 1990).

407. *See* Restatement (Second) of Torts §611 comment f (1977).

408. Schiavone Constr. Co. v. Time Inc., 847 F.2d 1069, 1072, 1088, 1089 (3d Cir. 1978).

409. Dorsey v. National Enquirer Inc., 17 Media L. Rep. 1527, 1529 (U.S. C.D. Cal. 1990). *Compare with* Foster v. Turner Broadcasting, Inc., 844 F.2d at 961, which noted that the fairness of a report about a statement by a government official was shown by eight interviews in the same broadcast which challenged the *bona fides* of the official conduct described in the report.

410. Torres v. Playboy Enterprises Inc., 7 Media L. Rep. 1182, 1185 (U.S. S.D. Tex. 1980).

411. Street v. National Broadcasting Co., 645 F.2d 1227 (6th Cir. 1981), *cert. dismissed*, 454 U.S. 1095 (1981).

412. Hartnett v. CBS, Inc., 12 Media L. Rep. 1824, 1827-1829 (N.Y. Sup. Ct. 1986). A CBS docudrama told the story of John Henry Faulk, who was falsely accused of communist connections during the "McCarthy era" of the 1950's, sued his accusers, and won a substantial award. The docudrama which was based on Faulk's book about the trial, followed the events by almost 20 years. Nevertheless, one of the defendants who lost to Faulk at the first trial took the opportunity presented by the television program to bring his own defamation suit based on his portrayal in the film. The defendants in the CBS action successfully invoked New York's statutory public records privilege for that part of the telecast which recreated the original trial, notwithstanding certain condensations and omissions.

413. *See, e.g.*, WKRG-TV, Inc. v. Wiley, 495 So.2d 617, 13 Media L. Rep. 1680 (Ala. 1986), *cert. denied*, 479 U.S. 1088 (1987). *See also* Gertz v. Robert Welch, Inc., 680 F.2d 527, 535 (7th Cir. 1982), *cert. denied*, 549 U.S. 1226 (1983), interpreting Illinois common law.

414. Medico v. Time, Inc., 643 F.2d 134, 138 (3d Cir.), *cert. denied*, 454 U.S. 836 (1981). *See also* Hogan v. Herald Co., 84 A.D. 2d 470, 477, 8 Media L. Rep. 1137 (N.Y. App. Div.), *aff'd mem.*, 58 N.Y. 630, 8 Media L. Rep. 2567 (1982).

415. Bufalino v. the Associated Press, 692 F.2d 266 (2d Cir. 1982).

416. An article which reported that a grand jury was investigating a Brooklyn Congressman added a statement not characterized as grand jury testimony: that t gressman and others "are suspected of having split an alleged $25,000 payoff." Because the article did not explicitly attribute the "suspicion" to charges before the grand jury, it was held that the article did not pretend to be a report of proceedings before the grand jury and the fair reports privilege was inapplicable. Keogh v. New York Herald Tribune, Inc., 51 Misc. 2d 888 (N.Y. Sup. Ct. 1966), *aff'd* 28 A.D. 2d 1209 (N.Y. App. Div. 1967), *appeal denied*, 21 N.Y.2d 955 (1968). *See also*, White v. Fraternal Order of Police, 909 F.2d 512, 528 (D.C. Cir. 1990) (a television broadcast which failed to attribute its reports to a police department internal investigation was not privileged); Dameron v. Washington Magazine, Inc., 779 F.2d 736, 740 (D.C. Cir. 1985), *cert. denied*, 476 U.S. 1141 (1986) (a story about an air crash which failed to tie defamatory statements about an air traffic controller to any particular governmental report or proceeding on the crash was not privileged).

417. Edwards v. National Audubon Society, 556 F.2d 113, 120 (2d Cir.), *cert. denied*, 434 U.S. 1002 (1977).

418. In Harte-Hanks Communications, Inc. v. Connaughton, _____U.S. _____, 109 S.Ct. 2678, 2682, 2699 (1989), the majority opinion noted that the petitioner in the case did not invoke the neutral reportage doctrine and it was therefore not under consideration (at n.1) but Justice Blackmun's concurring opinion noted: "petitioner has eschewed any reliance on the 'neutral reportage' defense. For this Court to adopt the neutral reportage theory, the facts of this arguably might fit within it." (The facts of the Harte-Hanks case are described at pages 82–86 above).

419. In 1989, the Ninth Circuit observed with some understatement that "The neutral reporting privilege is not a 'settled rule.' " Weaver v. Oregonian Publishing Co., 16 Media L. Rep. 2167, 2168 (9th Cir. 1989). According to a 1988 survey of the Libel Defense Resource Center, the doctrine has been recognized by at least one court in 12 jurisdictions and only 4 jurisdictions have definitely rejected the neutral reportage privilege (LDRC Bulletin, No. 24, at 52). In some jurisdictions, however, authority is divided. *See* R. Smolla, Law of Defamation §4.14[4], at 4-70 n. 328 (1990).

420. Edwards v. National Audubon Soc., 556 F.2d 113, 120, *cert. denied*, 434 U.S. 1002 (1977).

421. Ward v. News Group Int'l Ltd., 733 F. Supp. 83, 84, *adhered to*, 18 Media L. Rep. 1140 (C.D. Cal. 1990) (citing Barry v. Time, Inc., 584 F. Supp. 1110, 1122-28 (N.D. Cal. 1981)). *See also* (In re) United Press International, 16 Media L. Rep. 2401, 2407 (U.S. D.D.C. 1989) (also citing *Barry*).

422. (In re) United Press International, 16 Media L. Rep. at 2407; Barry v. Time, Inc., 584 F. Supp. at 1126.

423. (In re) United Press International, 16 Media L. Rep. at 2407.

424. Edwards v. National Audubon Society, Inc., 556 F.2d at 120.

425. *See*, *e.g.*, Davis v. Keystone Printing Service, Inc., 155 Ill. App.3d 309, 323, 14 Media L. Rep. 1225, 1232 (Ill. App. Ct. 1987), *appeal denied*, 116 Ill.2d 550 (1987).

426. Cianci v. New Times Publishing Co., 639 F.2d 54, 68 (2d Cir. 1980); Edwards

v. National Audubon Society, Inc., 556 F.2d at 120; Dresbach v. Doubleday & Co., 8 Media L. Rep. 1793, 1795 (U.S. D.D.C. 1982); Jones v. Palmer Communications, Inc., 440 N.W.2d 884, 893, 16 Media L. Rep. 2137 (Iowa 1989); Davis v. Keystone Printing Service, Inc., 155 Ill. App.3d 309, 323, 14 Media L. Rep. 1225 (Ill. App. Ct.), *appeal denied*, 116 Ill.2d 550 (1987).

427. Cianci v. New Times Publishing Company, 639 F.2d at 67, 68; Edwards v. National Audubon Society, Inc., 556 F.2d at 120; Jones v. Palmer Communications, Inc., 440 N.W.2d at 893; Dresbach v. Doubleday & Co., 8 Media L. Rep. at 1795; Ryan v. Herald Assoc., 566 A.2d 1316, 1321, 16 Media L. Rep. 2472 (Vt. 1989).

428. *See, e.g.,* Cianci v. New Times Publishing Co., 639 F.2d 54, 69 (2d Cir. 1980) which held against the publisher, among other reasons, for its failure to obtain the target's version of the facts. In another case, however, a federal court held that reporting "both sides" would not be necessary when it adds nothing to the neutrality of a simple and straightforward story. (In re) United Press International, 16 Media L. Rep. 2401, 2407 (U.S. D.D.C. 1989).

429. Cianci v. New Times Publishing Co., 639 F.2d at 69. In this case, the court also frowned on the reporter's harassment of the source to "get [her] to talk" as being inconsistent with the disinterested reportage which the privilege was meant to protect.

430. Edwards v. National Audubon Society, Inc., 556 F.2d 113, 120 (2d Cir.), *cert. denied*, 434 U.S. 1002 (1977); Cianci v. New Times Publishing Co.

431. *See* Price v. Viking Penguin, Inc., 881 F.2d 1426, 1434 (8th Cir. 1989), *cert. denied*, _____U.S. _____, 110 S.Ct. 757 (1990).

432. Edwards v. National Audubon Society, 556 F.2d 113, 120 (2d Cir.) *cert. denied*, 434 U.S. 1002 (1977).

433. *The American Heritage Dictionary of the English Language*, American Heritage Publishing Co., Inc. (1973).

434. *See* Gertz v. Robert Welch Inc., 418 U.S. 323, 339-340 (1974) ("Under the First Amendment there is no such thing as a false idea."); New York Times Co. v. Sullivan, 376 U.S. 254, 292 n.30 (1964) ("Since the Fourteenth Amendment requires recognition of the conditional privilege for honest misstatements of fact, it follows that a defense of fair comment must be afforded for honest expression of opinion based upon privileged, as well as true, statements of fact."). In Milkovich v. Lorain Journal Co., _____U.S. _____, 110 S.Ct. 2695, 2706 (1990), the Court reiterated, "a statement on matters of public concern must be provable as false before there can be liability under state defamation law, at least in situations . . . where a media defendant is involved," (citing Philadelphia Newspapers, Inc. v. Hepps, 475 U.S. 767 (1986)).

435. Milkovich v. Lorain Journal Co., _____U.S. _____, 110 S.Ct. 2695 (1990).

436. *Id.* at 2706.

437. Ollman v. Evans, 750 F.2d 970, 978 (D.C. Cir. 1984), *cert. denied*, 471 U.S. 1127 (1985).

438. Between 1984 and 1990, many decisions relied on a balancing test articulated in Ollman v. Evans, to separate fact from opinion, with four points of inquiry: (1) the specific language used; (2) whether the statement is verifiable; (3) the general context of the statement; and (4) the broader context in which the statement appeared. Other decisions attempted a less mechanistic approach based on the "totality of circumstances," described in Judge Bork's concurring decision in Ollman v. Evans. The continuing vitality of both approaches is questionable following *Milkovich*.

439. *See*, *e.g.*, Justice Brennan's dissenting opinion in *Milkovich*.

440. Ollman v. Evans, 750 F.2d 970, 978 (D.C. Cir. 1984), *cert. denied*, 471 U.S. 1127 (1985).

441. Unelko Corp. v. Rooney, 912 F.2d 1049, 1055 (9th Cir. 1990), *cert. denied*, _____U.S. _____, 111 S. Ct. 1586 (1991). Notwithstanding that "It didn't work" stated fact rather than opinion, Rooney won the case because the plaintiff could not show that the statement was false.

442. Milkovich v. Lorain Journal Co., _____U.S. _____, 110 S.Ct. 2695, 2706 (1990).

443. The Supreme Court's conditions for constitutional protection of opinion are not far removed from the common law criteria for the defense of "fair comment." The common law of most states has applied fair comment to protect statements of opinion, excluding false statements of fact, for many years. This privilege was derived not from the First Amendment of the Constitution, but rather from a judicially recognized advantage to society in balancing "the need for vigorous public discourse and the need to redress injury to citizens wrought by invidious or irresponsible speech." Milkovich v. Lorain Journal Co., _____U.S. _____, 110 S.Ct. 2695, 2703 (1990). The fair comment privilege as applied usually has four conditions:

1. The statement involves a matter of public concern. This is a broad category— broader than the term "public controversy" which limits the application of limited public figure status. It includes commentary about public persons which is not about "purely private" matters as well as commentary about anyone who presents services or goods to the public.
2. The statement must be based upon true or privileged facts. Usually these facts either have to be disclosed or they have to be widely known or available in the community. In the case of opinions on artistic or culinary endeavors, the underlying "facts" are considered to be available for members of the public to judge for themselves.
3. The statement must represent the actual opinion of the speaker; if the opinion is not sincerely held, the privilege can be lost.
4. The statement cannot be made solely for the purpose of causing harm. The privilege can be lost through bad faith or bad motive or if it is otherwise unfair.

See Milkovich v. Lorain Journal Co., _____U.S. _____, 110 S.Ct. 2695, 2703 (1990), citing 1 F. Harper & F. James, Law of Torts, §5.28, at 456 (1956); Restatement (Second) Torts §566 comment a (1977). *See also* R. Sack, Libel, Slander and Related Problems, 158, 166, 169, 170, 173, 175 (1980). The "fair comment" privilege has been eclipsed in recent years by defenses based on the First Amendment, which according to *Milkovich* (insofar as media defendants are concerned) also requires that statements pertain to matters of public concern and that they contain pure belief or ideas or facts which cannot be proven false. Because the constitutional opinion privilege ignores completely any lack of sincerity or malicious motive of media defendants, common law fair comment is likely to retain a subordinate position in media cases.

444. Milkovich v. Lorain Journal Co., _____U.S. _____, 110 S.Ct. 2695, 2707 (1990). *See also* Unelko Corp. v. Rooney, 912 F.2d 1049, 1053-1055 (9th Cir. 1990), *cert. denied*, _____U.S. _____, 111 S. Ct. 1586 (1991).

445. In *Milkovich* the Supreme Court suggested that full constitutional protection for

statements of opinion which do not contain a provably false factual connotation might be limited to matters of public concern and to expressions of opinion in the media. 110 S. Ct. at 2706, 2707.

446. Buckley v. Littell, 539 F.2d 882, 893 (2d Cir. 1976), *cert. denied*, 429 U.S. 1062 (1977). *See also* Ollman v. Evans, 750 F.2d 970, 979, 981 (D.C. Cir. 1984), *cert. denied*, 471 U.S. 1127 (1985).

447. *See* note 434 above.

448. Milkovich v. Lorain Journal Co., _____U.S. _____, 110 S.Ct. 2695 (1990).

449. *See, e.g.*, Kelly v. Schmidberger, 806 F.2d 44, 48, 49 (2d Cir. 1986) in which a priest asserted that other priests had fraudulently put church property in their own names, in the context of a highly charged and opinion-ridden theological debate; Cianci v. New Times Publishing Co., 639 F.2d 54, 64 (2d Cir. 1980) in which a mayor was accused of rape and obstruction of justice; Rajneesh Foundation International v. McGreer, 303 Or. 371, 374, 14 Media L. Rep. 1215 (1987) involving assertions that an individual "lies a lot"; and Rinaldi v. Holt, Rinehart & Winston, Inc., 42 N.Y.2d 369, 381, 382, 2 Media L. Rep. 2169, *cert. denied*, 434 U.S. 969 (1977), which involved the statement that a judge was "probably corrupt." None of these statements qualified as opinion though exceptions to this general rule do exist. *Compare with* Liberty Lobby Inc. v. Anderson, 746 F.2d 1563, 1573 (D.C. Cir. 1984), *vacated on other grounds*, 477 U.S. 242 (1986), in which alleging "the use of lies and half-truths" was found to be a statement of undefamatory opinion in the context of a stream of invective. *See also*, Hawkins v. Oden, 459 A.2d 481, 484, 9 Media L. Rep. 750 (R.I. 1983) in which the allegation that a state senator was "stealing public money" and "dipping into the public till" were deemed to be opinion when clearly labeled as such and based upon fully disclosed facts.

450. Although *Milkovich* did not say disclosure of underlying facts was a sure-fire method of achieving protection, Justice Brennan's dissenting opinion interpreted the majority view to be consistent with this long-standing rule, citing also the Restatement (Second) of Torts §566 comment c (1977). Justice Brennan also observed that "a statement preceded by only a partial factual predicate or none at all" did not necessarily imply other facts, the "operative question [being] whether reasonable readers would have actually interpreted the statement as implying defamatory facts."

451. *See* King v. Globe Newspaper Co., 400 Mass. 705, 713, 714, 14 Media L. Rep. 1811 (1987), *cert. denied*, 485 U.S. 940, and *cert. denied*, 485 U.S. 962 (1988).

452. *See* Milkovich v. Lorain Journal, _____U.S._____, 110 S. Ct. 2695, 2708 ff. (1990), dissenting opinion of Justice Brennan. *See also* Restatement (Second) of Torts §566, comment c (1977) which contains a similar comparison of statements on which the one in this text is based.

453. Although each of these cases was decided before *Milkovich*, they still seem to offer valid examples of means of avoiding libel difficulties. As Justice Brennan's dissenting opinion in *Milkovich* pointed out, there is nothing inconsistent between prior decisions made on this basis and the Supreme Court's majority opinion.

454. Lewis v. Time, 710 F.2d 549 (9th Cir. 1983).

455. Naked City Inc. v. Chicago Sun-Times, 77 Ill.App.3d 188, 191, 5 Media L. Rep. 1806 (Ill. App. Ct. 1979).

456. Trump v. Chicago Tribune Company, 616 F. Supp. 1434 (S.D.N.Y. 1985).

457. Miskovsky v. Tulsa Tribune Co., 678 P.2d 242, 9 Media L. Rep. 1954 (Okla. 1983), *cert. denied*, 465 U.S. 1006 (1984).

458. *See, e.g.*, Chalpin v. Amordian Press, Inc., 128 A.D. 2d 81, 14 Media L. Rep. 1206 (N.Y. App. Div. 1987) (an article describing a rock star's agent as "an unbelievably unscrupulous character" based on disclosed but misrepresented facts, did not fit within opinion's protected precincts).

459. Time Inc. v. Johnston, 448 F.2d 378, 384 (4th Cir. 1971).

460. Briarcliff Lodge Hotel, Inc. v. Citizen-Sentinel Publishers, Inc., 260 N.Y. 106, 118, 119 (1932).

461. Milkovich v. Lorain Journal, Co., _____U.S. _____, 110 S.Ct. 2695, 2706 (1990).

462. Hustler Magazine Inc. v. Falwell, 485 U.S. 46 (1988).

463. Hustler Magazine Inc. v. Falwell, which includes an historical review of political cartoons and their effects, concluding, "[f]rom the viewpoint of history, it is clear that our political discourse would have been considerably poorer without them" (485 U.S. at 53-55).

464. Letter Carriers v. Austin, 418 U.S. 264, 285-86 (1974). *See also* Greenbelt Cooperative Publishing Association v. Bresler, 398 U.S. 6 (1970).

465. Milkovich v. Lorain Journal, _____U.S. _____, 110 S.Ct. 2695, 2709 (1990); Hustler Magazine Inc. v. Falwell, 485 U.S. at 57.

466. Ollman v. Evans, 750 F.2d 970, 980 (D.C. Cir. 1984), *cert. denied*, 471 U.S. 1127 (1985).

467. Buckley v. Littell, 539 F.2d 882, 894 (2d Cir. 1976), *cert. denied*, 429 U.S. 1062 (1977).

468. Fudge v. Penthouse International Ltd., 840 F.2d 1012, 1016 (1st Cir.), *cert. denied*, 488 U.S. 821 (1988).

469. McCabe v. Rattiner, 13 Media L. Rep. 2309, 2311, 2312 (1st Cir. 1987) (cited approvingly in *Fudge*, 840 F.2d at 1016).

470. Henderson v. Times Mirror Co., 669 F. Supp. 356, 359 (D. Colo. 1987), *aff'd mem.*, 876 F.2d 108 (10th Cir. 1989).

471. Miskovsky v. Oklahoma Pub. Co., 654 P.2d 587, 593, 7 Media L. Rep. 2607 (Okla.), *cert. denied*, 459 U.S. 923 (1982).

472. Holt v. Cox Enterprises, 590 F. Supp. 408, 411 (N.D. Ga. 1984).

473. Loeb v. New Times Communications Corp., 497 F. Supp. 85, 89, 91 (S.D.N.Y. 1980).

474. *Id.*

475. Mr. Chow of New York v. Ste. Jour Azur S.A., 759 F.2d 219, 221, 222, 229 (2d Cir. 1985).

476. Mashburn v. Collin, 355 So. 2d 879, 888, 889 (La. 1977) (cited in Mr. Chow of New York v. Ste. Jour Azur S.A).

477. Mr. Chow of New York v. Ste. Jour Azur S.A., 759 F.2d at 229.

478. Innes v. Payne, 12 Media L. Rep. 1403, 1405 (N.Y. Sup. Ct. 1985).

479. Catalfo v. Jensen, 657 F. Supp. 463 (D.N.H. 1987).

480. *Id.*

481. Letter Carriers v. Austin, 418 U.S. 264, 285, 286 (1974).

482. Greenbelt Cooperative Publishing Association v. Bresler, 398 U.S. 6, 14 (1970).

483. Ollman v. Evans, 750 F.2d 970, 982 (D.C. Cir. 1984), *cert. denied*, 471 U.S. 1127 (1985), commenting on Myers v. Boston Magazine Co., 380 Mass. 336, 6 Media L. Rep. 1241 (1980).

484. King v. Globe Newspaper Co., 400 Mass. 705, 14 Media L. Rep. 1811 (1987), *cert. denied*, 485 U.S. 940, and *cert. denied*, 485 U.S. 962 (1988).

485. Donoghue v. Hayes, Irish Exchequer, 265, 266 (1831) [Ireland], *quoted in* Frank v. National Broadcasting Co., 119 A.D. 2d 252, 257, 13 Media L. Rep. 1801 (N.Y. App. Div. 1986), and in Salomone v. MacMillan Pub. Co., 97 Misc.2d 346, 351, 4 Media L. Rep. 1710 (N.Y. Sup. Ct. 1978), *rev'd on other grounds*, 77 A.D. 2d 501, 6 Media L. Rep. 1655 (N.Y. App. Div. 1980).

486. Salomone v. MacMillan Publishing Co., Inc., 97 Misc.2d at 350 (citing Triggs v. Sun Printing and Publishing Assn., 179 N.Y. 144 (1904), and Lambertini v. Sun Printing and Pub. Assn. n111 A.D. 437 (N.Y. App. Div. 1906)).

487. Polygram Records v. Superior Court, 170 Cal. App.3d 543, 556, 557, 11 Media L. Rep. 2363 (Cal. Ct. App. 1985), *quoted in* Frank v. National Broadcasting Co., 119 A.D. 2d 252, 260, 13 Media L. Rep. 1801 (N.Y. App. Div. 1986).

488. Polygram Records v. Superior Court, 170 Cal. App.3d at 546, 547. The court's opinion noted that it was unclear that the comedian even intended to mention the plaintiff's product and may have been referring instead to a wine of his own invention named "Reggie." 170 Cal. App.3d at 547 n.3, and 556 n.15.

489. Raye v. Letterman, 14 Media L. Rep. 2047 (Cal. Sup. Ct. 1987).

490. Hustler Magazine Inc. v. Falwell, 485 U.S. 46, (1988).

491. Dworkin v. Hustler Magazine, Inc., 867 F.2d 1188, 1194 (9th Cir), *cert. denied*, _____U.S. _____, 110 S.Ct. 59 (1989).

492. *See* Hustler Magazine Inc. v. Falwell, 485 U.S. at 53. *Compare with* Brooks v. Stone, 170 Ga. App. 457, 10 Media L. Rep. 1517 (Ga. Ct. App.), *aff'd*, 253 Ga. 565 (1984), in which the court failed to find the humor in the following statement which it interpreted to imply promiscuity: "Our mothers were German Shepherds; our fathers were Camels, so naturally we love to hump bitches in heat. Say, Ms. Brooks, when do you come in season?" Ms. Brooks was a private person and there was no particular debate in evidence.

493. Frank v. National Broadcasting Co., 119 A.D. 2d 252, 261, 262, 13 Media L. Rep. 1801 (N.Y. App. Div. 1986).

494. *See*, for example, Ault v. Hustler Magazine, Inc., 860 F.2d 877, 881 (9th Cir. 1988), *cert. denied*, _____U.S. _____, 109 S.Ct. 1532 (1989).

495. Dworkin v. Hustler Magazine, Inc., 867 F.2d at 1195.

496. Cowan v. Time Inc., 41 Misc. 2d 198, 200 (N.Y. Sup. Ct. 1963).

497. Ault v. Hustler Magazine, 860 F.2d 877 (9th Cir. 1988), *cert. denied*, _____ U.S. _____, 109 S.Ct. 1532 (1989).

498. Kirkland v. Peekskill, 634 F. Supp. 950, 951 (S.D.N.Y. 1986).

499. Fleming v. Kane County, 636 F. Supp. 742, 746, 747 (N.D. Ill. 1986).

500. Haberstroh v. Crain Publications, Inc., 189 Ill. App.3d 267, 271, 272, 16 Media L. Rep. 2423 (Ill. App. Ct. 1989).

501. Miskovsky v. Oklahoma Pub. Co., 654 P.2d 587, 593, 7 Media L. Rep. 2607 (Okla.), *cert. denied*, 459 U.S. 923 (1982).

502. DeMoya v. Walsh, 441 So.2d 1120, 1121, 9 Media L. Rep. 2527 (Fla. Dist. Ct. App. 1983) (the epithets were deemed "pure opinion based on disclosed facts").

503. Leidholdt v. L.F.P. Inc., 860 F.2d 890 (9th Cir. 1988), *cert. denied*, 489 U.S 1080, 109 S.Ct. 1532 (1989).

504. Dale v. City of Chicago Heights, 672 F. Supp. 330 (N.D. Ill. 1987).

505. *E.g.,* Ollman v. Evans, 750 F.2d 970, 980 (D.C. Cir. 1984), *cert. denied*, 471 U.S. 1127 (1985).

506. Costello v. Capital Cities Media Inc., 125 Ill.2d 402, 15 Media L. Rep. 2407 (1988). *See also* Fleming v. Kane County, 636 F. Supp. 742, 747 (N.D. Ill. 1986) and Rajneesh Foundation International v. McGreer, 303 Or. 371, 374, 14 Media L. Rep. 1215 (1987).

507. Vern Sims Ford, Inc. v. Hagel, 42 Wash. App. 675, 683, 684, 12 Media L. Rep. 2248 (Wa. Ct. App. 1986), *review denied*, 105 Wash.2d 1016 (1986).

508. Yancey v. Hamilton, 786 S.W.2d 854, 856-859, 17 Media L. Rep. 1012 (Ky. 1989).

509. Rinaldi v. Holt, Reinhart & Winston, Inc., 42 N.Y.2d 369, 381, 382, 2 Media L. Rep. 2169, *cert. denied*, 434 U.S. 969, 3 Media L. Rep. 1432 (1977).

510. Milkovich v. Lorain Journal Co., _____U.S. _____, 110 S.Ct. 2695 (1990).

511. Sweeney v. Sengstacke Enterprises, Inc., 180 Ill. App.3d 1044, 1048, 16 Media L. Rep. 1506 (Ill. App. Ct. 1989).

512. Hellman v. McCarthy, 10 Media L. Rep. 1789 (N.Y. Sup. Ct. 1984).

Other Sources

These sources, all of which have been cited in this book, are recommended for journalists and (especially) their lawyers when litigation threatens or occurs:

Slade R. Metcalf, Robin Bierstedt, and Elisa Spungen Bildner, *Rights and Liabilities of Publishers, Broadcasters and Reporters* (two looseleaf volumes), Shepard's/McGraw-Hill, Inc., Colorado Springs (updated annually).

Robert D. Sack, *Libel, Slander, and Related Problems*, Practicing Law Institute, New York (1980).

Rodney A. Smolla, *Law of Defamation* (one looseleaf volume), Clark Boardman Company, Ltd., New York (updated annually).

Table of Cases

All case citations checked through the AUTO CITE® service*; numerical references following case citations pertain to notes in which the cases appear (see Notes section).

*AUTO CITE® is the electronic citation service of Lawyers Cooperative Publishing, available exclusively through the LEXIS® service. LEXIS is a registered trademark for information products and services of Mead Data Central, Inc.

Index

About the Author

NEIL J. ROSINI is a partner in the New York law firm of Franklin, Weinrib, Rudell & Vassallo, P.C. He specializes in the areas of defamation, copyright, rights of privacy, trademark licensing, and television.